The Course Companion for BHS Stages III & IV

THE COURSE COMPANION FOR BHS STAGES III&IV

MAXINE CAVE BHSSM+T

J. A. ALLEN
London

British Library Cataloguing-in-Publication Data.
A catalogue record for this book is available from the British Library.

ISBN 0.85131.656.5
© J. A. Allen & Co. Ltd., 1996

Published in Great Britain in 1996 by
J. A. Allen & Company Limited,
1 Lower Grosvenor Place, Buckingham Palace Road,
London, SWIW OEL.

Typeset by Setrite Typesetters Ltd., Hong Kong
Printed by Dah Hua Printing Co. Ltd., Hong Kong

Reprinted 1996

Edited by Lesley Young
Illustrations by Maggie Raynor
Designed by Nancy Lawrence

Contents

Introduction

This book covers the horse care and knowledge elements of the BHS Stage examinations III and IV, and should be used in conjunction with the *Course Companion for BHS Stages I and II* to ensure that all background knowledge has been covered.

Each chapter has headings and divisions which indicate whether the material contained in them is required at Stage III or IV, and in some cases refers to Stages I and II. If a section is indicated as Stage II, III and IV, for example, then a basic understanding of that subject matter is required at Stage II level, a little more depth of understanding at Stage III and thorough understanding and experience for Stage IV. However, it is still very important that each student studies the contents of the BHS syllabus before taking any exam, as to separate the syllabi completely within each chapter and each book would entail being very repetitive. Every student should also realise that at each new level they should have confirmed and improved their knowledge from the level before. For example, the superficial muscles are included in the Stage III syllabus and are examined at that level. At Stage IV, however, the student should check that they have not forgotten this work as they may be questioned again. This can happen at each level with any subject.

The practical skills outlined within the book must be developed through "hands on" experience. There is no substitute for practical work. At Stage IV level particularly, there is an even greater need for practical experience. The candidates need to show that they have developed a feel and a good eye which cannot be developed through book work alone. They will need to have worked in the horse world for several years, among a range of horses, ponies and different disciplines, in order to gain enough experience for this level.

In the section "Helpful Hints and Exam Technique" I have tried to high-light areas where, as an examiner, I frequently find candidates in trouble through misinformation, lack of preparation or misunderstanding of the requirements of the examination situation.

1 Identification

STAGES III and IV

1. Means of Identification

a. Freeze branding is another way of marking and identifying horses. Branding irons are cooled in liquid nitrogen. When applied to the skin, they destroy the pigment cells so that white hair grows through, leaving a permanent mark. This is a pain-free process. Companies which provide this service will supply a registration document for each horse. The name of the horse and its brand will be retained on their register. This can be of great help when identifying stolen horses.

b. Hot-iron branding is also used. Applied to the skin, it is mostly used for native ponies and some traditional breeds from abroad, such as the Hanoverian. A new form of hot-iron branding, pain-less to the horse, involves branding the owner's post code on to the horse's hooves. Owners have branding irons made up and their farriers apply them. As the marks grow out, they are reapplied, approximately every six months.

c. A microchip is used to identify horses as well as dogs and other animals. The microchip is injected by a vet into the skin in the horse's neck. Here it soon attaches itself and remains undetected unless a scanner is used. Each horse's details are entered on the "HorseSafe" computerised register. Major sales, slaughter houses and some police forces have the appropriate scanners and can check a horse's identity.

2. Identification Documents

a. When a horse is registered with a particular breed society, it will be issued with an identification document. This document will detail the horse's name, date of birth, colour, markings, position of whorls, height and the owner's name and address. When buying or selling a registered horse, both vendor and purchaser can thus be sure of the identity of the horse being bought or sold.

b. When horses are given influenza inoculations, they will be issued with a registration card. This card bears a description of the horse, along with a series of outline diagrams on which the horse's markings are drawn and the position of whorls noted. The date of the injection given is written in, the veterinary surgeon signs the card and stamps it with an official stamp from their surgery. This card then provides proof of the horse's flu vaccination status, as well as working as an identity record. Again, this is helpful when buying or selling horses. At official competitions, which require the horse to have up-to-date inoculations, this card must be produced on demand. The horse's tetanus inoculations are also included on this card.

c. The BHD (British Horse Database) will register all horses. This is another way of providing your horse with some type of identification documents.

Helpful Hints and Exam Technique.

1. If asked to describe a horse, make sure you are observant and look at both sides of the horse so that you don't miss a freeze mark or any other marking.

2 Psychology and Behavioural Problems

By learning about the natural instincts of the horse and how domesticated horses of different types and ages may behave in various situations, and also why they do so, we can begin to understand equine behaviour. This, in turn, will aid safe and effective working practices with the horse as well as helping the individual to cope with horses which have developed behavioural problems. It will also encourage us to create a happy environment for the horse, which will help to minimise the likelihood of horses developing behavioural problems in the first place.

STAGES III and IV

1. The Stabled Horse Turned Out to Graze

a. Many horses are stabled and only turned out to graze for a few hours each day. This can create a number of problems, especially as some horses may have vices or characteristics which make them unsuitable to turn out with other horses.

b. Turning out a variety of different horses together each day will lead to excitable behaviour (squealing, kicking, biting and cantering around) as the horses introduce themselves to each other and establish who is "boss". This is an undesirable situation for turning out fit and valuable horses as they may easily sustain an injury and be off work for weeks or months.

c. Some horses may behave well when turned out on their own. They will, however, miss out on social contact with other horses, which can be relaxing and beneficial to a fit horse in hard work.

3

   d. Other horses, when turned out on their own, will pace the fence, gallop around the field calling, and generally show signs of distress. This is of no benefit and is likely to be harmful to the horse if it uses up large amounts of nervous energy or possibly attempts to jump out of the field.

   e. If the horse is normally happy turned out on its own, don't forget to consider the weather. If it is wet and windy and the horse is miserable, it will cease grazing and stand at the gate or in the most sheltered part of the field, head down, tucked up, gradually getting colder.

   f. Turning the horse out with a mature and quiet companion (that is unshod behind) can be a good solution. The same companion may not get on well with all the horses you need to turn out. If you have a large yard, be prepared to select a different companion for some horses.

   g. It is ideal if you have two or three horses which get on well and can be turned out regularly together.

   h. It is generally safer to turn mares and geldings out separately if you have several of each. This will avoid the problems caused by geldings fighting over the mares when they are in season.

   i. One gelding turned out with several mares will probably be a workable combination, but one mare with several geldings will probably not work.

   j. If the horses don't appear to get on, try to determine which horse is causing the problem. It may be that one of them is particularly dominant and inclined to kick and fight. A horse of this type is a candidate for turning out with one tough companion!

   k. Horses which gallop around, risking injury, for the first few minutes of their turn out time, will benefit from being turned out after exercise when they are less full of energy. Brushing boots will also help to protect their limbs and if they are hungry they are more likely to settle quickly and graze.

   l. Only mix young and old horses together in the field if there are several youngsters and several older horses. The youngsters can play, while the older horses have a quieter time. Turning out a single youngster with an old horse may lead to the older horse being harassed, which, in turn, may lead to it kicking and injuring the youngster.

m. A horse seen to crib or wind suck in the field will be a bad influence on others. Again, it would be better to turn it out separately.

n. Rigs and stallions pose a different problem. They could savage a gelding turned out in the same field and can only be turned out with mares if you intend to breed from them. Ideally, a stallion can be turned out in a secure paddock overlooking the yard where it is normally stabled. Here he can watch over his herd while enjoying a certain amount of freedom.

STAGES III and IV

2. Stable Vices

Weaving

a. A highly strung horse, prone to weaving, should not be stabled where there is a tremendous amount of activity taking place.

b. Weaving usually starts when a horse is stabled where it can frequently see other horses leaving the yard, going to the field or going out for exercise. In its desire to go with these horses, it begins to weave from side to side as it cannot get through the barrier of its stable door which is stopping it from following.

Anti-weaving bars with optional inset which can be fitted to create a full grid

c. Once it begins to weave habitually, it will be seen to do this whenever there is activity it would like to be involved in or whenever anything exciting is happening, for example at feeding times, or when a nearby hunt can be heard.

d. If stabled in a peaceful corner, with a companion, it is more likely to feel relaxed and therefore stand quietly.

e. Horses which weave excessively can put strain on their forelimbs and wear their shoes unevenly.

f. In most cases weaving bars fixed to the stable door will prevent the problem, but those with a particularly bad habit may stand behind the bars and continue to weave.

Cribbing/Windsucking

a. In more natural circumstances, the horse would be grazing for most of the day. When we replace part of its hay/grass diet with concentrated feed and keep the horse in the stable, we deprive it of the opportunity to graze.

b. The horse's instinctive need to be chewing can lead to chewing at any available woodwork. Once this has become a habit, it can lead on to sucking at the wood and, ultimately, windsucking.

Crib-biting and wind sucking

c. When windsucking, the horse tenses its neck muscles while gripping the stable door or some other solid object with its teeth, and then swallows air down into its stomach.

d. Some horses develop the windsucking habit to the extent that they swallow air without having to grip anything with their teeth. They just arch their necks and gulp the air down.

e. In the early stages the problem can be combated by covering all wooden or chewable surfaces with metal strips or foul-tasting substances.

f. Once the horse has begun to swallow air, a cribbing strap can be fitted. This strap buckles around the horse's throat where it sits comfortably until the horse tries to tense its muscles ready to swallow air. The muscles are restricted by the strap so the horse is unable to complete the process. However, in practice this strap often works initially then the horse seems to become accustomed to it and learns to complete the procedure despite it.

g. As a final resort, in particularly bad cases, there is an operation which involves removing pieces of muscle, and the nerve which supplies them, from the underside of the neck. The operation is not always successful.

Anti-crib-biting/windsucking strap

h. Cribbing can be dangerous to the horse if it gets splinters in its mouth or swallows them. It will also cause abnormal wear of the incisor teeth.

i. It is sometimes thought that windsuckers suffer from colic and unthriftiness. However, this is rarely the case. The most detrimental effect is likely to be the overdevelopment of the underline neck muscles.

j. Try to prevent these problems in the first place by feeding little and often, turning out frequently and providing companionship.

k. Some horses benefit from playthings in their stable, for example a rubber ring or small car tyre, which the horse can pick up or chew without coming to any harm.

Box Walking

a. This is a less common stable vice shown by some horses who become very restless when confined for long periods and take to walking round and round their boxes.

b. The bedding becomes trampled and churned up while the horse can lose weight and put undue strain on its limbs as it is constantly turning in a small space.

c. Once again, the horse needs more freedom and companionship.

3. The Horse when Ridden

Many different factors will affect the horse's behaviour when ridden, for example the mood and character of both horse and rider, as well as the situation and task to be tackled. Remember that, when handling horses, we take the place of the leader of the herd. If the horse is confident in us as its leader, it will do as we ask. When it loses confidence in us, problems begin.

STAGES III and IV

Schooling

a. The problems encountered when riding out can also occur when schooling, whether you are riding in an indoor/outdoor school, working in the field or jump schooling.

b. Remember the horse's instincts when you are schooling. It is instinctive for it to run away from danger. If you frighten or confuse it, therefore, it is bound to try to take flight. This may take the form of a sudden spook.

c. Spooking can be particularly irritating when you are trying to get a horse to concentrate on dressage. Think the problem through rather than just reacting with a reprimand. For example, if the horse repeatedly spooks in one corner of the school and you reprimand it with the stick each time, the horse will begin to anticipate being hit and will make even more of a fuss.

d. When the horse spooks, ride it firmly forward, turning its head away from the spooky corner. Avoid the area initially while you regain the horse's concentration, then gradually work towards the problem corner, using a movement like leg-yield or shoulder-in so that the horse doesn't have a chance to think about the imaginary "bogey man".

e. There may sometimes be a genuine problem, like an object the horse hasn't seen before. In this situation, it is only fair to let the horse have a look at the object that is worrying it.

f. The instinct to follow others and to communicate with strange horses when they meet will also affect schooling. When you first school a young horse among a group of other horses, it will be confused and worried by horses passing from different directions. Again, a reprimand will only serve to panic the horse. Work to reassure it and it will quickly settle.

g. Likewise, when the horse first goes to a show it will be looking at all the strange horses, sights and sounds. It will gain confidence from a firm but reassuring rider.

h. Confusing situations will lead to tension in the horse. Tension can also be due to overfeeding, long periods in the stable, poor stable management, etc. When the horse is tense, it will react sharply and find it difficult to concentrate. Again, the rider needs to be aware that the horse is tense, and not make too many demands on it until the tension has subsided.

i. Tension, confusion, and therefore fear, are also the reason why a horse will rush its fences when jumping. A young horse, asked to jump big fences before it has gained balance and confidence over small fences, will rush and use speed to try and launch itself over the fence.

j. Likewise, if the horse experiences pain when jumping, it may rush. The pain could be due, among other things, to an unbalanced rider or pain in the horse's back.

k. This, in turn, can lead to the horse refusing to jump. Often, older horses, which have jumped happily for many years, can develop soundness problems with age that lead to pain when jumping. For example, in its early stages navicular disease may not make the horse obviously lame but the horse may feel pain when it lands after a fence. Hence it refuses to jump.

l. Once again, the rider needs to consider why the horse rushed or refused to jump the fence. Was the horse in pain, frightened, confused?

m. If the horse behaves in a different manner from normal in any schooling or riding out situation, the rider should immediately question why. Could the horse be unwell, suffering discomfort, be in season or physically stressed?

n. A mare in season can behave as normal but some become sensitive and inclined to buck, while others become quiet and lazy. If they are affected by being in season, don't expect them to perform at their best.

o. Any horse could suffer permanent damage, either physical or mental, by demands being made when it is not in good health.

Follow-up Work to Confirm Knowledge and Experience

1. Keeping the horse's natural instincts uppermost in your mind, observe horses in as many different situations as possible – in the stable yard, in the field, at shows, at stud farms, at sales – and keep asking yourself why those particular horses are behaving in that particular way.

2. When working with your own horses, if you come across any problems, try to analyse how you could improve the horse's environment with due regard for natural instincts and see if you can successfully solve the problem.

Helpful Hints and Exam Technique

1. When answering questions in a theoretical situation, try to picture horses with which you have had experience. Whenever possible, answer the questions by using real examples. In this way your answers are more likely to have an authentic ring to them, showing the examiner that you really are experienced and have a good understanding of the subject.
2. Try not to disagree with other candidates' answers. If someone makes a statement with which you disagree, state your own opinion but remember that they may have experienced different situations to you and it may be that you are both correct. There are many situations in which there is no one correct answer, where everyone's comments can be valid.

3 The Field-kept Horse and Grassland Management

The needs of a horse at grass are many and varied. Through good management and regular maintenance, we can provide a horse with a suitable environment and good grazing

STAGES III and IV

1. Improving the Grazing

The improvement and maintenance of pasture should be carried out by, or with advice from, an expert. By learning a little about the expert's job, you will know when to seek advice and when to take action.

Where to Go for Advice

a. Many companies which have commercial interests in agriculture will offer an advisory service. However, their expertise is often more closely linked with cattle and sheep, rather than with horses. It is important to discuss your specific requirements with the advisor.

b. ADAS (The Agricultural Development and Advisory Service) is one body which can be approached. (Use the telephone directory to find your local advisor.) They will visit, look at the area, note the types of grass and herbs present and take soil samples for analysis. This will be followed by a report advising you of the action to be taken.

c. Other bodies to approach include seed merchants, fertiliser companies and farming contractors, or you may be lucky enough to have an independent equine grassland consultant in your area. Their specialist knowledge should prove invaluable.

STAGE IV

2. Soil Analysis

a. There are many different types of soil. As laypeople, the main categories we are likely to recognise are clay, sandy, gravelly, chalky and peaty

b. Top soils vary in depth, so the type of subsoil may not be immediately apparent.

c. Clay is heavy and dense. It holds nutrients well, but can become waterlogged. Being dense, it is difficult for air, and therefore oxygen, to get into the soil.

d. Chalk also holds water. However, providing the top soil is free-draining, the chalk will provide nutrients and water for the grasses to utilise.

e. Sandy/gravelly soil allows water to drain through easily. However, this can lead to it becoming too acidic as nutrients are washed out.

f. Grass grows best in soil with a pH of approximately 6.5. This is a measure of the soil's acidity.

g. Peaty soil tends to be acidic. It is formed in naturally wet areas and holds water like a sponge, making it unsuitable for grazing pasture.

h. The best type of soil for horse grazing is that which has plenty of nutrients for plant growth and drains well without becoming too dry or too acidic.

STAGES III and IV

3. Drainage

a. For good grass growth there must be a suitable balance of air and water in the soil. Air is necessary for microbes which are constantly breaking down organic matter, and the water is necessary for plant life. Too much or too little water will upset the balance. Hence the need for good drainage.

b. Ditches around the field allow water to drain away providing they are kept clear. Regular maintenance is necessary. Check for blockages in pipes leading into ditches as well as in the ditches themselves. Make sure ditches in neighbouring fields are also cleared as blockages there will also prevent water from running away.

c. In some heavily grazed paddocks the soil becomes so compacted that water no longer drains through. In this situation subsoiling may be a fairly simple way of improving the drainage. Plough shares are pulled through the subsoil to break it up, causing a minimum of disturbance to the surface turfs, but allowing water to drain through again.

d. If fields are very wet, underground drainage may be needed. This is a major undertaking. First, the top soil is removed. Then channels are dug, often in a herring-bone pattern, in which pipes are laid. The pipes may be made of clay or plastic, with small holes in them to allow water through. The pipes are then covered with gravel and the top soil will be put back. Water should now drain through into the pipes which will lead away to ditches.

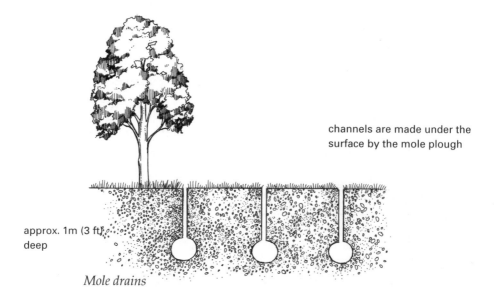

channels are made under the surface by the mole plough

approx. 1m (3 ft) deep

Mole drains

e. In clay soils "mole" drainage may be used A mole plough will pull the moles through the soil approximately 1 m (3 ft) below the surface. The channel made may remain viable for several years. However, in drought conditions the clay may dry out and crack open and this would destroy the mole drains. This type of drainage is not suitable for sandy soils as, unlike clay, the soil would immediately collapse back into the channels.

STAGES III and IV

4. Fertiliser

a. Organic fertiliser, produced from living creatures, contains a range of nutrients which are released slowly into the soil. Specific nutrients required cannot be accurately applied this way.

b. Farmyard manure (FYM) is one type of organic fertiliser. Poultry manure may contain too much nitrogen which will scorch the grazing, while pig manure contains too much copper. Cattle manure is best for horse grazing, although it may take some time to rot down into the soil.

c. Organic seaweed fertiliser may also be used, although nutrient levels vary in each batch.

d. Compound inorganic fertilisers usually contain the three main elements referred to as N (nitrogen) P (phosphorus) and K (potash). These nutrients are released quickly into the soil for the grass to utilise. This can lead to grass growth which is too lush for horses.

e. Fertilisers containing only one of these nutrients are referred to as "straights".

f. Nitrogen is basically responsible for the leaf growth of the grass, and phosphorus and potash for general nutrients and root growth.

g. Semi-organic fertilisers combine some of the good points from the types above. Nutrients are released fairly slowly and, being partly organic, this fertiliser encourages natural activity within the soil. At the same time, the amounts of NPK needed can be fairly accurately applied.

h. Fertilisers can be applied by broadcast scattering or by direct drilling. Direct drilling puts the fertiliser at root level where it is really needed, and can be done in combination with direct drill seeding.

i. Soils which become too acidic will need a dressing of lime every three years or so, depending on how quickly nutrients are being washed out of the soil. Weak and patchy growth of grass, along with the appearance of weeds, may be signs that the soil is too acid. Lime should be applied in dry weather to help to prevent it from sticking to and coating the grass. As horses will need to be kept off the field, apply lime in autumn or early spring, when horses may be stabled or confined to one area of winter grazing.

j. Having applied lime or fertiliser, you hope for gentle rainfall to wash it into the soil. The horses will need to be kept off the field until it has all washed in.

k. Always seek professional advice before fertilising and remember that severe growth and digestive disorders can result from overfertilising grazing intended for horses.

STAGES III and IV

5. Weed Control

a. Where weeds are present in only small amounts, they should be pulled or dug up before they go to seed. The plants should then be burnt to prevent their seeds from germinating elsewhere.

b. Larger quantities of weeds will need to be sprayed with a herbicide. Different varieties need to be sprayed at various stages of growth. For example, ragwort should be sprayed early in the growing season, when at the rosette stage, but nettles should be sprayed in midsummer when the plant is well developed.

c. The herbicide supplier, or ADAS, will be able to recommend the type and quantity of herbicide required for the job.

d. As well as other factors, weather conditions need to be taken into account to make sure harmful chemicals are only spread over the intended area. For this reason, spraying, whether with tractor-drawn equipment or a back-pack sprayer, should only be undertaken by a qualified expert.

e. Horses will need to be kept off the sprayed area for a period of time, preferably until the weeds have disintegrated, to avoid them eating the wilted remains.

f. Weed control is an ongoing problem. Seeds of the offending plants may remain in the ground for several years. However, repeated attempts to remove them should lead to reduced numbers each year. Of course, problems will arise if neighbouring fields are badly infested with weeds as the seeds will blow over and spread on to your fields.

g. Some of the most common weeds, like docks and ragwort, are covered by a regulation called the Injurious Weeds Order. Landowners must keep these weeds under control. Failure to do so may lead to them being fined.

STAGES III and IV

6. Grasses and Herbs

a. Good grazing will consist of grasses which are palatable to the horse, hardy, disease-resistant and digestible. The yield should not be too high, however, as horses shouldn't have lush grazing. The various grasses should have staggered flowering dates in order to provide continuous grazing throughout the growing season.

b. To provide these qualities, a good grazing mixture will include more than one variety of perennial rye grass, creeping red fescue, crested dog's tail, meadow grass and wild white clover. Timothy and cocksfoot may also be included.

c. Perennial rye grass grows almost everywhere in Britain. It is very persistent providing it is well fertilised.

d. Creeping red fescue copes well in the conditions found on hill pastures. It is of good nutritional value and palatable to the horse.

e. Crested dog's tail is very palatable.

f. Meadow grass is palatable and gives a good base to the sward. (The "sward" is the term used to describe the collective growth of grass and other herbage.)

g. Wild white clover is deep rooted and improves the soil as the roots introduce more nitrogen.

h. Only small amounts of clover are required as an excess can provide the horse with too much protein.

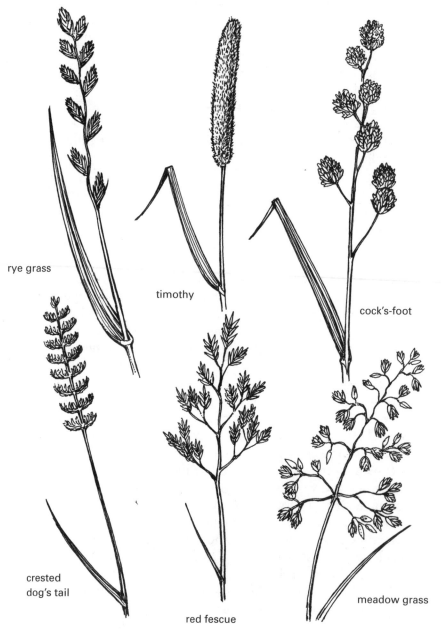

rye grass

timothy

cock's-foot

crested
dog's tail

red fescue

meadow grass

Nutritious grasses

i. Many horses enjoy grazing herbs. These can be included in the seed mixture or planted as a strip along one edge of the field. Herbs which may be included are dandelions, wild garlic, plantains, chicory, sheep's parsley and comfrey. They help to provide the horse with nutrients and some people feel that herbs have healing qualities which may help the horses to resist disease.

j. Seed mixes used will vary according to requirements. For example, stud farm grazing, riding areas, hay crops and general grazing will all require slightly different qualities from the grasses. Many seed merchants will supply mixes especially designed for your needs.

k. Seeds may be sown by broadcast or drilling methods. Various types of machinery are used to scatter the seed (broadcast) over the surface or drill the seed directly into the soil. If the seed is broadcast, it must then be rolled into the soil. The drilling method is more accurate.

l. Reseeding does not only take place on newly ploughed soil. Established pastures can be reseeded by either method in order to introduce more and/or better grasses to the existing herbage. The whole pasture may need reseeding or maybe just patches which have become poached.

STAGES III and IV

7. Further Procedures Requiring the Use of Machinery

Ploughing

a. Occasionally a pasture deteriorates into such poor condition that it will need to be ploughed up.

b. As it takes several years for grasses to become established enough to provide good grazing, the ploughing option is only undertaken in extreme conditions.

c. First, the existing herbage is destroyed. A substance such as Paraquat, which will kill all types of grass and weeds, will be used. This will help to prevent the poor grasses and weeds from growing back after ploughing.

e. In the spring, the field will then be sown and fertilised.

f. Once the grass has grown to a few centimetres in length, it is a good idea to introduce sheep to graze the field. They don't cause as much damage as horses and cattle. Keeping the grass short will encourage a thick sward.

Harrowing

a. Chain harrows can be pulled behind a tractor, Land-Rover, horse or any vehicle with a tow bar and the ability to cope with the terrain.
b. When there are several horses in a large field, it is not practical to shovel up droppings. Harrowing the field will accelerate the rotting process.
c. Harrowing pulls dead tufts of herbage out of the soil. This leaves room for the healthy grass to flourish.

Chain harrow

Rolling

a. After broadcast seeding, the seeds are rolled in order to push them firmly into the ground. This will help to prevent them from being blown away or eaten by birds, as well as helping the seed to germinate and take root.

Two rollers – one heavy, one light

b. Rolling presses the roots of existing grass firmly into the soil. This encourages tillering. Tillering is the process by which grass sends out side shoots, thus creating a thicker sward.
c. Grass likes to grow in quite firmly packed soil, whereas many weeds flourish in loose soil. Therefore, rolling can improve grass growth while discouraging weeds.

Topping

a. Topping is the process of cutting the grass, either by mowing with a tractor-drawn mower or by grazing with livestock.
b. Keeping the grass short encourages it to tiller and grow more thickly. Again, this creates a dense sward.
c. If you are lucky enough to have a rested field of quite lush grazing, sheep and/or cattle will top it well. They will remove some of the lush growth, help to reduce the worm burden and graze fairly evenly. This will leave the pasture less lush for the horses to graze and encourage them to graze the area evenly.

STAGES III and IV

8. Acreage and Year-round Maintenance

a. The size of field required will depend on many factors. For example, the size and number of horses and ponies, quality of the grazing, whether the horses live out all year round and weather conditions.
b. As an approximate guide, a small pony will need a minimum of a 0.2–0.4 hectare ($\frac{1}{2}$–1 acre) area to live in, and a horse will need 0.4–0.8 hectare (1–2 acres).
c. These plots need to be divided into two or more paddocks which can be rested in turn. This gives the rested area a period of time for regrowth. At the same time, you can carry out any necessary maintenance.
d. Horses will inflict a great deal of damage on the field in winter weather conditions. For this reason, it is better to damage just one paddock so that the other paddocks can be preserved for spring

and summer grazing. The winter paddock can then be repaired and rested in the spring.

e. When dividing fields, there are several points to consider, for example access, water supply, shelter and fencing. So plan your fence lines to incorporate all of these into each paddock.

f. If installing a water supply or shelter, position them in the fence line between two fields, in order to service both fields at once.

g. If you have more acreage than you need for grazing, it may be possible to take a crop of hay from one field. This is a risky business, however, as weather conditions in the UK are often unsuitable for drying the hay. If you are relying on contractors to do the work, you will find that they have many fields to cut, turn and bale. If your hay is last on the list, it could be the batch that gets rained on prior to baling, which could render it useless as horse hay – a very expensive exercise for no return.

h. If some of your grazing is low lying and inclined to be very wet in the winter, don't forget to plan your rotation of grazing so that this area is used when dry. Hill pasture may be drier in winter but is also more exposed and colder. Once again, plan ahead before moving your horses from one field to another.

i. Keep a check on drainage channels and ditches throughout the year. They are likely to become blocked with leaves and other dead herbage at the end of autumn so make a point of clearing them before the winter sets in.

j. Fertiliser is most effectively applied in spring and autumn. Again, weather conditions will dictate. Taking a tractor on to a waterlogged pasture will just churn up the turf so begin fertilising as soon as the pasture is dry enough. This may be as early as February. Look out for a wet autumn so that you don't leave it too late to get the tractor on to the field before wet weather sets in.

k. Early spring is the best time to reseed as the improving weather conditions will encourage good growth. Alternatively, reseed in the autumn and the new grass will flourish the following spring.

l. Keep checking for the appearance of weeds. If they are becoming fewer in number each year, your plan of action must be working.

m. Harrow the fields regularly throughout the year, especially after the horses have been moved on to another pasture.

Follow-up Work to Confirm Knowledge and Experience

1. Observation of the methods, procedures, systems and materials in use around you, at different farms and equestrian centres, is the only way to gain first hand experience.
2. If you live in a suitable area, observe the year-round procedures taking place on surrounding farmland or at any equestrian centres you visit. Question these procedures and make sure you understand what is taking place and why.

Helpful Hints and Exam Technique

1. Always try to use your own experiences to help you to put your points across. For example, if discussing types of soil at Stage IV, talk about the soil type you keep your own horses on. This should help you to recall information when nerves are slowing your thinking process.

4   Feeding

In order to be able to feed suitable types and quantities of feed to a variety of different horses and ponies, it is necessary to recognise different feedstuffs, good and bad quality and understand the horse's nutritional needs.

STAGES III and IV

1. Nutrients Required in the Horse's Diet

Water

a. Water is essential for all of the body functions.
b. Approximately 70 per cent of the horse's bodyweight is water.
c. Water is lost via the skin when the horse sweats, via the lungs when the horse breathes, and via urine and faeces.
d. The water lost is constantly replaced when the horse eats feeds like grass which has a high water content, and when drinking.
e. An insufficient supply of water will lead to dehydration.

Fibre

a. As the horse's digestive system works at its best when supplied with plenty of fibre, it is an important element in the diet.
b. Without fibre, cereals can form into a doughy mass which is difficult to digest. By mixing fibre with the concentrates, the feed passes through the system in a more easily digested form.
c. Fibre which is digestible is also a source of energy.

Carbohydrate

a. Carbohydrates provide the horse with energy.
b. Some feeds provide carbohydrate in the form of sugars and starches. These are fairly easily and quickly digested in the small intestine.
c. Another source of carbohydrate is cellulose. This is more difficult to digest and is broken down more slowly in the large intestine.
d. Feeding too much carbohydrate for the horse's needs will make it overweight as the excess will be stored as fat.

Protein

a. Proteins are used for growth and repair. All body cells are made from proteins.
b. Youngstock need more protein in their diet in order to be able to grow and develop.
c. Mares in foal need more protein for the development of the foal and the production of milk.
d. Mature horses need enough protein to maintain normal healthy tissue.
e. Too little protein will lead to poor growth and development, while an excess of protein will be converted and stored as fat.

Vitamins and Minerals

Vitamins and minerals are essential for normal body functions. Their roles are many and varied. The following is a summary of some of the most obvious and important roles that they play.

VITAMINS
Vitamins are divided into two main groups: water-soluble and fat-soluble vitamins.

Fat-soluble vitamins include:
- Vitamin A – This is necessary for good vision, reproduction, strong feet and growth in general, resistance to disease and healthy mucous membranes.

- Vitamin D – This aids the utilisation of calcium and phosphorus and is therefore essential for healthy bone.
- Vitamin E – Needed for good performance and fertility. It is also linked with helping to prevent problems such as azoturia.
- Vitamin K – Essential for effective blood clotting.

a. A shortage of any of these vitamins will lead to weakness and poor development in the areas mentioned.
b. Vitamins which are fat soluble can be stored in the horse's body.

Water-soluble vitamins include:
- The vitamin B complex – These play many important roles linked with appetite, energy and growth.
- Folic acid – Closely linked with the B complex and needed for red blood cell production.
- Biotin – Needed for the formation of good horn.
- Vitamin C – Needed for healthy skin, bone, cartilage and connective tissue.

a. Again, a shortage of any of these vitamins will lead to poor performance. For example, a lack of B12 and folic acid will cause loss of appetite and anaemia.

MINERALS
Minerals needed in the horse's diet are divided into major minerals and trace minerals.

The major minerals include:
- Calcium – Needed for bone formation, nerve and muscle function.
- Phosphorus – Also needed for bone formation. It can inhibit the uptake of calcium. For this reason, the horse should receive a calcium to phosphorus ratio of approximately 2:1.
- Sodium, chloride and potassium – All are needed to keep the body fluids balanced. A shortage could lead to dehydration.
- Magnesium – Linked with many body functions.

The trace minerals include:
- Copper, zinc, manganese, iron, iodine, cobalt and selenium.

a. A deficiency of any of these trace minerals can lead to problems such as weight loss, poor appetite, lameness and anaemia.
b. An excess of any minerals may have a toxic effect. This will result in the horse's system being poisoned, causing as much, or more, harm as a shortage of any of the minerals.
c. As vitamins and minerals interact with other elements in the horse's diet, too much or too little of them can have an adverse effect on the horse's health.

Fats

a. Fats provide a very concentrated form of energy.
b. They are a good energy source for endurance horses.

STAGES III and IV

2. Feeds and their Nutritional Value

Grazing

a. Young grass consists of a large proportion of water.
b. Fibre is present, some of which is digestible and some not. As the grass gets older, more stemmy and less leafy, it will contain more indigestible fibre.
c. There is carbohydrate and protein in grass. Again, as the grass ages, the nutrient levels fall.
d. Apart from some of the B group of vitamins, which the horse synthesises for itself in the gut, grass provides all the necessary vitamins.
e. Most minerals will also be available, but a mineral lick can be provided to make up for any which are not present.
f. If the horse is provided with good quality grazing, it should be receiving all necessary nutrients for the maintenance of good health.

Hay/Haylage

a. Hay will contain most of the nutrients found in good quality grazing. It will not have the high water content, and the carbohydrate and protein levels will depend on how leafy the grass was at the time of cutting.

b. Protein levels in the grass drop after it has gone to seed, so hay should be cut just before this happens. This is difficult to judge with meadow hay as the variety of grasses contained in it will go to seed at different times, but it is easier to judge with seed hay. For this reason, seed hay usually has a higher level of protein than meadow hay.

c. Grass grown for making haylage is cut earlier than grass being used for hay, therefore haylage contains more protein and carbohydrate .

d. Haylage also contains a higher percentage of water than hay.

e. Providing a horse is fed good quality hay or haylage and is provided with a salt/mineral lick and plenty of water, it should be receiving a good balance of nutrients for the maintenance of general health.

Cereals – Oats/Barley/Maize

a. These grains contain approximately twice as much energy as hay.

b. They are all low in calcium and have a high level of phosphorus, therefore horses fed on grain need their calcuim intake made up elsewhere in the diet.

c. Oats have quite a high proportion of fibre because of the separate outer husk which can be seen with the grain.

d. Compared with barley and maize, oats have a slightly higher percentage of oil and protein.

e. Barley has a similar feed value to oats but is slightly lower in oil, protein and fibre, and higher in energy.

f. Maize has similar feed values to barley but has a slightly higher oil content.

g. Cereals will provide the working horse with energy but need to be combined with other feeds if the horse is to receive a balanced diet.

COOKED CEREALS

a. Whole barley is sometimes boiled and fed. The cooking process makes the grain more digestible.

b. The cooked starch can be broken down and digested in the small intestine, which is preferable to it being fermented in the large intestine.

c. The large intestine is not designed to break down large quantities of starch and its presence there can be lead to serious digestive upsets.

d. Pre-cooked cereals can be purchased in the form of flaked maize or barley. A steaming process is used to cook the grain.

e. Micronised barley is cooked by a microwave process; extruded barley is cooked using steam, water and a rapid heating process.

f. The cooking processes make these feeds more nutritionally acceptable to the horse's digestive system.

Sugar Beet

a. As sugar beet must be soaked before feeding, it provides the horse with water and a succulent feed.

b. It is high in fibre and a good source of energy and protein.

Cubes and Coarse Mixes

a. Each different type of cube or coarse mix is formulated to meet the feeding requirements of horses in a variety of work.

b. They provide a good balance of nutrients for the horse's needs.

c. Some may be fed on their own, while others are designed to be fed as part of the ration.

d. In general, they range from high-fibre/low-energy feeds for ponies to low-fibre/high-energy and protein feeds for performance horses.

e. If you are competing with your horse, check that the feed you are giving is guaranteed to be free from substances prohibited under BSJA, FEI and Jockey Club rules.

Bran

a. Bran is low in nutritional value. The fibre and protein which it contains tend to be rather indigestible.

Some Less Common Feeds – Straw/Hydroponic Grass/Lucerne/ Naked Oats

a. Straw has a very low nutritional value but is a source of fibre. It is less likely to contain fungal spores, which makes it cleaner than hay.
b. Hydroponic grass is grown from barley grains in a specially controlled environment. Its feed value is similar to that of young grass. It can be a useful dust-free part of the stabled horse's diet.
c. Lucerne may be fed as a hay or as cubes. Compared to seed or meadow hay, it provides more protein, energy, calcium and some vitamins.
d. Naked oats are grown in such a way that we end up with a grain without the outer husk that we usually see as part of the product. These oats have higher protein and energy values and are designed to be fed in small quantities to high-performance horses.

STAGE IV

3. Additions to the Diet

The following is a selection of supplements, additives and extras which can make useful additions to the feeds of horses in a variety of work.

Vitamin and Mineral Supplements

a. If you think your horse is lacking something in its diet, you should seek veterinary advice. If your vet thinks it is necessary, he or she will advise which supplement to use.

b. Supplements can be purchased from most saddlers and feed merchants. Each different type will list the vitamins and minerals included in it on the packet.
c. Never mix two different supplements of this sort as you may end up overdosing your horse.
d. You may be better off feeding a supplement which provides one particular element rather than a wide range mixed together.

Biotin

a. Biotin is one of the supplements which provides a more specific addition to the diet.
b. It is often fed to promote healthy hoof growth.

Salt

a. Most horse diets are likely to be deficient in salt.
b. Add common salt to the feed daily. A horse in medium work should have approximately 20 g (roughly 1 tablespoon) and a horse in hard work approximately 40–60 g (roughly 2–3 tablespoons).
c. It is always a good idea to provide a salt lick for both stabled and field-kept horses.

Oil

a. Vegetable and corn oil can be purchased from a supermarket. As much as 200 ml ($\frac{1}{4}$ pt) may be added to the diet daily.
b. Cod liver oil is often used. However, it has a strong smell which discourages many horses from eating it, even when only small quantities are added to the feed.
c. Oils improve the general condition of the horse, as well as providing vitamins and a concentrated source of energy.
d. Again, check the type and quantity of oil with your vet.

Keep Blocks

a. These are rather like coarse mixes or cubes. They are solid blocks, which provide a concentrate ration that the horse can lick and chew at.
b. Keep blocks are useful for horses kept at grass in the winter. Instead of bringing the horses in two or three times a day for feeds, they can help themselves in the field.
c. Just like cubes or coarse mixes, the keep block will contain a ration which, with the addition of hay, should provide the horse with a balanced diet.

Molasses

a. Molasses will provide an additional source of energy because of its sugar content.
b. However, it is generally fed simply as a sweet and tasty extra to encourage the horse to eat up.
c. It is used with chaff to make mollichaff and is added to most coarse mixes.

Chaff

a. Chaff is chopped hay or straw or a mixture of the two. It is often molassed as mentioned above.
b. It is a useful addition to any concentrate ration as it encourages the horse to chew the feed thoroughly, and mixes with the ration to promote thorough digestion.

Soya Bean Meal

Soya bean meal is a good source of protein for those horses which require a high protein ration.

Linseed

Feeding linseed is another way of adding oil to the feed to improve the coat. It is also a source of protein and vitamin B.

Milk Pellets

Youngsters are sometimes fed milk pellets to provide them with more protein. Horses lose the ability to digest milk when about three years old.

Peas and Beans

Coarse mixes often contain peas and beans which have been micronised. They are high in protein and energy.

Limestone Flour

As already mentioned, cereal diets are low in calcium. Limestone flour will provide extra calcium.

Electrolytes

a. Electrolytes are the salts lost when a horse sweats excessively. They need to be replaced in order to prevent dehydration.
b. Your vet is the best person to provide you with electrolytes to put in the horse's drinking water or feed.
c. Electrolytes are also lost if a horse has diarrhoea as this causes the loss of large amounts of water.

Probiotics

a. These are purchased in the form of a paste or mix to add to the feed.
b. Probiotics are bacteria (of various types) which are fed to the horse to aid the bacteria already present in the horse's gut.
c. The hard-working horse is subjected to abnormal stresses which can upset the normal balance of microbes in the gut. Feeding probiotics can help to re-establish a good balance.
d. Live yoghurt has a similar effect and may be fed if your vet advises.

e. The balance of gut microbes is also affected by antibiotics which may be given when a horse is unwell. This will affect the horse's supply of vitamin B which is normally synthesised by microbes in the gut. Probiotics can help to return the balance to normal.

f. Yeast may also be used to encourage microbes which digest fibre in the gut.

g. Seek veterinary advice before feeding probiotics.

Herbs

a. It is thought that modern farming methods have reduced the number and variety of herbs that were once present as part of the horse's grazing.

b. You can plant herbs and encourage them to grow in your fields and/or they can be fed dried as an addition to the concentrate ration.

c. Feeding herbs may be a way of helping to provide the horse with a more natural diet or at least to provide some of the natural elements that horses may once have eaten as part of their daily diet. This should help to improve the general health of the horse and its ability to resist disease.

d. There is little or no scientific evidence to back up claims made about herbs and their uses. Quantities recommended for horses are based upon the amounts found to be suitable for humans and then increased to take into account the extra bodyweight of the horse.

e. As a result, some companies which specialise in producing herbs for horses are now researching herbs to try to find scientific evidence to back up their claims.

f. Garlic is probably the most commonly used herb. It is said to help horses which suffer from respiratory disorders, be effective against some worms and have a cleansing effect on the blood.

g. Other herbs and herb mixes can be purchased. The beneficial effects of each will be detailed on their packaging.

h. Some coarse mixes have herbs included.

STAGES III and IV

4. Feeding for Individual Requirements

The usual rules of feeding apply when planning a feed chart for a particular horse. Work, type, temperament, etc. all need to be considered. If the diet is not correctly balanced for that horse, various problems may occur. The horse could become too lively, too fat, too thin. Its bones may be brittle and weak, its hoof growth poor or it may get colic and any number of other diet-related ailments.

Brood Mares

a. For the first two-thirds of the pregnancy, a brood mare should receive all her needs from good quality grazing.
b. In the last third of the pregnancy, the foal grows and develops more quickly and makes more demands on the mare.
c. The mare will require more protein and energy but should not be overfed to the point of getting fat.
d. Stud cubes should provide her with the correct balance of nutrients.
e. Limestone flour could be given to provide her with calcium which may otherwise be lacking in her diet.
f. As the foal gets larger and occupies much of the abdominal cavity, the mare may find that her appetite for bulky food decreases. If she eats less hay, her concentrate ration should be increased.
g. When the brood mare has foaled and is feeding her foal, she will need a little more protein in order to be able to produce a good supply of milk. Good spring grass should supply her with all she needs.
h. If spring grass is not available, soya bean meal may be added to her feeds as an extra source of protein.

Youngsters

a. Try to give them access to plenty of good grazing during the spring and summer.

b. In winter, a cube or coarse mix specially formulated for young-sters will help you to ensure that they are receiving a balanced diet.

c. They will need a higher level of protein and calcium than a mature horse but, as always, it is important not to overfeed. Too much concentrate may result in bone-related growth problems.

Competition Horses

a. When horses are required to work faster and harder, their concentrate ration is increased and their hay/fibre ration decreased. This is because large amounts of fibre in the gut lead to a large "grass belly". This is not conducive to fast work as it makes the horse more cumbersome and puts a strain on the heart and lungs.

b. It is during fast and hard work that horses may sweat and become dehydrated. It is important with all competition horses to ensure that they have a plentiful supply of fresh water. Endurance horses will need to drink during a ride, not just before and after.

c. The needs of each different type of competition horse will vary. All will need more carbohydrates for energy and more protein in their diets than a mature horse at rest. Again, cubes or coarse mixes which have been formulated for competition work will provide a balanced diet. Use a brand which states that it is free from substances prohibited under BSJA, FEI and Jockey Club rules.

Old Horses

a. In old age, one of the horse's main problems is its teeth. Providing its teeth are in good condition, it can continue to feed and maintain weight. Once its teeth are worn or lost, to the extent that it can no longer feed normally, it will lose weight rapidly.

b. Give softer, more easily digested feeds like flaked barley and soft meadow hay or haylage.

c. A horse will need more protein and calcium to maintain health in its old age.

Grass-kept and Resting Horses

a. If the horse or pony is not working, good grazing and a mineral lick should provide it with all its needs.
b. Many native ponies will need to have their grass intake rationed in order to stop them from getting too fat. They were bred to roam over mountains and moorland where grazing is sparse, so their systems are very adept at putting every mouthful of food to good use.
c. During the winter, when grazing is poor, hay will need to be fed. To make up for any nutrients which the hay lacks, feed low-energy cubes/coarse mix or a keep block. Remember that horses will drink more water when feeding on hay than when they were grazing good grass.
d. If the horse or pony is being worked, restrict its intake of grass if it is getting fat and feed a small concentrate ration for extra energy and protein; for example, 30–40 per cent of the horse's ration could be concentrate (work this out by estimating the horse's daily feed requirement in the usual way), while grazing provides the rest of the ration.
e. It is difficult to estimate how much grass the horse may be eating. If it is still getting too fat, try to restrict its grass intake. The best way to do this is to put the horse on poorer pasture or pasture which has already been well grazed by cattle or sheep. If you stable the horse to prevent it from grazing, you will find it will just gorge itself when turned out.
f. Most small ponies in light work will not need any extra feed.

STAGES III and IV

5. Additional Information

a. Feed should be stored in a cool, dry atmosphere. If it becomes damp or mouldy, it should not be fed.
b. Do not order and store more feed than you can use within three to four weeks. After this time its nutrient values will start to deteriorate. Some feeds will have a use-by date, as will vitamin and mineral supplements.

c. The feed room should be as vermin-proof as possible. All feed bins and containers must also be vermin-proof.

d. Make sure you have a routine for storing new feed so that older feedstuffs are used first.

Follow-up Work to Confirm Knowledge and Experience

1. When visiting different yards or trade stands at shows, look at all the different types of feed on offer to help you to become familiar with a wide range of feedstuffs.

2. Find out about feeding programmes in use with any horses you come across. Compare how different people feed horses of various sizes and types in different types of work. Look at these horses and their performance records to help you to decide if their feed programmes have been well worked out.

Helpful Hints and Exam Technique

1. In an exam situation candidates often come to grief when describing how much concentrate and hay they will feed a variety of horses. This is mainly caused by not relating what they actually feed to horses on a day-to-day basis to a quantity they can describe in words.

    It is vital that students practise weighing out quantities of all different types of feed, including hay and haylage. If students only give feeds that have been measured out for them, they may develop a good eye for the right quantity but how will they describe that quantity to their examiner?

2. Another common mistake is to refer to quantities required by the horse as percentages but then to be unable to work out the mathematics to convert these percentages into actual amounts of feed. Don't use this process if you cannot follow it through!

    You need to be able to express amounts in pounds or kilograms, it doesn't matter which, so some basic mathematical ability is required. For example, if you think a horse needs 12.7 kg (28 lb) of feed a day and half of that should be hay, then the horse will receive 6.3 kg (14 lb) of hay and 6.3 kg (14 lb) of concentrate. You then need to be able to divide the 6.3 kg (14 lb) of concentrates into three or four feeds. Three feeds of 1.8–2.3 kg (4–5 lb) is accurate enough.

5 Fitness Work / Preparation / Roughing Off/Different Disciplines

By working horses progressively and following a programme suited to the aims for that horse, we can keep horses healthy and sound in wind and limb while working them at the level required.

STAGES II and III

1. Bringing a Horse Up from Grass/Rest

An event horse will usually have a winter break and a hunter a summer break. An injured horse will be forced to rest during the healing of the injury and some horses may simply have a break when their owners go on holiday.

The time of year and type of rest period will influence the procedure to be followed in order to prepare the horse for work again. A summer holiday at grass means that the horse is likely to be a little overweight and in soft condition. However, its muscles, tendons and ligaments will be firmer than those of a horse that has been confined to box rest because of injury. Horses on winter holidays will have been given concentrate feeds and hay to make up for a lack of grazing, while horses on summer grazing will have to be reintroduced to this type of feed.

    a. Prior to starting the fitness programme, arrange for the vet to give any vaccinations due, for example, flu and tetanus. The vet can also recommend what type of wormer you should dose your horse with at this stage.

    b. Either the vet or a horse dentist should check the horse's teeth.

    c. Contact the farrier and have the horse shod. Stud holes may be needed from the beginning so that road studs can be used.

d. Order feed, hay/haylage and bedding.

e. Check that your stables are clean and in good repair.

f. Check that all your tack, rugs and accessories are clean, repaired where necessary and ready to use.

g. The horse that has been at grass should be brought into its stable for a short period each day. This will help it to adjust to standing in again. It can gradually be kept in for longer and longer periods. As it has been in a fresh outdoor environment, take care to keep the stable well ventilated and free from dust in order to avoid respiratory problems.

h. While standing in, the horse can also gradually be reintroduced to concentrate feed and hay. Start with small amounts, damp the feed and soak the hay.

i. Horses on winter holidays will probably have been stabled at night and are therefore already accustomed to points (g) and (h) above.

j. Begin grooming as it will take some time to clean all the grease from the coat, especially if the horse has a winter coat which you will need to clip in a few weeks' time. Do not clip until the horse has completed one or two weeks of its fitness programme. It will need its coat to keep it warm while it is only at the walking stage.

k. The mane and tail can gradually be pulled and the feathers trimmed.

l. Rub surgical spirit into areas of soft skin that need to be hardened ready to take the girth, saddle and bridle.

m. Introduce light rugs. This will help to improve the coat if you are coming into the summer months, and will prepare the horse for heavier rugs if you are heading for winter.

n. Finally, if you are hunting or competing, make sure you have paid your subscription, membership or entry fees.

STAGES II and III

2. The Fitness Programme

a. With the horse in a correct outline, steady and purposeful walking on firm ground will tone up muscles, tendons and ligaments, making them strong and ready for the work to follow. As work progresses, the efficiency of the heart and lungs will gradually improve.

b. Horses that are recovering from injury need a slow beginning to their fitness programme, with many weeks of walking. If recovering from tendon/ligament injury, they may need anything from four to eight weeks or even more, depending on the severity of the injury. Your vet will advise you.

c. Mature, experienced horses will need one to two weeks of walking. Start with half an hour and increase the time each day until you are walking for one to one and a half hours.

d. Always be aware of the type of ground you are working on. Soft, deep going will pull and strain tendons/muscles, especially when the horse is still in soft condition. A horse is also likely to overreach when its feet are held by deep mud.

e. Only walk, or trot very gently, for short periods when on hard ground and roads. The concussion created when the horse's hooves meet the hard ground can lead to strain and inflammation. Roads are also very slippery, which means that trotting can be dangerous.

f. Stony ground can cause bruised soles and uneven ground may cause a slip or trip, leading to strains.

g. Although lungeing is a strenuous activity, generally used when the horse is fairly fit, it may be necessary to lunge a very fresh horse before you ride it. Some horses take time to settle into the working routine. If they are inclined to buck and generally misbehave, it will be safer to lunge for 10–15 minutes first.

h. Continue to turn your horse out whenever possible. Providing it does not have access to large amounts of grass, is not inclined to pace the fence line or gallop about and appears content, it will benefit from the fresh air and space to move. Horses confined to the stable for 20 or more hours a day are likely to stiffen up, suffer from circulatory problems and develop stable vices.

i. The best way to increase fitness without increasing concussion is to introduce hillwork. Start with gentle slopes, then gradually work up steeper and longer hills each day. Providing the horse is kept in a good outline, it will really have to use its topline muscles. Also, the greater effort required for walking or trotting uphill will make the horse physically stronger while developing the efficiency of its heart and lungs.

j. Each rider's routine will vary according to where they live. Some may have to cover many miles of road to reach good riding country, while others may have easy access to woodland, hills, etc. It may be necessary to travel by horse box to a good area for cantering or hillwork. This can be good practice for younger horses, teaching them to enjoy travelling and remain relaxed.

k. Throughout the programme, observe your horse's respiratory rate, making sure its breathing quickly returns to normal after any period of work. If not, you are doing too much work too soon. Check the horse's legs, which should be cool, firm and free from swelling. Any deviation from normal may indicate that you have progressed to fast work too quickly or that you are overfeeding concentrate feed.

l. All being well, introduce trotting into your daily programme. Start with approximately one minute, preferably on a gentle upward slope. Include two to four short trots spaced out over the one to one and a half hours' work. Each day, the length of time spent in trot can be gradually increased. Again, avoid concussion by using slopes and hills where possible.

m. In the early stages of the programme, some riders will not give their horse a day off. They may just ride it gently for a short period so that it has an easier day. This routine is helpful if you have limited turning out facilities, although most riders work their horses for six days a week and give one complete rest day.

n. Once the trotting phase has been well established over a period of two to three weeks, canter work can be introduced in exactly the same way. Keep the canter steady, with the horse working in a good outline.

o. Always make sure the horse is well warmed up before trotting or cantering. A purposeful walk for at least a quarter of an hour is essential for loosening and warming up the muscles, especially if the horse has come straight out of the stable.

p. Either just before, or just after, canter work has been introduced, work in the school can be included. Excitable horses may be calmer about having their first short canter in the school rather than out in the woods.

Always work the horse in a good outline when riding out. Hill work is particularly beneficial

q. Start with 15–20 minutes' school work, using mainly walk and trot and keeping to large circles and simple movements. Gradually increase the school work according to your horse's needs. (An event horse will need more than a hunter, for example.) Some horses will work and concentrate better if you go straight into school work before hacking out to do your fitness work. Most horses will benefit from the warming- and loosening-up effect of the fitness work prior to going into the school.

r. At this stage you may start to split the work up into two sessions. The horse may be working from one to two and a half hours a day, depending upon the type of work done. More intensive work in the school will result in a shorter working session, while steady walk and trot work will mean longer sessions.

s. Introduce show jumping and cross country practice as necessary once you have built up the schooling over a period of one or two weeks.

STAGES III and IV

3. Further Aspects of Fitness Work and Different Disciplines: Phase One

a. The first few weeks of any fitness programme will be very similar. Whatever the ultimate aim, the horse must go through a period of steady build-up work in order to tone up muscles, tendons and ligaments. Before starting work, the horse should be in good condition. This means it should be healthy, free from disease in any of its systems and sound in wind and limb. A horse in good condition is not necessarily fit but a fit horse needs to be in good condition. Condition shows in the look of the horse. It should have a shine to its coat, bright eyes, and generally display all the signs of good health.

b. If the muscles, tendons and ligaments are given time to build and strengthen, they will provide the horse with a strong framework with which to carry out the subsequent weeks of work. As a result, the horse is less likely to suffer problems with soundness and more likely to be able to continue a healthy working life for many years.

c. The effect of exercise is such that it also encourages bone to increase in strength and become more dense. Conversely, when the horse is resting for a period, the bone will become less dense and therefore weaker.

d. Likewise, muscles, tendons and ligaments need "practice" in order to begin to use their potential strength efficiently. Exercise gradually improves the supply of blood to the muscles and the efficient use of oxygen. If not used, muscles will waste away.

e. The start of this toning up work is purposeful walking exercise on roads or firm tracks, which provides the necessary stimulus to the bones, muscles, tendons and ligaments.

f. One to one and a half hours of walking exercise is generally a good length of time to aim for. However, there is no reason why some days the horse shouldn't work for two hours or more, and maybe another day work for only three-quarters of an hour, as long as the longer periods are worked up to gradually and the shorter periods are not repeated too frequently.

g. There is no set pattern to follow, as each horse is an individual and each rider's aims will vary. For example, to get fit for:

- Light hacking – one week of walking – half an hour on the first day, gradually increasing to one hour per day.
- Hunting or ODE – two weeks' walking – begin as for hacking, then increase to one and half hours per day during the second week.
- Racing, long distance riding or recovering from injury – four to six weeks' walking – begin as for hacking, then increase to one and a half hours during the third week and keep this up to the end of the period.

NB: If a horse is excessively fat, then it may need four to six weeks' walking before going on with a hacking programme. It may also be able to walk for only half an hour a day for the first week or so. The vet could advise that a horse recovering from a tendon injury needs eight weeks' walking, the first two or three weeks being for only half an hour per day.

h. Point (g) shows just how much variation there can be. Whatever the situation, there is no substitute for the walking phase and it should never be missed out or cut short. An average horse walks at approximately 6.5 kmph (4 mph) so you should be covering at least 6.5 km (4 miles) every day.

i. This initial build-up period progresses to include trot work. The trot increases the demands made on the horse and therefore strengthens muscles, tendons and ligaments and further improves their efficiency. The average horse trots at around 9.5–11.25 kmph 6–7 mph).

j. Although the horse may already have been working up and down hills, hillwork is particularly beneficial when trot work starts. The effort required by the horse to propel itself and its rider uphill is far greater than that required to continue along level ground and, as already mentioned, there is less concussion to the forelimbs as the hillwork lifts the forehand and encourages engagement of the hindquarters.

k. As the hillwork requires more physical effort, the heart and lungs will also be working harder. This gives them a chance to improve in efficiency before faster work is undertaken at a later stage.

l. The trot work should be gradually increased so that each one to one and a half hours of work is interspersed with periods of trot that may be one minute long to begin with, then increases to five, ten, 15 minutes and so on.

m. While you should aim to trot on firm and springy, not rock-hard, ground, each individual will have to work with the facilities that are available to them. Some of us may have endless bridleways and tracks to work on but others may have more road work to cope with than they would like.

STAGES II and III

4. Associated Ailments

Ailments most commonly associated with fitness work include:

a. Respiratory problems brought about by being stabled in a poorly ventilated environment, and by being fed hay contaminated with mould spores.

b. Strains to muscles, tendons and ligaments due to working an unfit horse too hard too quickly.

c. Bruised soles from trotting or cantering over uneven or stony ground.

d. Galls caused by tack that may be dirty or ill fitting, rubbing against soft skin.

e. Overreach wounds caused by the horse working in an unbalanced manner or moving too fast through deep going.

f. Bruising and inflammation from the effects of concussion, brought about by working too fast on roads and very hard ground.

All of the above can be avoided through good management and progressive ridden work. The unavoidable does happen, however. For example, a setback may be caused by the horse treading on a stone while out in the field, resulting in a bruised sole. The fitness programme may then need to be extended by one or two weeks. Allow for this when planning your first competition. Count back the required number of weeks from the competition date to the start of the fitness programme, then go back one or two more weeks to allow for injury.

STAGES II and III

5. Care after Hard Work

On return from hunting, eventing or other strenuous activity, the horse will need special attention. It needs to be made comfortable so that it can rest while its systems return to normal. At the same time, being tired, it will benefit from the minimum of fuss.

- a. Try to return home with a cool, dry horse. If it is wet, warm and sweaty, it will need to be walked in hand until dry and cool. Some stables may be equipped with infra-red lamps for drying horses. Whichever method is used, the first priority is to get the horse dry but not to allow it to become chilled.

- b. In some areas of the country horses return from hunting so caked in mud and clay that the only solution is to bath them immediately. A supply of warm water, shampoo and a washing-down area out of the wind are required. The bathing/rinsing process should be quick and thorough. Again, the first priority is to keep the horse warm and get it dry as quickly as possible.

- c. The horse may be thirsty but should not be allowed to drink large amounts of cold water. Add a small amount of hot water to a bucket of cold water (just enough to take the chill off). Offer water to the horse every 15–20 minutes, allowing it to drink only 2 or 3 litres (4 or 6 pt) at a time. Once it has quenched its thirst, it can be left with a normal supply of water.

- d. Any obvious wounds should have been noticed and dealt with accordingly. The horse now needs to be carefully checked for any hidden cuts, bruises or swellings. Early discovery and attention will aid a quick recovery.

- e. The horse should have a deep, warm bed and be rugged with light, warm rugs suitable for the time of year. A tired horse will often feel the cold more. Stable bandages will keep its extremities warm, at the same time giving support to tired limbs.

- f. If the horse was not bathed, a light grooming will remove enough dried mud and dried sweat to make it comfortable. Always pick out the feet.

- g. Feed the usual hay ration and also a light, easily digested concen-

trate feed. A bran mash with linseed would be warming and enjoyable.

h. Having settled the horse, return at intervals to check its behaviour. Some horses break out in a secondary sweat and will need
to be walked and dried again. Others may suffer a colic attack.
Hourly checks should be sufficient unless you suspect a problem,
in which case check every 15–20 minutes.

i. The following day, the horse may be stiff or even lame. It
should be led out in hand to help it to loosen up. Then trot it up to
check for soundness. All being well, it will benefit from a day in
the field where it can rest but also gently exercise its tired
muscles.

STAGE III

6. Ride and Lead

a. An alternative way of exercising several horses during these early
stages of walk and trot work, is to ride one and lead one. In polo
yards grooms frequently ride one and lead four! While this is rather
extreme and should only be practised by experienced grooms with
horses familiar with this form of exercise, riding one horse and
leading one other is a helpful way of exercising two horses in the
time it normally takes to exercise one.

b. Ride and lead can also be used to exercise a horse which, for some
reason, cannot be ridden but is otherwise sound. For example, it
may have a girth gall or saddle sore. It is also useful in hunting
yards when a groom may need to bring the master and another
hunt servant second horses or bring a tired horse home. Small
children or novice riders may be taken out on a hack by being led
in this way. A rider out on a hack may need to ride and lead if
another rider falls off and is injured, leaving their horse riderless
and needing to be taken home. So there are many situations when
being able to ride and lead is a useful skill.

c. First of all, the two horses to be taken out together need to be
compatible. Their strides need to be fairly evenly matched and
you need to be sure that they will not kick or bite each other.

d. The horse being led needs to be quite forward-thinking, other-wise you will end up riding and dragging! For this reason, if you find yourself with this problem, it is probably best to ride the slightly lazier horse and lead the more forward-going of the two.

e. While you should always try to wear highly visible clothing when riding on the road, remember that you will be a greater hazard to traffic when riding and leading, and will also probably have slightly less control than normal. It is therefore a good idea to wear reflective clothing yourself and equip both horses with fluo-rescent and reflective leg bands, exercise sheets, etc.

f. Again, as you have less control when coping with two horses, the likelihood of either horse stumbling and falling on its knees is probably greater than normal. For this reason, both horses should wear knee boots for road work.

g. As both horses will be moving very close together, and will pos-sibly be a little off balance at times, it is also a good idea if they both wear brushing boots all round.

h. The led horse should wear a bridle, to give the rider good control, and can be led from the reins or a lead rein with a coupling to the bit. If the reins are used, it is a good idea to thread the nearside one through the offside bit ring to prevent it being caught up around the horse's nose or being chewed.

i. The led horse may or may not wear a saddle. Obviously, if it is the master's second horse, it will be wearing a saddle. If the horse is just starting a fitness programme, then wearing a saddle may help to begin hardening soft skin in that area. Some horses may be-have in a more disciplined manner when saddled, and perhaps feel more free without one, which could lead to behaviour that is difficult to control. However, a saddle can also be a hazard as it is one more item that can get caught up on something or damaged if the horse scrapes it against a tree. If a saddle is worn, the stir-rups should be looped up and secured or removed altogether.

j. If you are working several horses through a fitness programme using ride and lead, make sure, where possible, that each horse has an equal amount of ridden work, as they are obviously work-ing harder when carrying the weight of a rider. It is not a good idea, however, to swap horses while out on a ride. It would be easy to lose control, especially once the horses are fairly fit and full of energy.

Horses equipped for ride and lead

k. Before setting off, carefully check the tack of both horses and tighten the girth of the led horse if it is wearing a saddle. Put the led horse on the near side of the ridden horse, with the reins or lead rope in the rider's left hand. In this way, when any road work is undertaken, the led horse is sandwiched between the verge and the rider, where control is easiest.

l. When mounting, make sure you are positioned where it will be easy to move off in the required direction with the two horses. In order to have room between the horses for mounting, stand the led horse at right angles to the horse you are riding with its head by your horse's shoulder to help to prevent them from nipping at each other.

m. When ready to move off, don't forget to use your voice so that the led horse knows what you are about to do next, for example, "Walk on" etc.

n. You will find that it is necessary sometimes to have the led horse's reins in one hand and the ridden horse's in the other, and at other times to have the led horse's reins in your left hand and the ridden horse's reins in both hands for steering and control.

o. Make sure you always keep the led horse well up by your knee. If the led horse starts to hang back, it will get dangerously close to the hind legs of the ridden horse, which may lead to kicking and loss of control.

p. With practice, the horses should trot and canter happily together but the rider should always be aware of the fact that he or she is trying to control two unpredictable animals and so should be very careful in their choice of tracks and think well ahead. For example, when trotting, take sitting trot for extra control and security if you feel the horses are about to spook or play up in some way.

q. If approached sensibly, ride and lead can be a very useful way of exercising during both the early stages of fitness and when the horse is fully fit and still in need of daily work to maintain fitness.

STAGES II, III AND IV

7. Lungeing

a. Another alternative to ridden exercise is lungeing. Although this is a fairly strenuous activity, it may be necessary to lunge a fresh horse prior to riding in order to settle it into a more sensible frame of mind.

b. Once the horse is fit, or partly so, it is a useful way of varying the exercise routine and improving suppleness and discipline.

c. Twenty minutes' active work on the lunge can be equal to one hour's ridden work. It is important, therefore, to start with just five or ten minutes and build up gradually, as with all fitness work.

d. Too often, horses are put on the end of a lunge line with no tack other than the lunge cavesson or a head collar, and are just allowed to trot and canter round as they please. This is not a beneficial form of exercise and will not improve the horse's way of going. It is merely a way of letting the horse stretch its legs.

e. To be exercised and improved in its fitness and way of going, the horse needs to be tacked up and worked by the lunger just as if they were actually riding it.

f. Firstly, when the horse is sent out on to the circle, obedience should be considered. Unless the horse is so fresh that it is likely to kick and buck, putting the lunger at risk, it should be asked to walk out on to the circle, moving away from the lunger calmly. If you were riding the horse, you would not tolerate it trotting away the minute you sat in the saddle, so, in the same way, you do not tolerate it rushing off into trot the minute you let it out on the lunge. However, for the sake of safety, you may need to let a very fresh horse move off quickly, then bring it back to walk and start again when it is in a calmer frame of mind and ready to pay attention.

g. As the person lungeing, you should never back away from the horse as this only encourages the horse to come towards you, causing a loss of control. You should walk forward with the horse, keeping level with its shoulder, and gradually let the horse move away from you, encouraging it to do so with voice and lunge whip. In fact, if the horse does fall in or come towards you, you should move towards it, at the same time pushing it forward more. This will encourage it to go forward and out on to a larger circle.

h. While sending the horse out on the circle, it is essential to keep a good steady contact on the lunge line. Each time you lose contact you are losing control.

i. Once the horse is on the circle, maintain contact with the lunge line and keep yourself positioned opposite, or just behind, the horse's shoulder, with the lunge whip pointing towards the horse's

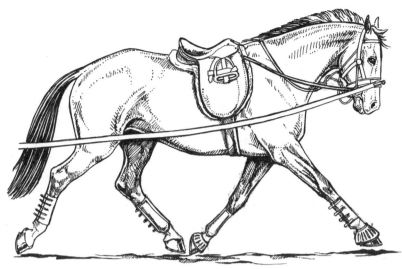

A horse equipped for lungeing

hindquarters. Your body should form the apex of a triangle with the horse's body as the base and the lunge line and whip the other two sides.

j. Using your voice, backed up by the whip as necessary, you give commands to the horse. Just as, when you ride the horse, you give aids to prepare for different movements and transitions, so, now, you use your voice to prepare the horse on the lunge. For example: (the preparation) "Dobbin, aaand" (the command) "Terrrot". Using the horse's name is a good way of gaining its attention. Keep commands simple and consistent to avoid confusion.

k. The horse should be worked actively forward into a contact with the side reins (which may be attached once the horse has worked in), in a good outline, being asked to track up in trot and remain steady and balanced in canter. The walk isn't used so much as, once the side reins are adjusted for trot and canter work, they will be too short for walk and therefore restrictive.

l. The size of the circle used can be varied but remember that constant circle work is strenuous and it is preferable to keep the circle at around 18–20 m. As the lunger, you can walk a small circle in the middle but be careful not to wander as the horse may catch you off balance or you may encourage crookedness or a lack of balance in the horse.

m. The lunger needs to practise standing and moving in a balanced way. For example, when lungeing on the left rein, the right leg should step forward and around the left leg, and vice versa on the right rein. If you remain in balance, you can move with the horse easily if it pulls or shoots off, or you can stand your ground if the horse gets strong. It is advisable to remove spurs before lungeing in case you trip yourself up!

n. You should also wear gloves for lungeing, to protect your hands and aid grip. It is advisable to wear a hard hat as young, fit or excited horses can easily fly-buck and kick out at head height.

o. Practice is needed in handling the lunge line and whip. The line should be kept smooth and evenly coiled. Avoid long loops of line that may catch around your feet and trip you up, and also avoid having small loops around your hand which can quickly tighten and trap you if the horse suddenly pulls. If the line is kept straight and not twisted, then it can be smoothly let out or coiled in and a good contact can be maintained. The whip should be kept tucked under your arm facing behind you when you are close to the horse, adjusting tack, etc. and should be passed round behind you when changing hands, otherwise the horse may think you are waving the whip at it. Do not put the whip on the ground if you can possibly avoid it as, when you bend down to pick it up, the horse can easily take fright or take advantage of the situation and get out of control. When using the whip, keep it pointing slightly downwards, towards the horse's hocks, and swing it forward so that it follows up behind the horse.

p. The key to effective lungeing is to treat it like riding the horse. You are simply using a different set of aids but are looking for the same qualities in the horse's work. The horse should go freely and actively forward, keeping a rhythm and remaining straight and balanced in a good outline.

q. If you intend to lunge the horse and then continue its work by riding it, use its normal tack but make sure you put brushing boots on all four legs as, when working continuously on a circle, and possibly putting in an occasional buck or losing balance, the horse can easily knock into itself. Secure the stirrup irons by looping them up in the leathers, and secure the reins by twisting them and looping the throatlatch through them. Attach side reins so that you will have a contact to work the horse into, and use a lunge cavesson for control. Sometimes overreach boots are used for protection on young, unbalanced or particularly boisterous horses.

r. If you do not intend to ride the horse then a lungeing roller can be used instead of a saddle to attach the side reins to. You could also remove the noseband from the bridle to help the lunge cavesson to sit more comfortably.

s. When carried out effectively, lungeing is an excellent way of improving the horse's level of fitness throughout the training programme. It is also a helpful way of maintaining fitness and can be used as an alternative form of exercise from time to time. As with ride and lead, there may be occasions when a horse cannot be ridden but can be lunged, for example if it cannot wear a saddle or if it hasn't yet been backed!

STAGES II and III

8. Roughing Off

After a season of hard work, most horses will need a rest. This may be a complete rest, turned out to grass 24 hours a day, or a period of gentle activity, perhaps partly stabled and ridden out for an enjoyable hack most days.

a. Begin by reducing the concentrate ration and increasing the bulk.

b. Reduce the amount of exercise gradually. (Stop schooling, jumping and fast work straightaway.)

c. If the horse is having a winter break in the field, allow its coat, mane and tail to grow for warmth and protection. (It may need a New Zealand rug.) Also groom less so that grease returns to the coat to make it waterproof.

d. Reduce the number or thickness of rugs worn. This will encourage the coat to grow.

e. Begin turning the horse out in the field for longer periods. This process should be gradual if the horse has not had access to much grass and is now going to have a summer holiday.

f. If vaccinations, worming or tooth rasping are due soon, now is a good time.

g. If the horse is not going to be ridden, you may have all or just the hind shoes removed.

h. For those horses that will be staying out at night, pick the best possible weather for their first night out.

i. If the horse has not been turned out daily during its working season, it is likely to be very excitable when first let loose. Ride it first to make it a little tired, put brushing boots on all four legs for protection and turn it out hungry so that it is keen to settle and eat the grass.

j. This whole process will take approximately two weeks.

STAGES III and IV

9. Further Aspects of Fitness Work and Different Disciplines: Phase Two

a. The first phase of fitness work may have taken anything from approximately four to six weeks, or even longer if the horse was recovering from an injury or illness. It is after this initial stage that programmes will become more varied according to the final aim.

b. Dressage, canter work and jumping both natural and coloured fences can all be introduced at this stage, starting gradually and building up according to the horse's needs.

c. The horse may now work for longer each day or be worked more intensively during any session. It is vitally important that the horse is always well warmed up for each period of work, especially if it has just been brought out of a stable where it has been standing overnight. Aim to use purposeful walking exercise for at least ten minutes before progressing to more demanding work. This will aid good circulation and give the horse a chance to loosen up, thus helping to prevent injury. It may also suit your routine to split the horse's work into two sessions. This also has the advantage of breaking up the length of time the horse may be left standing in its stable.

d. Throughout the fitness programme, the aim is to increase the horse's ability to carry out the work required without becoming unduly stressed, and to remain sound in wind and limb. Progressively increasing demands on the horse, by building up walk, trot, then canter work, using hills to increase demands, but keeping the work steady and purposeful, will increase endurance and condition heart and lungs. The canter work will help to take the fitness work a stage further by asking a little more of the horse.

e. Heart and lung efficiency will be gradually improving due to this progressive work. Being a muscle, the heart will increase in size at it is used more, thus making it stronger and more efficient at pumping blood around the system. Greater use of the system increases the number of capillaries which supply blood to all parts of the body, including the lungs. As well as receiving an improved blood supply, the lung capacity will increase with use. More alveoli will be recruited as alveoli which have been out of commission and have become partly blocked with debris will be cleared out during your progressive fitness programme.

f. As the heart and lung efficiency increases, the horse's system is able to use oxygen more efficiently. This delays anaerobic respiration which produces lactic acid and quickly causes fatigue.

g. This second phase may take anything from two to four weeks or more, again depending on the aims of your fitness programme. Young horses requiring a lot of schooling will need the extra weeks during this phase, as will endurance horses, while experienced horses, or those aiming for a lesser level of fitness, will not need as much time.

h. Towards the end of this second phase, the horse should be fit enough to be taken out to some small shows or to go cub hunting. This gives the horse a chance to gain experience, to have a change of scene to keep it interested and to be tuned up for different disciplines. The rider will then have a better idea of how the horse is progressing and where more work is needed. Each outing is also work which contributes towards the fitness programme.

STAGES III and IV

10. Further Aspects of Fitness Work and Different Disciplines: the Final Phase

a. By now the horse should be reaching its correct level of fitness for the work required. This will not necessarily be peak fitness as the horse should go on improving as its competition season gets underway, each outing hopefully contributing towards its improvement.

b. Each horse will need to continue its basic working routine but this last two to four weeks is when the finishing touches are needed. This depends on the horse and the rider's aims. For example, riders who wish to go hacking every day will now have a horse fit enough to do the job. If they would like to progress to a longer hack, perhaps a day ride, then all they need to do is gradually increase the distance they cover each day.

c. A long-distance competitor will need to know what distance they will have to cover in competition and at what speed. They can then practise covering set distances at this speed to give themselves experience at judging pace and distance.

d. Event riders need to study their rule books and check the speed required for different levels of competition, including roads and tracks and steeplechase for three-day events. To gain experience in judging pace and distance, they will need to time themselves (with a stop watch) working over a measured distance. A measuring wheel can be used to measure a distance in a field or an all-weather track may be used.

e. Showjumpers, and any competitors required to jump, should check the height of fence required and the types of fences they need to have experience of.

f. Obviously, this type of preparation should not have been left to the last minute as all competitors should have studied their rule books thoroughly at the outset and have made themselves aware of the speeds and distances required of them. These are the goals they are progressively working towards throughout their programme.

g. Fast work should not be carried out every day but can be included once or twice during each week of this final phase. Some work at three-quarter speed, followed by a short full-speed gallop (often called a pipe opener), will give the horse a chance to use and expand its lungs really well. This, in turn, will help to clear out any debris that would reduce the efficiency of the lungs in future work.

h. The speed and distance required will vary from horse to horse, not just because each will be preparing for different goals, but also because different breeds and temperaments respond in various ways to work, and different riders will have their own preferences about the type of programme they follow.

i. For pure dressage or showjumping, the work has many similarities. For both disciplines the horse needs to work towards greater degrees of collection, while also being able to extend when asked. The horse needs to be fit enough to work in for its competition and then perform in the arena, quite intensively, for a period of a few minutes. At any one competition, the horse may be entered for several classes. These horses will not need fast work in their fitness programmes and should be fit enough to compete after approximately eight weeks' preparation. This, as usual, depends on experience, length and type of holiday, etc. Indeed, these horses may compete all year round as competitions can be held indoors as well as out. They need plenty of walk, steady trot and canter work, combined with schooling several times a week (probably every day for the dressage horse) to build up the muscles required for collection, through which they can produce the impulsion required for the job.

j. For hunting and endurance riding, assuming the rider's interest lies in just one of these areas, there is unlikely to be any schooling. These horses will be worked and brought to their required level of fitness purely by being ridden out around the countryside. Serious hunters need very similar work to endurance horses initially, as they need to be able to stay all day. The latter stages of their programmes may differ more. The endurance horse and rider will need to go on working on judgement of pace and distance, whereas the hunter can look forward to taking the day as it comes. Endurance riding preparation programmes may take 16 weeks or more, while a hunter can be ready after just six to eight weeks.

They both need a tremendous amount of stamina to be able to keep up trot and canter work for several hours at a time, especially the endurance horse.

k. Event horses, whether riding club, Pony Club or BHS level, have a greater variety of activities to practise and really must combine a little of all of the above. Although a great deal of schooling is required for the dressage and showjumping phases, event horses are not required to work to the same degree of collection. As they need to combine these disciplines with an ability to gallop across country, the rider must be aware of not overdeveloping opposing sets of muscles, making it difficult for the horse to carry out the required work. For Pre-novice and Novice events, a programme of 10–12 weeks should be sufficient, providing the horse is not starting with any major drawbacks, for example being very fat or recovering from an injury, etc.

l. Riding school horses will need to be able to carry out a variety of different types of work and need to be at least hacking fit before starting work in the school. This generally takes approximately four weeks. After this time, the continuing fitness programme will depend upon the level to which the horse is required to work. For beginner lessons, the horse will be fit enough at this stage, but for more advanced jumping and dressage lessons, the horse will need another four to six weeks. As most riding school horses work for several hours each day, they are generally quite fit and could easily, for example, enjoy a few hours' hunting, providing they were not carrying too much condition and bearing in mind that they probably wouldn't have had a "pipe opener" recently.

STAGES III and IV

11. Keeping Fit

a. Once any horse has reached a level of fitness suitable for the work required, it must be kept fit but not be overworked which would cause it to become "stale".

b. After a competition, the horse should be given a day off, preferably an enjoyable day in the field. If it has been a particularly strenuous competition, for example lasting over two or more days, or involving a lot of travelling, then the horse may need two or three days off to relax completely.

c. If a suitable area for turning out is a problem, then the horse could be led out in hand to graze for a while, preferably several times during the day, to give it a chance to stretch and loosen up.

d. Work for the next few days will depend upon when the next competition is planned. Horses competing at Novice levels may well be going to a competition nearly every week or once a fortnight. In this case, a normal work routine needs to be resumed after the horse's day off. The first day may consist of an hour's hack out and perhaps a short schooling session. The rest of the week should follow a normal pattern depending on the particular discipline. Hunters and eventers will not need fast work if their outings are close together. If the eventer has a break of two weeks between events, some fast work midweek before the competition will be beneficial. Generally, periods of longer, steady work will maintain fitness, whereas too much fast work can quickly send the horse over the top.

e. Horses competing at more advanced levels will have longer gaps between competitions in most cases. At advanced levels, each competition will take more out of the horse, so they need more time to recuperate in between. For these horses, several days of hacking out will keep the horse ticking over after its initial rest day or days. As the next competition approaches, a normal work routine is resumed, for a couple of weeks, to bring the horse back to form.

f. Different types of horses keep fit better than others. The keen, forward-thinking type often puts in more effort and works itself with little encouragement from the rider, thus keeping itself on form. In fact, it may be too keen and require less work to prevent it from burning up too much energy. Horses of a calmer disposition may be lazy and need a lot of work to encourage them really to use themselves and improve their fitness. A horse with a "stuffy" attitude to its work can benefit from going cantering with a Thoroughbred, which may encourage it to compete and open up a little more. Likewise, an excitable type may benefit from the calming effect of a quieter horse.

g. If a horse has an injury, for example a bruised sole, and an important competition is imminent, it may be possible to take the horse swimming to help to keep it fit while the injury heals. Swimming will exercise muscles and work the heart and lungs without putting strain on the lower limbs. Although helpful, it cannot, however, be a substitute for normal work as the horse is using different muscles and not experiencing the hardening effect of working on firm ground.

STAGES III and IV

12. Additional Information

a. A rider who does not succeed in getting their horse fit for the job lays themselves and their horse open to accident and injury. A tired horse is likely to make mistakes which could lead to disaster. Riders must be aware of signs of fatigue, such as gulping and gasping for breath, slowing of pace or stumbling.

b. Experienced riders will know when their horses are fit, especially if they know that particular horse very well.

c. For the less experienced, or the rider who likes to be certain, it is possible to approach fittening work more scientifically by studying recovery rate, pulse and respiration.

d. First, the rider needs to know the horse's normal pulse and respiration rates. These should be between 35 and 45 beats per minute at rest for the pulse, and eight to 12 breaths per minute for respiration. These rates will obviously increase a little when the horse begins work. The rider should take the pulse and respiration rate after a warm-up period of walk and trot and make a note of this as the horse's normal rate. Bear in mind that these rates will also increase if the horse is upset or excited for any reason.

e. After a period of trot or canter work, the pulse and respiration can be checked, then checked again after ten minutes of walk. This gives the horse's recovery rate. If the rates have returned to normal, the horse is fit enough to progress with its progamme and be asked to work a little harder. If the horse's rates have not returned to normal, then you have worked the horse too hard for its level of fitness so far and should do a little less for a while. This way of checking up on your horse's progress can be incorporated into any fitness programme.

f. For those who wish to take this process further, interval training can be used. This system can begin during the trot work phase when the horse is a few weeks into its programme. The aim of interval training is to give the horse a set piece of work, followed by a short rest at walk, followed by another set piece of work. The short rest at walk allows the horse to recover partially and therefore delays a build up of lactic acid which would quickly cause fatigue. The second piece of work asks the horse for a little more effort than before, thus gradually increasing the horse's tolerance to stress.

g. Not all types of horse will take to this form of training. Some lazy horses, especially, are inclined to "switch off", and may be better suited to more traditional programmes.

h. The distance covered, the speed at which it is covered and the type of terrain will all affect how much effort is required from the horse. The rider can adjust any of these three factors in order to make the sessions more or less stressful.

i. Riders using interval training will develop their own combination of work and rest periods depending on the horse and level of fitness required. Interval training should be carried out just twice per week.

j. If available, a distance of 1.6 km (1mile), marked off into 400-m (437 yd) sections, is used. If this is not possible, then mark out one 400-m stretch.

k. Having warmed up in walk and trot for at least half an hour, cover the 400-m distance in canter, aiming to take just over one minute, which will be a speed of approximately 350 m per minute (mpm) (383 ydpm), equivalent to a steady canter. Walk for three minutes, then repeat the canter. Check the pulse and respiration rates. If they are close to normal, repeat the work. Check the pulse and respiration rates again then and again after ten minutes. If they have returned to normal, the horse is ready to progress. If not, it needs to stay with this work out until its recovery rate has improved. Once ready to progress, the length of time spent in canter, and the speed, can be increased. The horse should canter comfortably at 400 or 425 mpm (437 or 465 ydpm). Once the horse has worked up to five lots of three-minute canters at 400 mpm and has a good recovery rate, it would be fit enough for a Pre-novice or Novice one-day event.

l. Point (k) outlines the basis of an interval training programme. Horse and rider would need to build up progressively from the one-minute canter sessions to the three-minute canters, over a period of four to five weeks.

m. Remember, longer, slower canters and gallops improve staying power, while shorter distances covered at a higher speed develop speed and strength. Fast work is very strenuous and can bring a horse to peak fitness too soon, after which time it may quickly deteriorate. The longer, slower work produces a horse that will maintain its fitness level for longer.

n. After a work out, the pulse rate should have been raised to between 80 and 150 beats per minute. This rate, along with the respiratory rate, should have dropped by at least 30 per cent in the following ten minutes. Failure to do so is an indication that you have overworked your horse. The respiratory rate should never exceed 100 breaths per minute and work should stop before it reaches this level.

Follow-up Work to Confirm Knowledge and Experience

1. Stand at the finish of a one-day event and compare how the horses finish, looking to see how much they are blowing, whether they finish full of running or not, and consider what type of horses they are.

2. Practise riding and leading with a pair of quiet horses, then see if you can cope with two fit horses. This will soon make you aware of the advantages and disadvantages of this type of exercise.

3. For Stage IV level particularly, it is vital to have a good range of experience. It will also help to have copies of the current rule books for the main disciplines. Study the speeds required for different phases and watch horses working and competing at those speeds.

Helpful Hints and Exam Technique

1. Candidates often make the mistake of learning a basic fitness programme for a hunter then cannot adjust to describe how they
   would work a horse that simply needed to be fit enough for general hacking. If they really had some experience, they would be
   aware that the first three or four weeks of the hunter fitness programme would produce a horse fit enough for hacking.

2. It is important to be flexible and aware that there are many different methods of producing fit horses. For example, some trainers
   may lunge their horses in the early stages; others may feel strongly
   that this is not a good idea. This doesn't mean that either person
   is wrong. Circumstances often dictate which procedure should
   be followed.

3. Try to speak from your own experience. All horses need to be fit
   for their jobs, so think about the work your own horse or the horses
   you take care of do. Don't try to invent something that is beyond
   your own experience.

6 Saddlery, Its Use, Care and Fitting for Riding, Training and Competition

For horse and rider to work safely and in harmony, it is essential to select the right tack for the job in mind, to be able to fit it correctly and to be able to check it is in safe condition for use.

STAGES I, II and III

1. Fitting the Equipment

GP Saddle

The tree, around which the saddle is built, is made in various widths, usually narrow, medium and wide. Saddles are also made with different lengths of seat to accommodate various sizes of rider. The saddle should be fitted without a numnah then girthed up with the horse standing level.

- a. When placed on the horse's back, there must be a clear passage down the gullet. No weight should be taken on the horse's spine.
- b. There should be approximately a 10 cm (4 in) clearance between the pommel and the withers, without the rider.
- c. The saddle should be level, neither too low at the front nor at the back, which would tip the rider forwards or backwards.
- d. The full surface area of the panels should be in contact with the horse's back. These will distribute the rider's weight over the largest possible area.
- e. The length of the saddle should suit the length of the horse's back. There should not be any weight on the loins.
- f. The knee roll, panels and saddle flap should not protrude over the shoulder, as they may restrict the horse's freedom of movement.

g. The fitting of the saddle is not complete until seen with the rider on top. The rider's weight will reduce the amount of clearance over the withers and spine.

Snaffle Bridle

Bridles are made in different sizes: pony, cob and full size. There are also different widths and strengths of leather. For example, bridles for heavy-weight horses and hunters will be made of strong, broad strips of leather, while bridles for show ponies will be made from finer leather.

a. The job of the browband is to keep the headpiece from slipping back down the horse's neck. It should not pull the headpiece forward where it will rub, but should keep it in place just behind the ears.

b. The throatlatch, which is attached to the headpiece, has the job of stopping the bridle being pulled off over the horse's ears. It should not be tight when the horse flexes at the poll. When correctly adjusted, you should be able to fit the width of your hand between the horse's cheek and the throatlatch.

c. Apart from having the throatlatch attached to it, the headpiece also supports the cheekpieces.

d. The cheekpieces have the job of supporting the bit and should be long or short enough to enable you to adjust the bit to the correct level.

e. The reins are attached to the bit to give the rider control. They should not be too short, which may cause the rider to let go if the horse suddenly snatches its head down, nor should they be too long which may lead to them becoming tangled around the rider's foot.

f. The job of the cavesson noseband is as a point of attachment for a standing martingale. However, it is often worn just to make the bridle look complete. It should sit the width of two fingers below the projecting cheek bones and be loose around the nose to allow free movement of the jaws. Allow for the width of two fingers between the front of the horse's nose and the noseband.

g. The snaffle bit should be adjusted to a height where it wrinkles the corners of the horse's mouth. The mouthpiece should not protrude more than 6 mm ($\frac{1}{4}$ in) on either side of the horse's mouth, nor should the bit rings appear to pinch inwards. If the bit is too wide, it will slide from side to side when the rider uses the reins. If it is too narrow, it will pinch and rub the sides of the mouth.

Martingales

a. The neck straps of both the standing and running martingale should fit around the base of the neck, allowing for the width of one hand to be placed between the neck and the neck strap.

b. To fit the standing martingale, place the neck strap over the horse's head and attach one end to the girth. Then follow the line of the underside of the horse's neck with the martingale strap, up under its throat and down to its chin groove.

c. To fit the running martingale, place the strap over the horse's neck and attach the end to the girth. If both rings are drawn back along the line of the shoulder, they should be approximately 15–20 cm (6–8 in) short of reaching the withers.

d. Rein stops must be worn with the running martingale. They will prevent the rings from becoming stuck where the reins buckle on to the bit.

e. Both martingales have the job of preventing the horse from raising its head too high: the standing type by exerting pressure on the nose via the cavesson noseband; the running type by exerting pressure on the reins, which is then transferred to the bit.

f. The running martingale will only work if the rider has a contact on the reins.

g. Provided they are correctly adjusted, both types of martingale should allow the horse free movement of the head and neck while working on the flat or over fences. They should only come into action when the horse tries to raise its head too high for the rider to maintain control.

Breastplate and Breastgirth

a. Both hunting- and racing-style breastplates and breastgirths should fit securely in order to fulfil their job of preventing the saddle from slipping back.

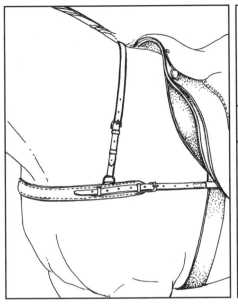

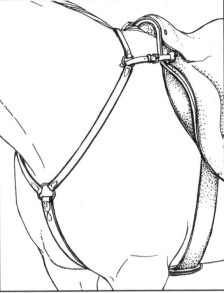

Breastgirth or racing breastplate   *Hunting*

b. Allow for the width of an upright hand between the withers and the wither/neck strap of both styles.

c. The racing style should fit close to the chest without restricting the shoulder movement.

d. The hunting style should follow the line of the horse's shoulder blades, with the centre ring sitting at the base of the neck in the middle of the chest.

e. The strap from the chest to the girth should hang 3–6 cm (1–1$\frac{1}{2}$ in) below the horse's chest.

f. A running or standing martingale attachment can be used with the hunting-style breastplate and with some designs of racing breastplates. Simply attach and then fit in the same way as described for the martingales.

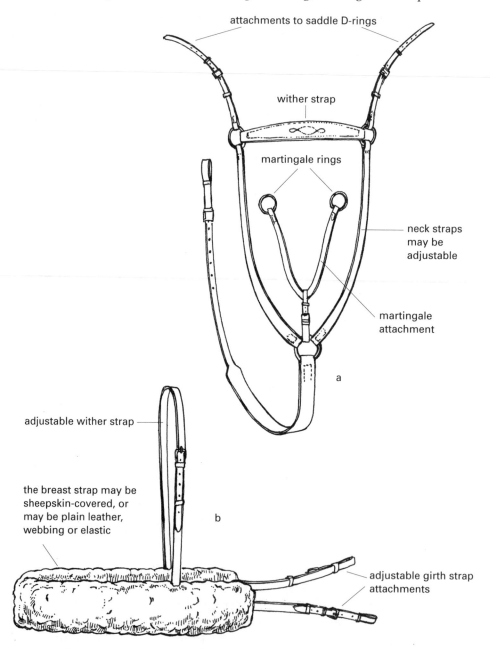

attachments to saddle D-rings

wither strap

martingale rings

neck straps
may be
adjustable

martingale
attachment

a

adjustable wither strap

the breast strap may be
sheepskin-covered, or
may be plain leather,
webbing or elastic

b

adjustable girth strap
attachments

a) Breastplate; b) breastgirth

Lunge Cavesson

a. Because of the force exerted on the lunge cavesson by the lunge line, it must be fitted firmly, hence the need for plenty of padding around the nosepiece.
b. The headpiece and browband (which is optional) should fit as described for the snaffle bridle.
c. The nosepiece should be fitted at the same height as a cavesson noseband (which is normally removed if the bridle is being worn), but should be firmly buckled, without pinching, to prevent the lunge cavesson from slipping.
d. The throatlatch, or jowl strap, which is fitted lower than on the snaffle bridle, is buckled firmly around the lower half of the horse's cheeks. It also helps to stop the lunge cavesson from slipping.
e. If being used, the bridle should be put on first, with the lunge cavesson placed on top. Then put the throatlatch and nosepiece under the cheekpieces of the bridle. This prevents the lunge cavesson from interfering with the action of the bit.

Some designs of lunge cavesson may not fit under the bridle cheekpieces without pulling them out of line. In this case, place the throatlatch over the bridle and the nosepiece underneath.

If the noseband is removed from the bridle, there will be more room for the lunge cavesson to sit comfortably.

Side Reins

These come in various different, adjustable designs.

a. Attach the loop end on each side of the horse by slotting the second or third girth strap through it. Then pass the side rein under the first girth strap.
b. Once attached to the girth strap, hold each side rein in a straight line towards the horse's bit. While the horse is standing at rest with its head held in a relaxed position, the side reins should just reach the bit. This guideline gives a good starting point to work from. Subsequent adjustment depends on how the horse goes when worked on the lunge.
c. When not in use, the side reins can be hooked on to the D-rings of the saddle.

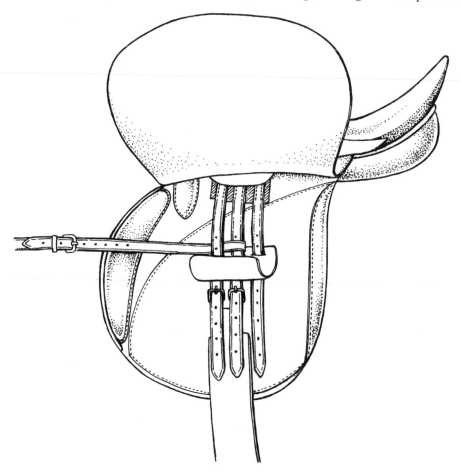

The correct way to attach a side rein to the girth strap

Boots

These come in many varied designs for different uses and are made from a variety of materials. The following general points will apply to the fitting of most boots.

a. The boot should not sit too high where it may rub the back of the knee or front of the hock when the joint is flexed. It should not sit so low that it rubs the heels when the foot is moving.

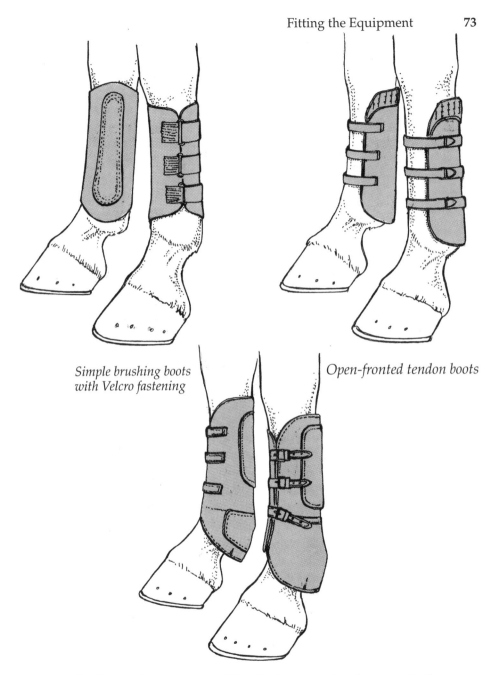

*Simple brushing boots
with Velcro fastening*

Open-fronted tendon boots

*Leather brushing boots, providing tendon support and extra protection
around the fetlock joint*

b. A firm fit is required to prevent boots from slipping down the leg.

c. With most designs, straps are secured by being drawn firmly across the cannon bone and fastened pointing towards the rear. This helps to prevent unnecessary tension across the tendons.

d. To make them easy to put on and take off, boots are fastened on the outside of the leg. This also helps to prevent knocks against the opposite limb.

e. Fasten the centre strap first to secure the boot. If the horse begins to fidget before the other straps are fastened, the boot will then remain in place.

f. Likewise, if the centre strap is unfastened last, the boot will not slip or flap if the horse fidgets when it is taken off.

g. Some designs of boot currently available include:

- brushing boots – for general leg protection against knocks
- tendon boots – open-fronted to give support to the tendons, or not open to incorporate all-round leg protection with tendon support
- speedy cut boots – to protect horses with this action fault
- polo boots – thick felt boots to give good all-round protection against the rigours of polo
- fetlock boots – to protect just this area
- sausage boots – to protect against low knocks round the coronet, or some designs are used in the stable to prevent capped elbow
- overreach boots – to protect the heels against overreaching.

Points to Remember when Removing Tack

a. When removing the bridle, start by undoing the noseband. This is essential if a drop or Flash noseband is used, due to its firm fitting. Then undo the throatlatch. Push the headpiece gently forward over the horse's ears. Lower the bridle slowly in order to allow the horse to drop the bit in its own time. If you pull the bridle away quickly, the bit could catch on the horse's teeth. The horse may then be nervous of having its bridle removed in future. Leave the reins round its neck until you have slipped on the head collar.

b. When removing the saddle, let the girth down gently. If it is dropped down, it will bang against the horse's legs and can cause injury as well as frightening the horse. Then lift the saddle up, slightly back and towards you. In this way you avoid pulling against the horse's spine, which would cause bruising and discomfort.
c. When returning from a long hack or a day's hunting, it is a good idea to dismount before reaching home and loosen your horse's girth a little. This allows the circulation under the saddle to return gradually and avoids a sudden rush of blood (and therefore congestion) to the saddle area.
d. Secure the horse, by buckling the head collar around its neck, before you remove the bridle, then slip the head collar on and tie up. Now remove saddle and boots. To remove a martingale, the girth needs to be undone. In this case, tie up with the head collar over the bridle and remove the saddle first.

STAGES III and IV

2. Training Aids

Although it would be nice to think that all horses could be schooled purely with the use of a snaffle bridle, a saddle and the rider's natural aids, this is not always the case, particularly with horses which have not been well schooled in the early stages of their training.

Side Reins

a. These are training aids that are used regularly by most trainers for lungeing, both in the early stages before a horse has been backed and afterwards for any work on the lunge.
b. Many different designs are available, made in leather and nylon, but three main ones predominate, all being adjustable in length. First the plain leather or nylon type, with a simple buckle for adjustment, which I prefer as they give an uninterrupted conta Those with a slip-through buckle adjustment should be avo

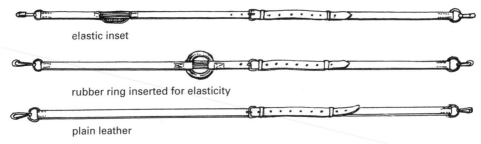

elastic inset

rubber ring inserted for elasticity

plain leather

Three designs of side rein

as they have a tendency to slip and are more difficult to adjust accurately.

Second, the type with a rubber, doughnut-shaped ring inserted for the purpose of giving some elasticity to the contact. In practice, I feel the rubber ring creates a weight which drags down slightly and interrupts the contact. At the same time, the elasticity is negligible unless the horse really leans on the contact, which should be discouraged anyway.

Third, the type with an elastic inset, with or without overcheck. Again, the inset is designed to give an elastic contact but, in practice, can be too elastic and encourage the horse to lean or pull. Certainly, the type with an overcheck would be preferable to prevent the horse from taking advantage of the elasticity.

c. The side reins are attached at one end to the bit and at the other to the girth straps. There will be variation in fitting and attachment at the girth end as they can be attached quite low, making a straight line from bit to saddle, or quite high, making an upward slope from bit to saddle. This is up to the trainer's preference for that particular horse. Some may prefer the straight line to create a little more pressure directly on the bars of the mouth. Others may prefer the higher level as the side rein then produces a contact similar to that which the rider will take when riding.

Likewise, the length of the side reins will vary according to the horse's level of training and way of going. Younger, novice horses should be worked in long side reins to encourage them to stretch and seek a contact, while older, more advanced horses will be worked into a shorter length of side rein and be asked to produce more collection.

d. When a rider is given a lunge lesson, side reins should be used to keep the horse under the instructor's control. At the same time, the rider should take only a light contact with the reins, otherwise the horse will be receiving two opposing contacts which could lead to resistance and adverse reactions from the horse.

e. Once the side reins are attached, they can only be adjusted if the instructor stops the horse and makes an adjustment. If a rider was taking a positive contact on the reins while the side reins are also attached, the horse may object, resist by backing off the contact and even end up rearing. The rider could react by leaning forward and giving the reins but the side reins will not adjust their contact. As a result, the horse could continue resisting and actually rear over backwards.

i. For the same reason, it is not safe practice to ride off the lunge with side reins attached, they should only be used for working the horse on the lunge.

Draw Reins

a. These are usually made of webbing or leather. They attach to the girth, then run up between the forelegs, through the bit rings and back to the rider's hands. The rider is then holding two pairs of reins. The draw reins should be long enough to allow complete

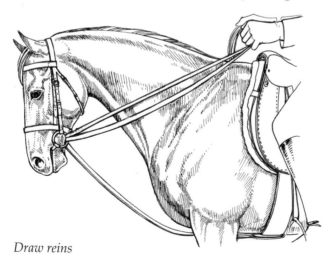

Draw reins

freedom of the horse's head and neck when the rider takes hold of the reins. The length is then adjusted by the rider as he or she works the horse.

b. These reins draw the horse's head down and the nose in and are used as an aid to produce a rounder and more collected outline.

c. In inexperienced hands, they tend to cause the horse to become overbent, behind the bit and inactive behind. If the rider is particularly restrictive when using them, they will also cause a lot of tension in the horse's neck and back, and therefore resistance.

d. In experienced hands, they may improve the outline of a strong or particularly difficult horse, providing the rider is aware of not allowing the horse to become overbent or behind the bit, and providing they keep the horse working actively from behind. They should be used as a short-term aid to help to correct a problem.

e. Draw reins are particularly popular with show jumpers and many can be seen working in draw reins before competitions. They are, however, prohibited tack for BSJA competitions, BHS dressage competitions and horse trials.

Running Reins

a. These are very similar to draw reins and also made from webbing or leather. In fact, one set of these reins can be used as running

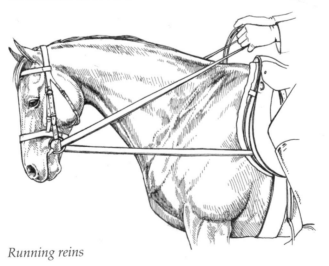

Running reins

reins or draw reins. The difference is that running reins attach to the girth straps at each side of the saddle, then run to the bit and back to the rider's hands. The length should be the same as for draw reins and, again, they will be adjusted by the rider as they work the horse.

b. This makes an action which draws the nose in but has less downward pressure.

c. Once again, they should be used only by experienced riders, on a short-term basis, and are prohibited tack for BSJA competitions, BHS dressage competitions and horse trials.

Market Harborough

a. This aid starts at the girth then divides into two branches from the chest, in a similar way to a running martingale, passing through a neck strap. The two branches run through the bit rings and then clip on to rings on the reins, therefore Market Harborough reins are required, with rings sewn on at intervals along them. The rings on the reins allow for variation in adjustment.

b. As with a running martingale, when correctly adjusted there will be no interference with the horse's way of going if it is working in a good outline. However, as soon as the horse raises its head and/

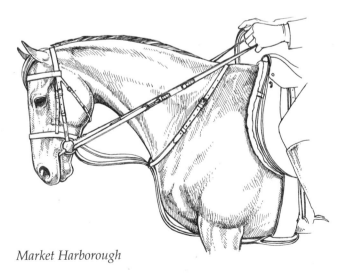

Market Harborough

      or pulls, the Market Harborough will exert a back and downward force on the bit.

c. It is really a cross between a martingale and draw reins, being more severe in its control than the former and a little less strong than the latter.

d. This can be a useful device for very strong horses but, again, it would be preferable for the horse to be better schooled in the first place. It can be used in BSJA competitions but only with a plain snaffle, and is not permitted in pony competitions. It is not permitted in BHS dressage or horse trials.

Chambon

a. Usually made of a combination of leather and cord, this training aid runs from the girth, between the forelegs up to each side of the poll, then down to the bit rings.

b. A padded strip sits over the poll, with a ring on each side for the cords of the chambon to run through.

c. The chambon encourages the horse to lower its head and neck without restricting downward or sideways movement. It should be fitted so that if the horse raises its head above the required level, the chambon tightens, lifting the bit up into the corners of the horse's mouth and applying pressure to the poll.

d. It is an excellent schooling device for encouraging the horse to lift

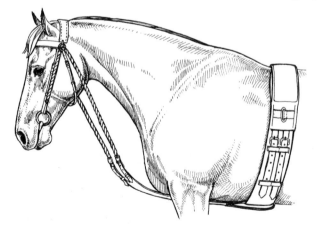

The chambon

its shoulders, round its back and work through with its hindquarters, therefore it can be very helpful when reschooling a horse with a weak back, to help build up muscles before it is asked to carry a rider, or one which has developed too much muscle on the underside of its neck.

e. Many trainers use the chambon in the training of all their horses, whether they have a problem or not.

f. Although some trainers may ride with a chambon, it should really only be used for schooling on the lunge. The added weight of the rider on the horse's back when it is stretching long and low to that extent could be damaging to the muscles.

De Gogue

a. This training aid has similarities to the chambon but can be ridden in as well as being used for lungeing. Again, it is generally made from leather and cord.

b. For lungeing, it runs from the girth to the poll, through a ring attached to the pad at the poll, down to the bit and back to the girth. When used for riding, it returns from the bit to the reins and thereby to the rider's hands.

c. There are little stops on the cord, which limit the leverage and help to prevent the horse from becoming overbent or behind the bit. Again, it should only be used by an experienced trainer.

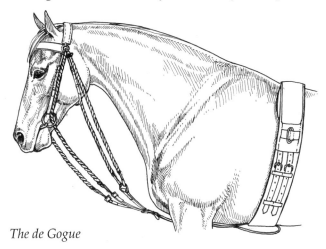

The de Gogue

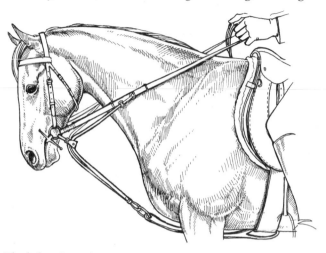

The balancing rein

Balancing Rein

a. Most commonly known as the Abbot-Davies balancing rein, this is a device which can be used in various positions and is made from a combination of rubber, cord, leather and pulleys.
b. It can be attached from girth to mouth to the rein; from tail to mouth to the rein; and from behind the ears to mouth to the rein. It is used for both lungeing and riding.
c. It is supposed to produce a round outline and encourage the horse to use all the correct topline muscles. However, in practice, I feel that it causes most horses to become overbent and behind the bit, perhaps because of the weight of the pulleys in combination with the various fittings.
d. In my opinion, it can be the most harmful of all the training aids in inexperienced hands.

Long Reins

a. For long-reining, most trainers will use two lunge lines, although some may prefer to select reins of a lighter material in order to avoid a drag on the horse's mouth.
b. There are various methods of long-reining but in the UK the long

Long reins

reins are most commonly attached to the bit, then taken through rings on each side of a roller. The trainer then walks behind the horse or stands as he or she would to lunge the horse, with the outside long rein round the horse's hindquarters.

c. In many cases, the trainer does not have access to an expensive roller and, instead, may make do with running the reins through the stirrup irons on the saddle. This method can cause some interruption in the contact with the horse's mouth.

d. Not all trainers use long-reining in their training programmes. However, for those who manage to master the art, it is an excellent way of developing the horse's outline, balance, understanding and confidence before it is required to cope with the weight of a rider. The horse can be schooled through movements at all gaits in the school or asked to go out along lanes and tracks.

e. Long-reining can be used in a reschooling situation as well and is not only for use with horses which have not yet been backed.

New Schooling Aids

a. New ideas appear from time to time. Most of them are variations on the above aids.

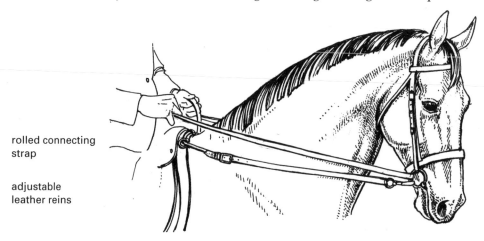

rolled connecting strap

adjustable leather reins

The Schoolmasta

    b. One of these new designs is the Schoolmasta. It is a variation on the side rein, with design features which make it safe for riding in. It has a specially designed numnah, to which the reins are attached. Clips allow for quick adjustment or detachment if necessary. In practice, it is not that easy to detach the clips quickly.

    c. In the manufacturer's advertisements, the Schoolmasta is said to be used and approved by many top riders and trainers.

    d. The Schoolmasta is designed to help to keep the horse in a good working outline, helping both horse and rider to work well together. Again, in the right hands this can be a useful aid.

STAGES III and IV

3. Tack for Cross Country

When galloping and jumping across country, the tack used can be put under a lot of strain. While we should always consider safety with regard to equipment used in any situation, for cross country riding it is vital that the equipment is particularly strong and in good condition. A broken rein, stirrup leather, etc. could lead to a disastrous accident.

The Bridle

a. Apart from the need to check the stitching and leather work carefully for any signs of weakness and to replace anything that shows undue signs of wear, the main parts of the bridle that may be altered for cross country are the reins, noseband and bit.
b. Although each individual rider will have their preferences, strong reins with good grip are required. Rubber-grip reins are most commonly used. Avoid the narrow variety, as the leather will be weaker, and opt for a fairly broad pair. Reins which attach to the bit with a billet hook are more likely to give way under pressure. It is difficult to tell when a billet and the surrounding leather may be about to give way. For this reason, it is preferable to use a buckle attachment or reins which are sewn on to the bit.
c. Plain leather reins will be too slippery for cross country. Plaited leather or nylon reins give more grip but become slippery when wet and are inclined to stretch. Continental reins are favoured by some but one's hands tend to slip between the notches. Laced leather reins are quite good but will become slippery if wet.
d. If a horse has a tendency to become strong and excited across country, it may be necessary to use a stronger bit and noseband. A greater variety of bits and nosebands is permitted for cross country competitions than for dressage. The choice will depend upon the horse's way of going.
e. In case of a fall in which the rider is thrown over the horse's head, which sometimes leads to the bridle being pulled off, many riders plait a piece of mane at the poll and secure it around the head piece of the bridle as a preventive measure.

Breastplate/Martingale

a. A breastplate is an essential piece of cross country equipment, especially at the higher competition levels when fit horses take on a more greyhound-like shape. Without a breastplate, as the horse stretched out at a gallop and over fences, it would be easy for the saddle to slip back to the narrower part of the horse's abdomen. The girth would become loose and the whole lot would slip under the horse's belly, taking the rider with it.

b. Most breastplates are made of leather, webbing, and/or tough elastic. There are two main designs: the hunting style and racing style which is often called a breast girth.

c. The hunting style is probably the most useful for cross country, as it has three points of attachment. It attaches to the girth, and the two D-rings that are riveted into the tree of the saddle at either side of the pommel. (Do not attach it to the D-rings which are only attached to the saddle by pieces of leather as these could easily pull away.) This style of breastplate facilitates the use of a martingale attachment and is useful for passing an overgirth through where it attaches to the girth. This helps to secure the overgirth and prevent it from slipping back.

d. The racing-style breastplate or breast girth only attaches to the girth on each side and is not always fitted with a loop for a martingale attachment. However, many riders choose this style of breastplate as it is a matter of the rider's preference.

e. A running martingale attachment is often used for cross country as it will help the rider to maintain control of a strong or excited horse by exerting downward pressure on the bars of the mouth, via the reins and bit, if the horse pulls and tries to raise its head beyond the point of control.

The Saddle

a. There are many different designs and makes of saddle. Obviously, the saddle must fit the horse, but otherwise it should be forward cut enough for the rider to feel he or she can ride comfortably with a short stirrup length. The rider needs to choose a saddle in which they feel comfortable. Knee rolls usually help to produce a snug fit. For eventing, many riders use a general purpose saddle design, which can be used for each phase if they cannot afford to have a dressage saddle as well.

b. The girth straps are the most important area to check for safety. The webbing to which they are attached must be in sound condition. The stitching must be sound. The straps themselves must be thick and strong, not stretched and thin. Each buckle hole in the strap should be examined. If one hole is stretching and spreading towards the next hole, the leather will be very weak and break easily.

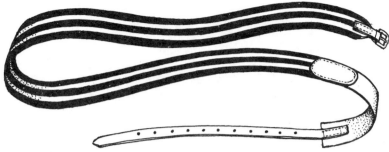

Overgirth

c. As an extra safeguard, an overgirth is worn for cross country. Made of a combination of webbing, leather and elastic, it is fitted over and around the saddle. Having an elastic inset allows for firm adjustment but also for expansion with the horse when it begins to breathe more heavily. It is threaded through the breastplate loop with the girth and is usually buckled up fairly low on the horse's side, in order to make sure the buckle does not interfere with the rider's leg.

d. Stirrup leathers need to be very strong. Buffalo or rawhide leathers are virtually unbreakable and very good for cross country riding.

e. Stirrup irons should always be made from stainless steel. Nickel, which is fairly outdated now but once was commonly used for stirrup irons, should be avoided as it can snap quite unexpectedly.

f. There are now many different designs of girth, and many different materials from which they can be made. The most important features are: strength, breathability (especially for three-day events when the horse is girthed up for relatively long periods) and a non-abrasive effect on the horse. Leather girths that are shaped to prevent rubbing in the girth area behind the elbows (the Atherston design), with an elastic inset at one end, are strong, soft against the horse's skin and allow for expansion of the rib cage when the horse is breathing heavily. However, this is only one design. The leather Balding design is also very popular, as is the leather three-fold (which must be used with the open side facing towards the rear to prevent rubbing and wrinkling). Each rider must select the type they prefer.

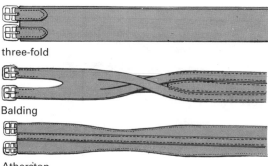

three-fold

Balding

Atherston

Three designs of leather girth

g. Most riders use a numnah to protect the saddle from sweat, absorb sweat, to help to keep the back cool and to provide some cushioning effect between the rider and the horse's back. Natural fabrics, like cotton or sheepskin, are most likely to provide these qualities. The numnah should be firmly secured to the saddle to prevent slipping.

h. If a weight cloth is required, it may be completely separate to the numnah or the two may be incorporated together. Weights may be carried towards the front of the saddle, the back of the saddle or evenly distributed along the horse's back. Some riders prefer the weights to the front as the horse's centre of gravity is further forward when galloping, thus helping the horse to remain balanced and carry the weights to good effect. Other riders prefer not to overload the forehand and use weights carried further back.

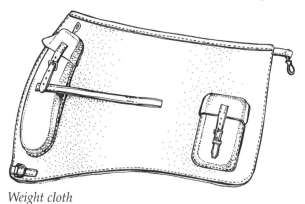

Weight cloth

The rider needs to make sure the weights do not interfere with the fitting of the saddle or their own comfort when mounted. It is vital to have the weight cloth well secured as the rider would be eliminated from the competition if it slipped back and came off.

Leg Protection

a. Anything worn on the legs must be well secured in order to withstand the rigours of the horse galloping through water and mud as well as knocking against solid fences or scraping through brush, etc. At the same time, it is essential that firmly applied boots or bandages do not restrict circulation or put uneven pressure on the limb.

b. If exercise bandages are worn, they should be applied over gamgee or Porter boots to ensure even distribution of pressure. They are usually sewn in place in case the horse knocks the bandage and tears it. If it came unravelled, it could be disastrous. One or two strips of plastic electrician's insulating tape, wrapped right around the leg, will help to secure the bandage. Some riders prefer to use only tape, rather than bother with needle and thread, especially if they use the type of bandage which sticks quite firmly to itself.

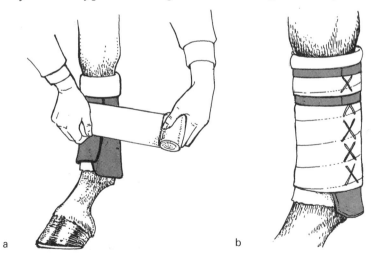

a
b

a) An exercise bandage being applied over a Porter boot
b) A well-secured and stitched exercise bandage

c. Exercise bandages are usually worn on the front limbs to give support to the tendons. As the tendons run right down the back of the limb from below the knee, the bandages should be applied to support as far down the leg as possible, without interfering with the movement of the fetlock joint. The close, firm contact afforded by an exercise bandage should provide more support than a tendon boot, providing they are expertly put on.

d. Some riders may only use exercise bandages if their horse has a history of tendon injury. Other riders may use them as a preventive measure on all their horses, or perhaps just when competing at more advanced levels.

e. If poorly applied, loosely or with uneven pressure, an exercise bandage will do more harm than good. If they slip down, they will restrict movement, be more likely to come unravelled or trodden on, and therefore become dangerous. If the pressure is uneven, they can cause ridges and bruising on the tendons and therefore damage them rather than give protection.

f. It is also thought that using exercise bandages can weaken the tendons by giving false support, rather than encouraging the tendons to strengthen and stand up to the required work independently.

g. Another school of thought is that exercise bandages give no support at all as tendons run north to south down the leg, while the bandage wraps around the limb, applying pressure but not supporting.

h. Boots are made from many different materials and with various fastenings. For cross country the fastenings must be very secure and particularly able to stand up to going through water. Buckles work well, providing the straps are in good condition. Simple Velcro fastenings may not be secure enough, although some are more secure in design than others. The material must be sturdy enough to provide protection and should not be too absorbent otherwise the boots would become very heavy in wet conditions.

i. Boots are worn to protect the horse from knocks, both from the fences and from the horse's own legs.

j. Overreach boots, also known as bell boots, are worn in front to protect the horse's heels from overreach injuries. Some riders prefer to risk going across country without these boots as a horse treading on its boot, on landing from a fence, may fall as a result of not being able to get its front limbs away quickly enough. Again, each rider must weigh up the pros and cons and make their own decisions.

STAGES III and IV

4. Tack for Dressage

There are probably more restrictions on the tack permitted for dressage than in the other disciplines, therefore it is important, as always, to check the rule book carefully.

The Double Bridle

a. The double bridle may be used from Elementary level upwards. It is used to enable the rider to give more refined aids as the horse progresses to more advanced levels. Used in combination with all of the rider's aids, it is an aid to collection and encourages the horse to remain light in the hand, in self-carriage, throughout all the required movements.

b. It is made up from the same pieces as a snaffle bridle but also has a "sliphead", which is the headpiece from which the bradoon bit is suspended. The sliphead is attached to the bradoon on the near side, passes over the head and buckles to a cheekpiece on the off-side.

c. As the noseband is designed to buckle up on the near side, the sliphead is buckled to its cheekpiece on the off side in order to even out the number of buckles on each side of the bridle. This helps the bridle to lie smoothly and fit comfortably.

d. When putting the bridle on, follow the same procedure as for a snaffle bridle but, when taking the two bits in your left hand, make sure the bradoon is lying over the top of the curb. This helps the horse to arrange the bits comfortably in its mouth once the bridle is in place.

e. When fitting a bridle which the horse has not worn before, first slip all the straps out of their keepers to facilitate quick

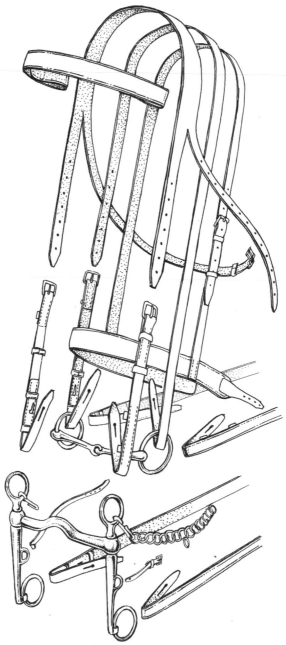

A double bridle

adjustment if necessary, then hold the bridle up to the side of the horse's head, in order to see if it is approximately the right size. Adjust if necessary at this stage, then make final adjustments once the bridle is on.

f. The bridle should fit in a similar way to the snaffle bridle, the difference being that the bradoon should sit a little higher in the horse's mouth than an ordinary snaffle, while the curb should sit just below it so that the two bits are just about touching in the horse's mouth.

   The curb bit also has a curb chain which should sit comfortably in the curb groove, tightening when the curb bit shanks are drawn back to an angle of approximately 45 degrees. To keep the curb chain in place and to help to prevent it from being lost, a lip strap is also attached to the curb bit and curb chain.

g. The double bridle is not only used for dressage. It can be useful for a strong horse going across country or hunting. If the rider is experienced, the double bridle enables them to keep the horse light in the hand and therefore under control, without having to pull at them and use degrees of strength which will only encourage the horse to become a puller. It is also correct tack for some showing classes.

h. Two widths of rein are used on the double bridle to help the rider to distinguish between the two. A thinner rein is used on the curb bit and a slightly broader one on the bradoon. For dressage, plain leather reins are usually used, but if the bridle was used for hunting or cross country then a rubber-covered rein would probably be used on the bradoon bit.

The Saddle

a. As the rider needs to ride with a longer, straighter leg and a deep seat for dressage, the saddles are made with deep seats and have straight-cut panels. This helps the rider to sit correctly and securely. At the same time, the stirrup bar is extended to place the stirrup leather further back in order to facilitate the rider's leg position which needs to be more underneath their seat.

b. There are many different makes of dressage saddle and each rider will have their particular favourite. Apart from the details men-

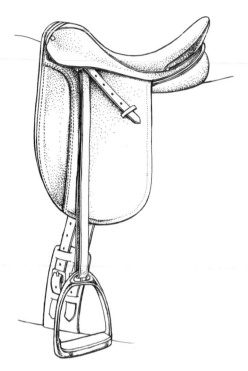

A dressage saddle with a short Lonsdale girth

tioned above, the saddle should not feel too bulky as the rider needs to feel close to the horse. For this same reason, dressage saddles are usually fitted with extra-long girth straps to which a short girth, known as a Lonsdale girth, is attached. These girths buckle up low on the horse's side where they do not interfere with the rider's leg and therefore aid close contact.

c. It is also a good idea to use quite a thin numnah for dressage, again to avoid any bulkiness under the saddle.

d. Important in the fitting of all saddles, but particularly for dressage, is to ensure that the horse's shoulders are completely free to move. Make sure the saddle is sitting comfortably behind the shoulder, not overlapping it and interfering with the movement.

A showjumper wearing a chest guard

STAGES III and IV

5. Tack for Showjumping

There are many similarities between tack suitable for showjumping and that used for cross country riding.

    a. Rubber-grip reins or one of the other designs which provide good grip are usually used and running martingales are frequently seen.

    b. Breastplates are not always used but a forward-cut saddle is essential to allow for the shorter length of stirrup required for jumping. For pure showjumping, the saddle is usually more forward cut than that used by event riders.

    c. An overgirth is sometimes seen in the showjumping arena but not always.

    d. Chest guards, which attach to the girth and protect the horse from its studs hitting its chest when it tucks up its forelegs over a large fence, are worn at more advanced levels.

e. The front legs are usually protected with open-fronted tendon boots. These boots are designed to provide tendon support but, by leaving the front of the limb exposed, the horse can still feel if it knocks a pole and should, therefore, still try to be careful. Over-reach boots are nearly always worn.

STAGES III and IV

6. Additional Information

a. A particular point to look for when choosing a saddle for any discipline is that it has plenty of width at the gullet. A wide gullet will distribute the rider's weight well away from the horse's spine, whereas a narrow gullet can pinch on either side of the spine.

b. There are now many different designs of synthetic saddle, which have the advantages of being light, easy to clean and less expensive to purchase. They can be used in competitions and are favoured by many people. For heavy usage, however, as in riding schools, they tend to wear out more quickly than leather saddles.

c. For long-distance riding, there are now some excellent saddles, specially designed for the job. They are made with horse and rider comfort in mind and are rather like a combination between a traditional saddle and a Western design. They provide plenty of padding to distribute the rider's weight over a large surface area and to provide the rider with a well-padded seat to sit on.

d. Long-distance riding needs other special considerations with regard to tack. Protective boots are not usually worn as mud and grit are likely to cause friction between the boot and the horse's limb. The tack, in general, should be simple and light to avoid friction, sores, etc. Bitless bridles are sometimes favoured as they can make it easier for the horse to drink *en route*.

e. In particularly wet and muddy conditions, cross country riders may plait the full part of their horse's tail, from top to bottom, then fold it up and secure it with tape. This prevents the tail from becoming clogged and heavy with mud during the competition. This is also seen on the polo field, where it prevents the tails from becoming tangled in the riders' sticks.

Follow-up Work to Confirm Knowledge and Experience

1. Stage IV level students should practise riding and schooling with the various training aids available. Providing the rider is under supervision, they should not do the horse any harm and they will provide first-hand experience of how these aids work and affect the horse's way of going.
2. Stage II and III level students should practise preparing horses for various competitions. If they can gain practice at a real competition, then they will learn to become efficient and cope with a horse that is likely to be unsettled and excited by its surroundings. Speed and efficiency are vital as few horses will stand quietly for long periods while someone fiddles with tack, bandages, etc.
3. Students should read and familiarise themselves with rule books for different disciplines as this information is vital for grooms and trainers as well as competitors. If all members of the team know the rules, mistakes are less likely to occur.

Helpful Hints and Exam Technique

1. A good way of keeping up to date with new items on the market is to visit the local saddlery shop and have a good look at all the items on offer.
2. Before starting on a task set, have a good look at the horse you are working with to see if it is likely to need a narrow saddle or a small bridle, for example.
3. A common mistake made by candidates is not checking both sides of the equipment once they have fitted it to the horse. For example, they may put on a bridle and not realise that the noseband is sitting much higher on one side than the other, or that the cheekpieces are not adjusted to the same height on each side.
4. Always adjust tack to fit the horse. Candidates often put an item on, then tell the examiner it doesn't fit. If there are adjustment holes available, the examiner will then ask the candidate to adjust the item to fit. The candidate would give a much better impression if they had made these adjustments without being prompted.

7   BITTING

Learning about the structure of the horse's mouth and how various bits and nosebands work will help in the selection of appropriate bitting arrangements for a variety of horses.

STAGES III and IV

1. The Structure of the Horse's Mouth

In order to understand the effects of different designs of bit, it is necessary to look at the structure of the horse's mouth and consider how it may differ from horse to horse.

    a. The bit should lie in the horse's mouth, in the gap between the molar and incisor teeth. This stretch of the jaw, without teeth, is known as the "bar".

    b. The bars are sensitive structures. If a bit with leverage is used, it will apply pressure downwards on the bars of the mouth. If a snaffle bit is used, it will apply pressure on the bars if the horse is carrying its head in a good working position.

    c. All bits lie across the tongue and some horses will have thicker tongues than others. The tongue will spread itself and partly protect the sensitive bars of the horse's mouth.

    d. Thicker-tongued horses may find some designs of bit uncomfortable. Bits with ports or tongue grooves will allow more room for the tongue, as will a jointed bit.

    e. When a horse tries to evade a bit, presumably through discomfort initially, it may try to get its tongue over the bit, which

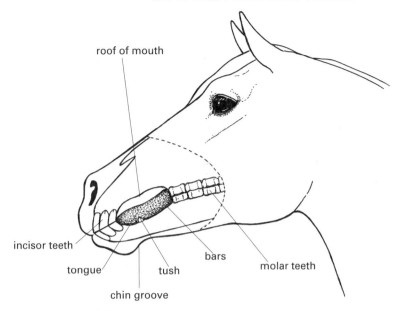

roof of mouth

incisor teeth

tongue

chin groove

tush

bars

molar teeth

The structure of the mouth

becomes apparent when a horse hangs its tongue out to one side of its mouth. Once the horse has moved its tongue in this way, the rider will lose a certain amount of control.

f. Some horses may not evade the bit but, if their tongue is thick, it could be seen bulging out slightly between their lips.

g. The finer and more sensitive breeds of horse are more likely to have fine mouths, with smaller tongues and finer lips. The sensitive bars will therefore have less tongue to protect them. This type of mouth structure will be more sensitive than the thick, fleshy mouths of some of the heavier breeds.

h. Those with thick and fleshy mouths will sometimes find bits with very thick mouthpieces too much to fit in their mouths and therefore be uncomfortable.

i. Horses with very long, or very short, mouths will also have problems. When the bit is fitted in the corners of a mouth that is very long, it may lie too close to the molar teeth. This can lead to the horse taking hold of the bit between its teeth. Long-mouthed horses are considered by some people to be more likely to become pullers.

j. For a horse with a short mouth, it may be necessary to wrinkle the corners of the mouth more than is comfortable for the horse in order to get the bit to lie high enough. In this situation the horse may become particularly resistant if asked to accept a bit with a very thick mouthpiece which will stretch the lips even more, or a double bridle for the same reason.

k. The roof of the horse's mouth is particularly low just behind the incisor teeth. It can easily be bruised by a jointed bit which is too wide and hanging too low in the horse's mouth. Bitting should not incorporate pressure against the roof of the horse's mouth as this is too sensitive and will only cause resistance.

l. Wolf teeth are small teeth which come through (in some horses but not all) at around six months of age, in each side of the upper jaw and sometimes also in the lower jaw, just in front of the molars. They may then be shed, along with the milk teeth, without being noticed. However, they often remain indefinitely and, as they have quite short roots, they can cause the horse discomfort by moving around in the jaw if the bit knocks against them. Many horses are not affected by them at all. A vet or horse dentist can quickly remove wolf teeth if they are causing the horse to resist.

m. When using a bit with a curb chain, the chain should sit snugly in the curb groove. Some horses with long narrow jaws and long mouths can be a problem to fit with a curb chain as it tends to ride up their jaw line. This is a sensitive area, as there is only a thin covering of skin over the jaw bone, whereas, in the curb groove itself the jaw bones are not so exposed. The lip strap should help to keep the curb chain in place.

STAGES I and II

2. Basic Principles

The following basic principles of bitting should enable you to assess the action of almost any type of bit. In general, we aim to school the horse in such a way that it will respond to the simplest form of bitting.

a. There are five families of bits:

- snaffle
- curb
- Pelham
- gag
- bitless

All bits can be fitted into one of these categories

b. There are seven areas where pressure can be applied by various bits:

- tongue
- bars
- lips/corners of mouth
- nose
- poll
- chin groove
- roof of mouth (not used in modern day bitting)

c. A thick mouthpiece will spread pressure over a larger surface area and will therefore be more gentle, while a thin mouthpiece will work in the opposite way and be more severe.

d. Bits with loose rings or sliding mouthpieces give the bitting arrangement more mobility, while those with fixed mouthpieces and rings reduce the mobility. The horse's response will vary according to the arrangement used.

e. Bits with shanks – The longer the shank above the mouthpiece, the more leverage there is on the poll. The longer the shank below the mouthpiece, the more leverage on the bars.

f. A snaffle will apply pressure on the tongue, lips and bars of the horse's mouth.

STAGES III and IV

3. The Snaffle

a. There are many different designs of bit within the snaffle family which is the simplest of the five families of bits.

b. The snaffle bit should be adjusted to lie where it wrinkles the corners of the horse's lips. It incorporates a slight head-raising action as it lifts up into the corners of the horse's mouth. The degree to which it raises the head depends upon the level at which the horse is carrying its head at the time and where the rider is carrying his or her hands. For example, if the horse is working long and low, and the rider is carrying his or her hands well above the wither, there will be a greater degree of head-raising action. However, if the horse has raised its head very high and the rider drops their hands, then there will be very little head-raising action and little pressure on the corners of the lips.

c. The snaffle bit also lies across the lower jaw, thereby applying pressure to the tongue and the bars. The degree of pressure on the bars will, again, vary according to where the horse is carrying its head and the level of the rider's hands.

d. Loose-ring snaffles make for a more mobile bit which should encourage the horse to keep a relaxed jaw and mouth the bit. This can be helpful if the horse is inclined to try to fix its jaw. The disadvantage is that they can sometimes pinch or rub where the ring slips through the mouthpiece. Pinching can usually be prevented by putting rubber "biscuits" or guards on the bit, although these are not permitted for dressage competitions. The more fixed eggbutt design may be better for a horse that is inclined to mouth too much and play with the bit. It is also smoother where mouthpiece and rings meet, therefore there is no pinching or rubbing.

e. Straight-bar or mullen-mouthed snaffles (those with an unjointed but slightly curved mouthpiece) will apply pressure more across the tongue than on the bars and are very mild in their action.

f. The jointed snaffle allows more room for the tongue because of its slight nutcracker action, and puts a little more pressure on the bars.

g. Those with more than one joint, like the French link or Dick Christian, have less of a nutcracker action and distribute pressure over both tongue and bars. Being a little looser in the mouthpiece, they are sometimes effective in encouraging horses that are inclined to set against the bit, to mouth and accept the bit.

h. Bits with cheeks help when turning a horse as the cheek applies pressure to the cheek of the horse. This is especially helpful with

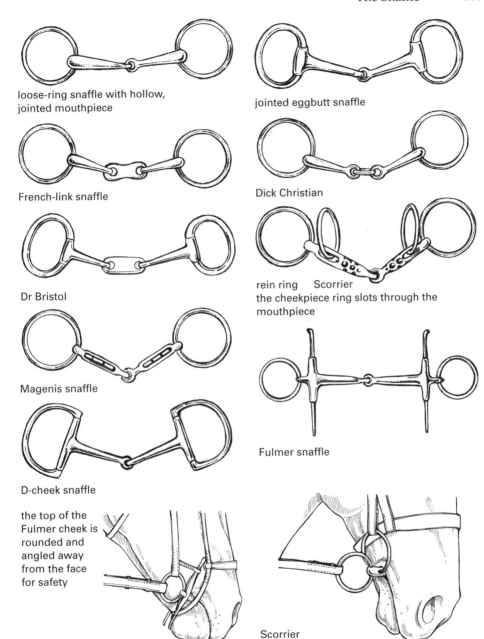

loose-ring snaffle with hollow, jointed mouthpiece

jointed eggbutt snaffle

French-link snaffle

Dick Christian

Dr Bristol

rein ring   Scorrier
the cheekpiece ring slots through the mouthpiece

Magenis snaffle

D-cheek snaffle

Fulmer snaffle

the top of the Fulmer cheek is rounded and angled away from the face for safety

Scorrier

Snaffle bits

strong, young or uneducated horses. The cheek will also prevent the bit from being pulled through the horse's mouth. The loose-ring snaffle with very large rings and the D-cheek have similar advantages and are often seen on racehorses.

i. Snaffles with cheeks should be used with keepers which attach to the cheekpieces to keep the bit in an effective position. Without these keepers the cheeks of the bit tilt forward and are no longer in a position to apply pressure to the side of the horse's face.

j. Bits with thicker mouthpieces are milder than those with thin mouthpieces but more effective. They spread the pressure over a greater surface area, rather than applying a thin line of pressure which, due to its intensity, can dull the horse's responses, leading to horses which become stronger and less responsive.

k. The Fulmer is an example of a snaffle which incorporates several of the above features. It is jointed, has cheeks, a fairly thick mouth-piece and loose rings.

l. Another feature which will affect the action and acceptance of the bit is the material from which it is made. Most bits are made from stainless steel. The softer synthetic materials of a plastic nature are good for horses with very sensitive mouths as they give the horse a different feel and this encourages some horses to be more accepting of the bit.

m. Within the snaffle family, at the more severe end of the scale, are the Dr Bristol, Magenis, Scorrier and various designs with twisted or roller mouthpieces. These bits are employed to help in the control of strong or difficult horses.

n. The Dr Bristol has a lozenge-shaped section in its centre which is set at an angle, thus applying sharper pressure to the tongue.

o. The Magenis has small rollers set into the mouthpiece, which are designed to slide over the jaw and help to prevent a horse from crossing and setting its jaw.

p. The Scorrier has two sets of rings, one pair set into the mouth-piece to which the cheekpieces are attached, and the normal pair to which the reins are attached. Along with a grooved mouth-piece, this creates a strong stopping device.

q. The many other designs with twisted and other types of mouth-piece are all designed to create stronger points of pressure in order to make the horse take notice of the bit.

r. Only the simple snaffles are permitted for dressage competitions so check the rule book carefully.

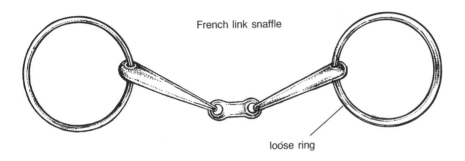

French link snaffle

loose ring

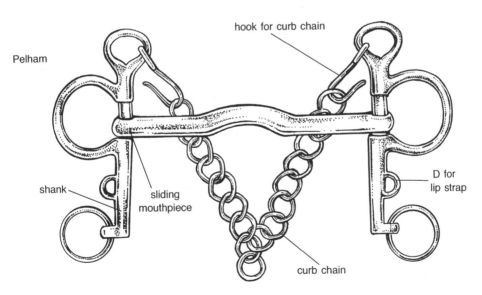

hook for curb chain

Pelham

shank

sliding
mouthpiece

D for
lip strap

curb chain

Parts of the bit

STAGES III and IV

4. The Double Bridle

a. For this family of bits, the horse is required to wear two bits, hence the name double bridle. Once again there are many different designs of these two bits which consist of the bradoon and the curb.

b. The bradoon bit should sit in the mouth a little higher than a snaffle bit would normally be positioned. The curb should sit just below the bradoon.

c. The bradoon is a snaffle bit and therefore acts in the way previously described. Its head-raising action helps the rider to keep the horse carrying its head at a good working level for the more advanced stage of work for which a double bridle is used.

d. Bradoon bits usually have smaller rings and thinner mouthpieces than conventional snaffles to make them less of a mouthful for the horse when it is having to cope with two bits.

e. In order for the two bits to lie comfortably, the bradoon needs to have a slightly wider mouthpiece than the curb bit.

f. There are variations in the design of curb bits but all need to have a curb chain in order to bring the bit into action. The curb chain is generally adjusted so that it tightens in the curb groove when the shanks of the bit are drawn back to an angle of 45 degrees.

g. There are several different designs of curb chain. The single-link chain, the double-link, leather, and elastic, or a chain with a rubber guard. In general, the milder chains are preferable, as they apply pressure without rubbing, pinching or causing general discomfort. If the horse is uncomfortable, it will only resist the bitting arrangement, so a soft curb chain is best. Each curb chain needs a fly link for the lip strap to help to keep it in the correct position.

h. The leverage action of the curb bit applies pressure to the poll. The longer the shank above the mouthpiece, the more pressure there is on the poll. Not all horses work well with poll pressure and those that don't should have a bit which is short in the shank above the mouthpiece.

i. The curb also applies pressure to the tongue and the bars. The degree of pressure on the bars depends on how thick the horse's tongue is and the design of the mouthpiece of the bit. Those with

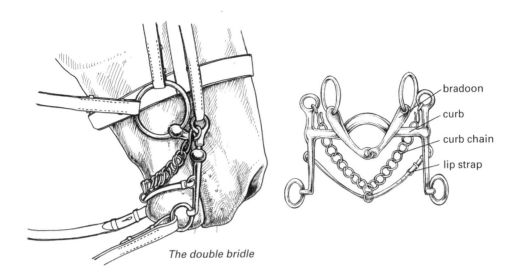

The double bridle

bradoon
curb
curb chain
lip strap

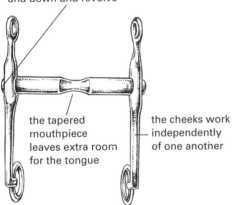

the mouthpiece fits into a slot in
the cheek so that it can slide up
and down and revolve

the tapered
mouthpiece
leaves extra room
for the tongue

the cheeks work
independently
of one another

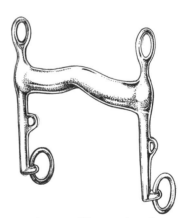

Banbury curb

German dressage Weymouth curb

larger ports or tongue grooves allow more room for the tongue and distribute more pressure on to the bars. A straighter mouthpiece will put more pressure on the tongue. The tongue will spread and partially cover the bars, making the pressure from the bit on to the bars less direct.

j. The longer the shanks below the mouthpiece, the more leverage there is on the bars.

k. The curb bit, often called a Weymouth as this is the design most often seen, may have a fixed cheek or a sliding mouthpiece. As with the snaffles, this makes the bit either less or more mobile. The choice depends upon whether your horse benefits from a little more mobility to encourage it to accept the bit or a fixed mouthpiece which can help to keep the horse quieter in its mouth.

l. The German dressage curb, which is basically a curb with a very thick mouthpiece, is also very popular.

m. The Banbury curb has cheekpieces which move independently and is not so often seen in use. However, its fairly straight mouthpiece, which can turn in the horse's mouth, has a less direct action on the bars and can suit some horses.

n. At more advanced levels, which require a greater degree of collection, the bradoon and curb bit together, combined with the rider's natural aids, help the rider to achieve a more advanced outline while maintaining a light contact.

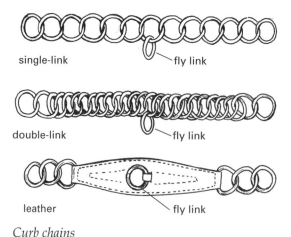

Curb chains

STAGES III and IV

5. The Pelham

a. This family of bits tries to combine the two distinct actions of the double bridle bits into one. Inevitably, by combining the two, the resulting action is less clear.

b. The Pelham looks very similar to a curb. It is used with a curb chain, has a loop for the lip strap to be attached to, but also has a ring to which the bradoon rein is attached.

c. The idea is that, with two reins attached to the one bit, the rider can either emphasise the bradoon or curb rein action. In practice, the two rein actions tend to merge into one, resulting in pressure on tongue, bars, poll and a little on the lips.

d. The Pelham is usually positioned a little lower than the snaffle and a little higher than a curb bit. The amount of pressure on the lips depends upon how much bradoon rein is used and the level of the rider's hands.

e. It is a bit which seems to suit some horses, particularly those with very small or thick-lipped mouths, which would find it difficult to accommodate the two bits of a double bridle. However, those with long thin jaws and mouths tend not to go well in Pelhams as they sit too high for the curb chain to work effectively.

f. Pelhams usually have unjointed mouthpieces with ports or mullen mouths. There are some jointed Pelhams but this makes a difference to the curb chain tension which needs to be tighter than normal to be effective. With a jointed Pelham many different effects are taking place at once, probably resulting in confusion and a gradual deadening of the sensitivity within the horse's mouth.

g. The Pelham has become a bit which is often used for a horse or pony which proves just a little too strong in a snaffle. It may be seen on ponies, when it is used to help their young riders keep control. As a result, it is often used with leather roundings and just one rein which is easier for a young person to cope with. In this situation, the two-rein action becomes even less distinct.

h. The Kimblewick is part of the Pelham family and also seems to be used on ponies for the same reasons. It requires only one rein as

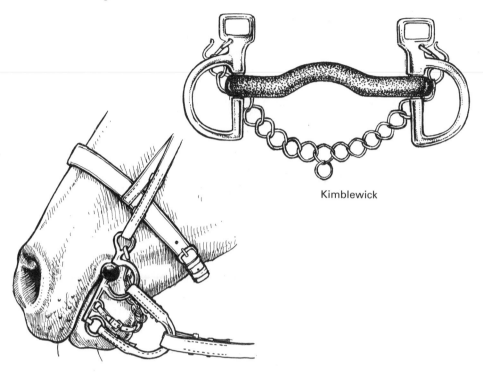

Kimblewick

A Pelham fitted with roundings

the usual two rings of a Pelham, along with the leather rounding, are all merged into one D-shaped ring in this bit. It applies pressure in the same areas and the idea is that the rein should move up and down the ring when the rider raises or lowers their hands, allowing for either more or less curb action.

i. Instead of the usual rings, the Kimblewick has squared-off slots to attach the cheekpieces to. This creates a greater degree of poll pressure, despite its short shanks.

j. Kimblewicks are used with curb chains but do not have a D-ring for a lip strap to be attached. They usually have unjointed mouthpieces with tongue grooves but jointed ones are available. As with a jointed Pelham, this creates a bitting arrangement which tries to combine too many actions in one.

k. Pelhams are not permitted in dressage competitions.

The gag snaffle   *The Duncan gag*

STAGES III and IV

6. The Gag Snaffle

a. As the name suggests, the gag snaffle looks very similar to an ordinary snaffle. The difference lies in the two slots, one in the top and one in the bottom, in each of the bit rings. A piece of cord runs through these two slots. The cheekpieces attach at one end of the cord and the reins at the other.

b. The gag snaffle therefore applies pressure to the poll, tongue, lips and bars. The emphasis of the action is on raising the horse's head, while the poll pressure helps to keep the horse in a controllable outline.

c. The size of the bit rings influences the amount of leverage which this bit has. The larger the rings, the greater the leverage.

d. Although not many riders do use gags in this way, they should be used with two reins, the gag rein and a rein attached as a normal snaffle rein. In this way, the rider can use the bit mainly as a snaffle and then employ the gag rein only when they feel the need. The horse is then more likely to take notice of the stronger effect of this rein.

e. The Duncan gag is a design which can only be used with one rein.

f. Gags are probably most useful with horses which become too strong for their riders when jumping across country. If the horse lands after a fence and takes a hold with its head low, the gag rein will help the rider to raise the horse's head and regain control.

g. Gag snaffles are not permitted in dressage competitions.

STAGES III and IV

7. The Bitless Bridle

a. Most bitless bridles are referred to as hackamores, although this is not the correct term for all. While a variety of bitless bridles are available and will more often be seen abroad, the Blair pattern bitless bridle is the one most often used in the UK and this is generally referred to as a hackamore.

b. This design of hackamore controls the horse by exerting pressure on the nose and in the curb groove, along with a degree of pressure on the poll. The nose is a very sensitive area and some designs of hackamore can be very severe.

c. The simple Blair pattern hackamore has a sheepskin-lined nose piece, and a leather strap in the curb groove, with relatively short metal shanks to which the reins are attached.

d. This type of hackamore can be useful as a temporary measure if the horse has a sore mouth, problems with its teeth or some sort of injury which makes bitting uncomfortable.

e. If used by more novice riders, who try to use the hackamore like a conventional bridle, the horse will often begin to lean on the

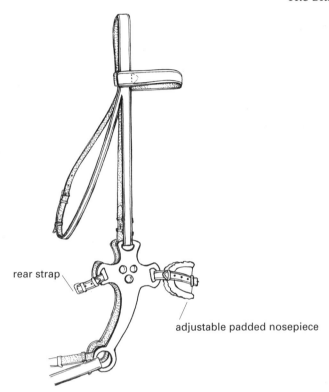

rear strap

adjustable padded nosepiece

Blair pattern bitless bridle

rider's hands as too much pressure is exerted by the rider on the reins.

f. There are some horses which go better when permanently in a hackamore rather than a bit, perhaps because of bad experience in the past with bitting, or perhaps because of an old injury.

g. Hackamores are not permitted for dressage competitions but can be used under BSJA rules for showjumping and under BHS rules for showjumping and cross country.

h. More severe hackamores have long shanks and a nose piece which tightens around the front of the nose when the contact on the reins is increased. The nose piece is covered with thick sheepskin. I have seen horses with swollen noses after being ridden in this type of hackamore, and prefer not to see them used.

STAGES III and IV

8. Nosebands and Additional Tack Affecting the Bitting Arrangement

a. The type of noseband worn with the bit can affect the bitting arrangement. The cavesson noseband is the simplest. It is often worn just to make the bridle look complete and does not affect the bitting at all if it is fitted to allow free movement of the jaws. The cavesson noseband is used to attach a standing martingale. It should be fitted to sit approximately the width of two fingers below the projecting cheek bone.

b. The Flash noseband is similar to a cavesson but has a second strap attached at the front which is fitted firmly around the nose and under the bit. The cavesson part of this noseband needs to be fitted firmly at the same height as an ordinary cavesson in order to stop the lower strap from pulling it down, and should therefore be thicker and more padded than an ordinary cavesson noseband, to prevent pinching and rubbing. The lower strap helps to keep the horse's mouth closed. This, in turn, makes it more difficult for the horse to evade the pressure of the bit. A standing martingale can be used with this noseband.

c. The drop noseband is fitted firmly around the nose, around the chin groove and below the bit. It is, therefore, fitted lower than the cavesson or Flash but should not restrict the horse's breathing – no lower than 10 cm (4 in) above the nostrils is a good guideline. This is probably the most effective noseband for keeping the horse's mouth closed and, at the same time, it exerts a certain amount of pressure on the nose.

d. The Grackle or cross noseband has a lower strap which fits below the bit, while the upper strap fits above. The two straps are fitted firmly to help to prevent the horse from crossing its jaws and opening its mouth to evade the bit. There is also some pressure on the nose at the centre point of the noseband.

e. The Puckle or Kineton noseband relies on nose pressure for its effectiveness. The front portion looks similar to a drop noseband but it does not encircle the nose. Instead, it has two metal loops

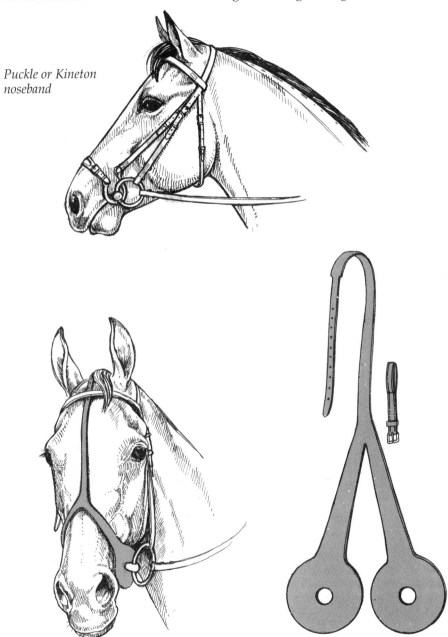

Puckle or Kineton noseband

Australian cheeker

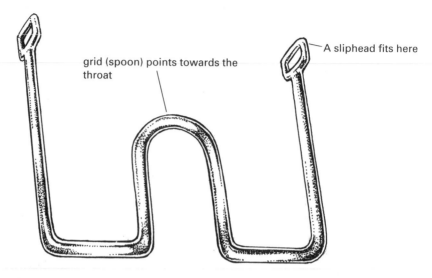

grid (spoon) points towards the throat

A sliphead fits here

A tongue grid

which fit around the bit. It should be fitted at the same level as a drop noseband. Each time a contact is taken on the rein, pressure is also applied to the nose.

f. The Australian cheeker is made of rubber and looks like two bit guards fixed together by a central strap which, in turn, attaches to the middle of the headpiece. This device is often used on race horses. It keeps the bit well up in the corners of the horse's mouth, which helps to prevent the horse from putting its tongue over the bit, and applies pressure to the nose when a contact is taken with the bit.

g. The tongue grid is a device which fits high in the horse's mouth, and prevents the horse from putting its tongue over the bit.

h. A tongue strap, which doesn't really affect the bitting, is a strap fitted around the lower jaw and over the tongue. This is generally used in racing to prevent a horse from swallowing its tongue during a race if it is found to be prone to this problem.

i. The running martingale, Market Harborough and other training aids already mentioned in the previous chapter all affect the bit and its actions.

Follow-up Work to Confirm Knowledge and Experience

1. To become familiar with a wide range of different bits, it may be necessary to visit the local saddlery shop and examine the range of bits available. Some of the yards which you visit or work at are bound to have a selection of bits but may not have a comprehensive range.
2. Where possible, ride a variety of horses in different types of bits and gain a first-hand feel of how they affect the horse and the way you ride it.
3. Fit as many different bits to as wide a range of horses as possible. A particular bit fitted to one horse with a particular type of mouth may look very different when fitted to another horse.
4. In order to become expert at putting on and fitting a double bridle, regular practice is vital.
5. Practise fitting the different types of noseband as well.

Helpful Hints and Exam Technique

1. Candidates are inclined to be muddled when describing the action of bits. Although you may think you understand the workings of the bit, it is important to practise talking about them in practice sessions so that you know you can put your thoughts into words clearly.
2. Candidates are rarely practised in putting on and adjusting double bridles. The only way to be good at the job is to practise it every day.

8   HORSE CLOTHING

STAGES II and III

1. Bandages

Bandages are made in different widths, lengths and materials, for different uses.

Tail Bandage

  a. Tail bandages are a little less stretchy than exercise bandages but are made from similar material, approximately 7–8 cm ($2\frac{3}{4}$–2 in) wide, with cotton ties.
  b. They are used to protect the tail while travelling and to help to improve the horse's appearance by keeping the top of the tail smooth, especially after it has been pulled.
  c. A tail bandage should not be left on for more than an hour. As it has to be applied firmly to prevent it from slipping down, it could interfere with circulation if left on too long. This may cause the hair to fall out!
  d. Damp the tail hair at the top of the tail before applying the bandage. This aids grip for the first few turns.
  e. For even pressure, keep the bandage smooth and overlap each turn evenly, as well as keeping the tension of the tapes, when tied, the same as the bandage.
  f. Bandage almost to the end of the dock for a pleasing appearance and a firm base to work around.
  g. When travelling, finish the bandage by winding it a few centimetres back up the tail, tie the tapes slightly to one side, and

fold the last turn of your bandage down over the tapes to cover them. This helps to prevent them being rubbed undone if the horse leans its tail against the wall in the box. If the bandage is finished and tied too high, the tapes and knot may rub against the horse and cause a sore.

h. Finally, with one hand under the tail, reshape it to follow the contour of the horse's hindquaters so that the horse is not left with its tail sticking out at an uncomfortable angle.

i. To remove the bandage, untie the tapes then slide the whole bandage off in one piece, from the top, down the horse's tail.

Stable/Travelling Bandages

a. Stable/travelling bandages are 10–12 cm (4–4$\frac{3}{4}$ in) in width and made from slightly stretchy material which may be wool, cotton or synthetic. They may have cotton ties or Velcro fastenings.

b. They can be used in the stable for warmth, for support after a hard day's competing or to secure a poultice.

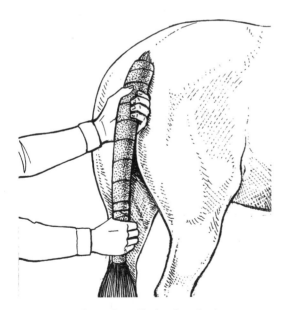

Shape the tail after bandaging

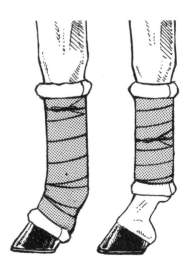

A travelling or   An exercise
stable bandage   bandage

c. Used for travelling, they provide support and protection.

d. Fybagee or gamgee is used under these bandages to help to distribute even pressure. When travelling, the Fybagee can be cut long enough to extend above and below the bandage to help to protect the coronet bands, knees and hocks. It is now possible to buy shaped pieces of padding for use under travelling bandages, which make it easier to protect the knees and hocks.

e. Roll the bandage around the leg in the same direction as the overlap of your Fybagee/gamgee. Otherwise the Fybagee/gamgee will be unrolling as you try to bandage.

STAGES III and IV

Exercise Bandages

a. Exercise bandages are very stretchy, approximately 10 cm (4 in) in width and made from an elastic and cotton mix, with cotton ties.

b. They can be used to give support when the horse is working. They are most frequently used in cross country or showjumping when brushing boots do not give as much support.

c. Always use Fybagee/gamgee underneath them.

d. For competition work, it is safer to secure the bandage with tape instead of ties and to sew the last turn to the rest of the bandage or sew down the complete length of the bandage.

e. Vetwrap bandages are often used as they are made of a material which sticks to itself as it is applied to the limb. The end result is a very secure bandage. However, these bandages can usually be used only once really effectively. This makes them expensive to use.

Further Points

a. For polo, thick bandages called polo wraps are often used to protect as much of the lower limb as possible from knocks and bruises. As they are particularly soft and thick, it is not necessary to use Fybagee/gamgee under these wraps. They are sometimes also used for working in for other disciplines such as dressage.

b. Other types of bandage appear on the market from time to time, intended for use in first aid situations. They may be impregnated with gel which will cool when exposed to the air, and will stay cool for several hours, or be used straight from the fridge, providing instant cold. Some designs are made from material which provides additional support to an injured limb.

STAGES II and III

2. Further Protective Equipment for Travelling

Make sure your horse is familiar with new equipment before the travelling day. For example, hock boots take time to get used to. Use a minimum of equipment for long journeys, to avoid sores and discomfort. Choose rugs that are suitable for the weather conditions.

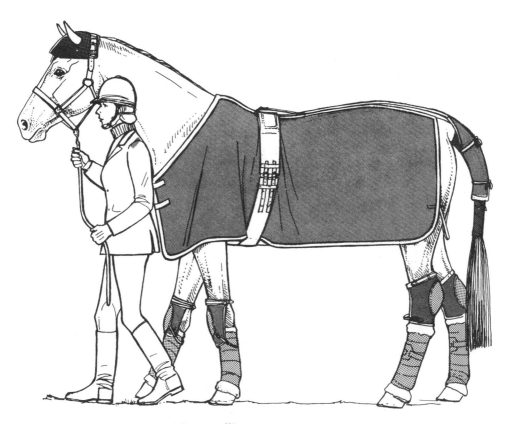

A horse equipped for travelling

Poll Guard

a. If there is not much head room in your box or trailer, and if the horse is tall or inclined to resist while being loaded, this is a useful item.

b. Some guards cover only the poll, while others extend to protect the eyes and forehead.

c. The poll guard attaches to the head collar. When fitting it, check that it will not rub around the ears and that the head collar will not slip back. If a browband is fitted to the head collar, this will prevent it from slipping back.

Tail Guard

a. This can be put over a tail bandage for short journeys but should be used on its own for long journeys.

b. This guard protects the very top of the tail. Horses often lean against the trailer ramp for support while travelling, causing this area of the tail to be rubbed raw.

c. Tail guards can be made from wool, cotton, leather or synthetic material, and may fasten with buckles, tapes, zips or Velcro. Attach it to the roller at one end, then position the top of the guard just above the top of the tail, wrap it around and fasten.

d. Many modern rugs which do not require rollers to keep them in place are fitted with a small loop of material to which the tail guard can be attached.

Knee and Hock Boots

a. The knees and hocks are vulnerable when travelling as the horse may lose its balance and stumble or knock its joints against the partitions etc.

b. These boots must be fitted firmly above the knee or hock to prevent them from slipping down. For this reason they must be well padded around the top strap, for comfort.

c. The lower strap needs to be quite loose to allow the joint to flex.

d. Knee boots are also made for exercise purposes, to protect the knees if the horse stumbles on the road. These are called exercise or skeleton knee boots. They consist of a simple knee cap, often with no lower strap and without the extra material found on the travelling type.

Travelling Boots

These come in many different shapes and sizes and are made from a variety of materials. They are a quick and simple alternative to bandages but do not give the same degree of support to tired legs. Most have Velcro fastenings. Some incorporate knee and hock protection.

Overreach Boots

a. Also called bell boots, these are designed to protect the bulbs of the heels from being trodden on from behind, therefore they are used on the front feet only.
b. They are usually made of rubber. Some fasten with buckles, rubber straps or Velcro and others are made to pull on.
c. They are mainly used for exercise but when used for travelling they help to protect the coronet band as well as the heels.
d. The pull-on variety can be difficult to get on. Soaking them in warm water for a few minutes will help.

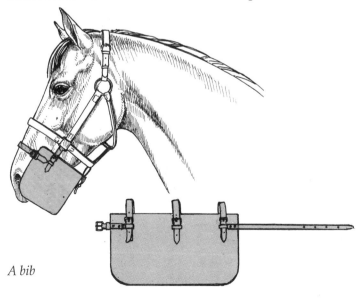

A bib

STAGES III and IV

3. Specialised Clothing

Bibs

A bib is attached to the headcollar and worn in the stable to stop a horse from chewing at its rugs. It can also be helpful if the horse is wearing bandages and tries to chew them. A bib can be made from leather or plastic.

Cradles

A cradle may be worn in the stable if a horse has been blistered or has any other ailment in which it must be prevented from rubbing part of its body with its nose. If it did rub a blistered area, for example, it would blister its nose and face. The other alternative would be to tie the horse up but this would be very restrictive. Care must be taken to ensure that there is nothing in the stable on which the cradle could get caught up.

A cradle

Muzzles

A muzzle may be worn in various situations to prevent a horse from eating or biting. It may be made of plastic or wire net, with a strap to attach it that is made of nylon or leather. When travelling to a show, a muzzle may be worn to prevent an unsociable traveller from biting its companions. At a competition, a muzzle may be worn to prevent a horse from eating grass, hay, bedding or from chewing the stable door. The muzzle must be designed to allow the horse to breathe easily and to drink without water becoming trapped in the muzzle.

Hoods

A hood can be made from various materials and will cover the head and neck. It may be worn in the stable or field to help to keep a horse clean or to keep it warm. Some turn-out rugs can be bought with neck attachments to keep the horse clean and dry.

A muzzle

A hood

Further Points

a. All equipment should be cleaned regularly. Any leather should be soaped and oiled in the usual way. Boots can be brushed or wiped clean depending on the material. Some can go in the washing machine.

Follow-up Work to Confirm Knowledge and Experience

1. It is advisable to practise putting on, checking the fitting and taking off as great a range of equipment as possible. As already mentioned, as so many different designs are now available, confidence will improve if the candidate is familiar with a wide range of designs. Visiting the local saddlery shop is helpful in this.
2. Speed and efficiency are important qualities to develop. A good way to do this is to be involved with horses going to competitions. Having to prepare horses for travelling, which must be ready for a certain deadline, or take care of a horse as it completes its competition, are good ways of improving these qualities.

Helpful Hints and Exam Technique

1. Check the available equipment carefully before you select what you are going to use for the task set. In an exam situation it is easy to miss something. Although you will be expected to be quick and efficient, it will be easier for you to do a good job if you have selected the right items to start with.
2. In your place of work, practise talking about the equipment you are fitting while you are fitting it. Although you do not have to talk while you work in the exam, there may be something you would like to point out to the examiner while they are observing your work. Practising this skill will help you to put over more information as you go along. However, you should remember that the ability to perform the practical skill is the most important part of the practical sections, rather than an ability to talk about it.

9 Conformation and the Superficial Muscles

STAGES III and IV

1. Type and Condition

a. The horse's condition is directly related to its state of health, the work it has been doing, its feeding programme and how it is being cared for.

b. A horse can be in good, but soft condition when it is unfit, in which case it may be lacking in muscle development. This should not be mistaken for poor conformation. Nor should an excess of fat be mistaken for good muscle development. For example, an excess of fat can lead to well-rounded quarters and a very prominent crest. By looking at the whole picture it should be possible to distinguish between the two.

c. Likewise a horse in poor condition should not be mistakenly thought of as having poor conformation when it may be quite good. This is when an experienced person should be able to picture how the horse would look if well cared for.

d. A fit horse, in good condition, should have firm, well-developed muscles but do remember that the muscle development will relate to the type of horse and the work it is fit for. A dressage horse will show more development of the muscles required for collection, whereas the race horse will show more development of muscles required for galloping and extension.

e. When first looking at the horse to assess its conformation, its type or breed should be a consideration, as this will obviously have a strong influence on the whole make up of the horse.

f. If the horse's breed is not known, then it may be described as Thoroughbred/cob/warmblood/pony/hunter "type", and so on.

g. It is necessary to be familiar with many different breeds of horse in order to be able to describe a horse as a certain type. For example, an Arab is expected to have a high tail carriage and dished face. These features may display themselves in a crossbred horse, giving away its part-Arab breeding. The quality of the Thoroughbred is used as a cross with a heavier horse to produce the hunter type, or with a pony to produce a hack or polo pony.

h. There can also be types within different breeds. For example the Dutch Warmblood may vary, from a heavier type suitable for riding and driving, to a more athletic type suitable for showjumping and dressage. The variations are endless but, whatever the breed, good conformation must be a priority.

2. The Head

a. The horse's ears are very good indicators of what the horse is thinking. When the horse is in a relaxed home environment, its ears can show us something about its character. If constantly laid back, the horse may have a mean and aggressive temperament, at least to handle, if not to ride. Pricked forward, they show intelligence and a pleasant disposition.

b. Long ears are sometimes thought to denote speed, and lop ears a kind temperament. However, the length of the horse's ears is really just a cosmetic feature which may make a horse more or less attractive.

c. The forehead should be broad and flat. A bulging forehead is sometimes linked with the horse behaving unpredictably, and the breadth of the forehead allows for the eyes to be set well apart.

d. The eyes need to be set well apart to allow for good peripheral vision. Large, clear, "kind" eyes seem to be linked with a kind, intelligent horse. Small eyes, often termed "piggy", frequently seem to go hand in hand with a "piggy" nature. Horses frequently showing a lot of white of the eye are usually frightened and may be aggressive. Of course, if the white of the eye is showing due to the horse having a wall eye or lack of pigment, then this is not related to the horse's character.

e. Horses with wall eyes, or very pale eyes, sometimes have problems in the summer as their eyes are very sensitive to bright sunshine.

f. The shape of the horse's nose is frequently related to its breeding and will make the horse more or less attractive. Welsh ponies and Arabs have dished faces; many horses have straight noses; some may have a Roman nose, which is generally linked with common breeding, as opposed to Thoroughbred blood.

g. Nostrils should be large and clearly defined in order to allow a free and generous intake of air.

h. The mouth should not be very short, which may cause difficulty in bitting, particularly if the horse is required to wear a double bridle. Likewise, the mouth should not appear to be very long. Long-mouthed horses are inclined to pull. If the lips are thick and fleshy, the horse may lack sensitivity.

i. When parting the lips to expose the teeth of the upper and lower jaw, the teeth should be seen to meet neatly together. If the upper set of teeth overlap the lower, this is termed overshot or parrot-mouthed. The opposite of this is an undershot jaw, where the lower set of teeth are further forward. If the teeth do not meet neatly, the horse can have problems with feeding and the wear of its teeth, which may lead to unthriftiness and resistance when being ridden. It can also be more difficult to tell the age of a horse with an over- or undershot jaw, due to uneven wear.

j. The horse should have a good width in its jaw. If you can fit a fist between the two jaw bones of the lower jaw (just in front of its throat), this is a good guideline and shows that the horse has plenty of room for the start of its respiratory tract.

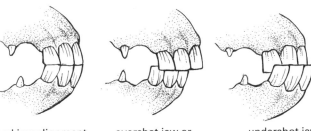

good jaw alignment   overshot jaw or   undershot jaw
                      parrot mouthed

Jaw alignment

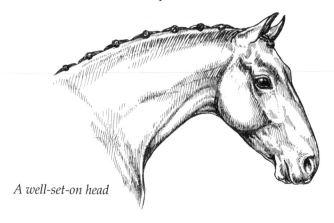

A well-set-on head

k. The overall size of the head should appear to be in proportion to the rest of the horse's body. A very large and heavy head, especially if it is set on the end of a long neck, will be inclined to make the horse heavy to ride and difficult to bring off its forehand. A very small head will not cause problems but may make the horse more or less attractive, depending on the overall type.

l. How the head is set on to the neck is very important. The head/neck junction should not appear to be thick through the jowl and gullet as this will make it difficult for the horse to flex correctly at the poll and can often lead to the horse being strong and resistant to ride. As a guide, you should be able to fit two fingers between the jaw bone and the wing of the atlas bone in the neck when the horse is standing relaxed. The throat and jaw line should be clearly defined.

3. The Neck

a. The horse uses its neck as a balancing pole. The length of its neck will affect its way of going and what it is like to ride.

b. When riding a horse with a good length of neck, you feel that you have plenty of horse in front of you, as opposed to a horse with a short neck, when you may feel that you could easily tip over its ears as you have very little in front of you. "A good length of rein" is the term used to describe a good neck that is also well set on to a good sloping shoulder.

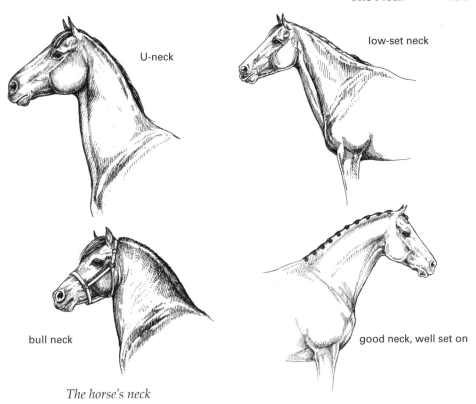

U-neck

low-set neck

bull neck

good neck, well set on

The horse's neck

c. The topline of the neck should be well developed, with a gentle upward curve from the withers to the poll. This shows that the horse will work in a good natural outline. If the topline dips down, the horse is said to have a U-neck or upside-down neck (sometimes also called a ewe neck). This goes hand in hand with a poor head carriage, making the horse more difficult to ride.

d. Along with the U-neck, you will see an overdeveloped underline, making it more difficult for the horse to work in a good outline.

e. A swan-necked horse will have a long neck which will dip a little in front of the wither then curve upwards to flex at the second vertebra rather than at the poll. The poll will then be lower than the highest point of the neck. This shows that the horse has difficulty in working in a good outline.

f. A short, thick neck, sometimes called a "bull" neck, is likely to make the horse strong and resistant to ride as the horse will find it difficult to flex and work in a good outline.

g. The neck should be set on to the shoulder in such a way that it appears to curve naturally upwards. A low-set neck will make it difficult for the horse to work with a light forehand, and is likely to develop into a U-neck, making the horse feel downhill to ride.

h. The trapezius muscle covers a triangular area stretching from halfway down the neck to a point just behind the withers and down the middle of the shoulder blade to form the point of the triangle. This muscle should be well developed as it lifts the shoulder and forehand (in combination with other muscles). A well-developed trapezius is an indication that the horse works in a good outline.

i. The rhomboideus muscle should be well developed as it is also involved in lifting the shoulder and forehand. It stretches from the ligamentum nuchae, running under the trapezius muscle on its way to attach to the shoulder blade. (The ligamentum nuchae is a large ligament which runs from poll to withers and helps to support the head.)

j. The splenius muscle turns the neck from side to side and also extends it. When well developed, it helps to make up a good topline as it occupies the space that stretches from behind the poll to where the trapezius begins.

k. The sternocephalic muscle lies directly under the horse's neck, running from the jowl region to the breast bone. It helps to move the head and neck and should not be overdeveloped. U-necked or bull-necked horses sometime have an overdeveloped sternocephalic muscle which bulges forward when they set themselves against the rider, making it difficult to get the horse to relax into a good outline.

l. The brachiocephalicus muscle moves the head and neck to either side and brings the shoulder and forelimbs forward. It runs from just behind the jaw, along the lower side of the neck, to attach to the humerus. It should be well developed in a fit horse as it is very important for good movement in front, whether the horse is racing, jumping or in dressage training. If the rider uses a restrictive rein contract, he or she will restrict the movement of the brachiocephalicus muscle and therefore restrict the horse from

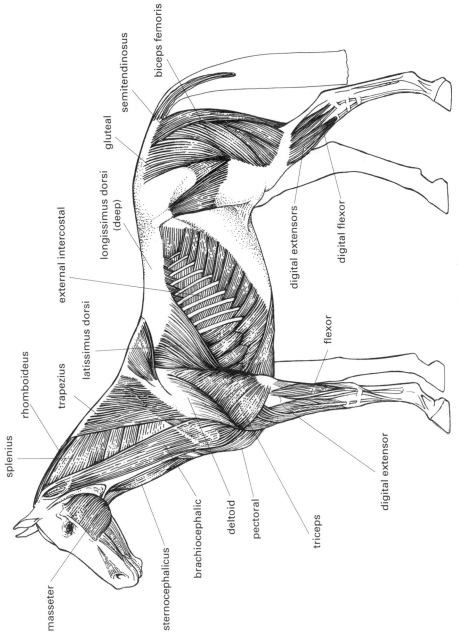

biceps femoris

semitendinosus

gluteal

longissimus dorsi (deep)

external intercostal

latissimus dorsi

rhomboideus

trapezius

splenius

masseter

sternocephalicus

brachiocephalic

deltoid

pectoral

triceps

digital extensors

digital flexor

flexor

digital extensor

The superficial muscles

moving freely. For example, if the rider does not allow the horse to stretch its head and neck forward when jumping a fence, the horse will not be able to use the brachiocephalicus muscle to draw its shoulders and front limbs up and forward to clear the fence.

4. The Shoulders and Withers

a. The withers, which are formed by the dorsal spinous processes of some of the thoracic vertebrae, lie at the top of the shoulder, between the base of the neck and the beginning of the horse's back.

b. Some horses, usually of Thoroughbred type, have very prominent withers. This can make saddle fitting difficult as there must be no pressure on the withers when the horse is ridden. Undue pressure can lead to fistulous withers.

c. The other extreme is very flat withers which can cause equal problems for saddle fitting as there is nothing for the saddle to fit over. It can be a common problem in small ponies which then need a crupper to stop their saddles from slipping forward up their necks.

d. The ideal is clearly defined withers which are neither too prominent or flat.

e. A horse which hollows away excessively on either side of the withers is lacking in development of the trapezius muscle.

f. The slope of the shoulder depends on the slope of the scapula or shoulder blade. If you draw an imaginary line down the middle of the shoulder blade, it should slope to form an angle of approximately 45 degrees with a line horizontal to the ground.

g. A well-sloping shoulder contributes to the horse having a good length of rein and allows the horse to take a naturally long stride. This has several advantages. It allows the horse to cover the ground smoothly with minimum concussion to the limbs. It helps the horse to extend for dressage, jumping or fast work. It also contributes to making the horse a more comfortable ride.

h. An upright shoulder leads to a short stride which will contribute to greater concussion for the limbs, a less comfortable ride and, usually, a horse with less scope for competition work.

i. Having said that, a shorter-striding horse can be good for beginners who are learning to ride as a less-extravagant movement is helpful while they learn basic balance and co-ordination.

j. The term "loaded shoulder" is used when a horse is very broad across its shoulders and appears very heavy in front.

k. The horse should be well muscled over its shoulders, without excessive development which would contribute to a loaded shoulder. These muscles include the neck muscles already mentioned, which extend into the shoulder area along with the deltoid, triceps and latissimus dorsi.

l. The deltoid muscle lies over the scapula and runs down to the humerus. It helps to flex the shoulder joint.

m. The triceps muscles form a bulge at the lower part of the shoulder, just above the elbow joint. They help to flex the shoulder and extend the elbow joint.

n. The latissimus dorsi runs from behind the shoulder and up on to the back. It also flexes the shoulder joint.

5. The Chest

a. A broad, deep chest allows for plenty of heart and lung room. When viewed from the front, therefore, the horse should appear to have a leg at each corner of its chest, rather than seeming to have both legs coming from one hole in the middle.

b. A good guideline, which stems from the showing world, is that you should be able to imagine fitting a bowler hat between the two forearms.

c. However, an overly broad chest can give the horse a rolling action and make it uncomfortable to ride.

d. With a broad chest and a leg at each corner, the horse is less likely to have problems with close action in front.

e. From a side view, a chest, which appears to bulge forward is referred to as a pigeon chest. This can make the horse a little heavy in front.

f. The superficial muscles, which we see forming distinct bulges over the front of the chest, are the pectoral muscles. These help to advance each forelimb.

6. The Front Limbs

a. When viewed from in front or from the side, the front limbs should appear to be straight and an equal pair. They will then be able to carry the weight of the horse evenly. Any crookedness in the limbs will lead to the weight being carried unevenly, therefore putting more strain on certain parts of the limb or foot.

b. The term "tied in at the elbow" is used when the horse appears to have elbows held in very tight against its sides. This can lead to restriction of movement and is an undesirable feature.

c. A long, well-muscled forearm, along with a short cannon bone, is a good feature. The cannon bone supports the majority of the horse's weight. If it is short, dense and broad in circumference, it will be more able to support the load. Cannon bones which are long and thin are likely to be weak.

d. When the horse has a good pair of cannon bones, it is said to have "good bone". The bone is measured around its circumference, just below the knee. The amount of bone which is desirable depends upon the size and type of horse.

e. It is generally accepted that a horse with around 20 cm (8 in) of bone will carry up to 82.5 kg (13 st). Around 23 cm (9 in) of bone will carry up to 95 kg (15 st). If the horse's bone measures more than 23 cm (9 in) then it will be a strong, heavyweight horse, capable of carrying a heavy rider.

f. As a guide, a quality 16 h.h. TB would be expected to have a minimum of 20 cm (8 in) of bone. A similar-sized hunter would certainly need 21.5 cm ($8\frac{1}{2}$ in) and a warmblood type about 23 cm (9 in) of bone.

g. There are several muscles in the forearm, but the digital extensor muscles at the front, and digital flexor muscles towards the back, are those which become tendons in the lower part of the limb. As their names suggest, their jobs are to extend or flex the limb.

h. Knees should be large and flat. A large joint is more able to absorb concussion as the surface areas within the joint are larger and therefore concussion is spread over a greater area. A flat joint is free from signs of swellings or other blemishes.

i. When a horse is said to be "calf kneed", it has knees which seem to bow in towards each other. This would put uneven strain on the lower limb and place extra weight on the inside of the foot.

j. The term "tied in below the knee", refers to limbs which appear to narrow excessively just below the knee. This makes the limb weak and leaves little room for tendons and ligaments.

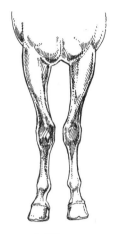
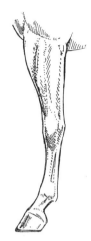
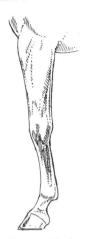

Calf knees   *Back at the knee*   *Over at the knee*

k. Viewed from the side, "over at the knee" is when the knee seems to be forward, with the cannon bone angled back from it. Some horses are equally over at the knee on both limbs, while others are more so in one limb than another. This fault can be the result of contracted tendons, in which case it may lead to tripping. If it is a feature of the horse's natural conformation, however, it rarely leads to tendon-related lameness and, as such, is a feature favoured by some people.

l. "Back at the knee", which is the opposite problem, is a less desirable feature. It will put more strain on the tendons at the back of the limb, therefore it is a weakness and likely to cause unsoundness.

m. Running down the back of a short, strong cannon bone should be clearly defined tendons with no sign of swelling or thickening.

n. The fetlock joint should be large, clean and clearly defined, not rounded.

o. The pastern and foot generally slope at a similar angle to the shoulder, so a horse with an upright shoulder usually has upright pasterns and feet. A pastern sloping at about 45 degrees is best, as either extreme can cause problems. An upright pastern will not be good at absorbing concussion, while a very sloping pastern will have too much give and put strain on the tendons.

p. The feet should follow on from the slope of the pastern. A broken foot/pastern axis is usually due to poor care of the feet and poor farriery. Once this axis is broken, there is weakness as the ability of these structures to absorb concussion is reduced.

q. The feet should be of equal size and in proportion to the size of the horse. Feet that seem small for the size of horse will have little room for internal structures and be less able to cope with concussion. Large "soup-plate" like feet often combine with a heavy-footed movement which only serves to increase concussion.

r. Flat feet are prone to bruising of the sole. Low heels are weak and inclined to get bruised. "Boxy" feet are a sign that there are internal changes taking place which will probably result in unsoundness.

s. Horses which stand "pigeon toed" will not move straight and will probably "dish". If they stand with their toes turned out, they will be more inclined to brush as, once again, they will not move straight.

t. Feet which appear to dip in at any point on the wall are certainly a cause for concern as internal structures may be cramped.

u. There are many seats of ailments in the front limbs, ranging from capped elbow to splints, tendon or ligament strain, sesamoiditis, ring bone, side bone, navicular and pedalosteitis. Some of these may be caused by direct injury or may be due to faults in conformation or be hereditary.

7. The Back and Barrel

a. "Deep through the girth" is a term used to describe a good deep chest, viewed from the side, which will allow plenty of room for the heart and lungs.

b. The underline of the horse, from the girth to the stifle, will vary according to condition and fitness. An overly fat horse will droop downwards, while a fit horse will curve smoothly upwards, giving a more "greyhound-like" appearance.

c. If the underline draws up very sharply towards the stifle, despite the horse being in good condition, it is said to be "herring gutted". If it draws up a little bit sharply, for example after a period of hard work, it is said to "run up a little light". This will be remedied with good feeding and a period of lighter work.

d. The shape of the horse's barrel depends upon its rib cage. "Well sprung" ribs are those which give the horse's barrel a well-rounded shape. This is a good feature, giving the rider a good base to sit on and allowing plenty of room for the internal organs.

e. If the rib cage is very rounded and broad, however, the horse can feel uncomfortably wide to sit on. Equally uncomfortable is the horse that is very narrow, with ribs that seem to drop straight down. This horse is called "slab sided" and will feel very insubstantial to sit on.

f. To assess the length of the horse's back, stand away from the horse and draw an imaginary line straight down through its girth. The horse should appear to be the same length nose to girth as it is from girth to point of buttock, when standing at rest. This can be a useful way of assessing how well proportioned the horse is.

g. A horse with a short back is said to be "short coupled" or "well ribbed up". It should be strong, find it easy to track up and be able to engage its hindquarters more easily for all types of work, providing the rest of its conformation is good.

h. A very short back can be a problem, however, when it comes to saddle fitting. If the rider requires quite a large saddle, they may find it sits too close to the horse's loins which should not be carrying the weight of the rider. It is also not a desirable feature in a brood mare as she requires a good length of back to allow for the abdominal room needed to accommodate a foal.

i. A long back is generally looked upon as a weakness. The horse will find it more difficult to track up and engage its hindquarters for all types of work.

j. Long-backed horses are sometimes referred to as being "short of a rib". This means that the gap between the last rib and the point of hip seems very long and therefore gives the impression that the horse is missing a rib. As a guide, one would usually expect to be able to fit a hand's span between the last rib and the point of hip.

k. A "roach backed" horse is one which appears to slope upwards to a slight hump towards and over the loins. This is not a good feature. The horse is uncomfortable to ride as it tips the rider forward and will be inclined to go on its forehand.

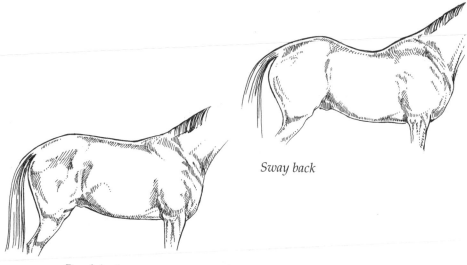

Sway back

Roach back

l. A "sway-backed" horse is one with a dipped back. This some-times occurs in a brood mare after she has had several foals, and sometimes occurs with either sex in old age. A horse which is sway backed as part of its natural conformation will tend to look rather odd and weak. However, when under saddle they often look quite normal and give a good, comfortable ride.

m. The loins, which lead into the hindquarters, should appear to be strong and well muscled. Long-backed horses often appear to have weak loins.

n. Running from the lumbar vertebrae/loin area, forward over the back and ribs to behind the withers, is the longissimus dorsi mus-cle which is the longest and largest muscle in the body. This is the muscle which carries the weight of the rider and, as such, is an important muscle to see well developed. It extends the back and is involved with turning from side to side.

o. Over the rest of the chest and abdomen are the intercostal mus-cles, which fill the spaces between the ribs and assist in breath-ing, and the abdominal wall muscles (of which there are several layers) which support the weight of the internal organs and at-tach to several structures, including the ribs and pelvic bones.

8. The Hindquarters and Hind Limbs

a. The hindquarters are the power house which propels the horse forward and, as such, should appear to be well muscled and strong.

b. When viewed from behind, with the horse standing square, the quarters should appear well rounded, with the horse's hips level.

c. The tail should be "well set on". This phrase refers to a tail which is not too low set as this often denotes weak, sloping quarters.

d. A very pronounced croup is sometimes referred to as a "jumper's bump".

e. If the horse has a fairly pronounced croup with quarters that slope away quite sharply, it is called "goose rumped".

f. Some people favour a jumper's bump with a slight goose rump as good conformation for a jumping horse.

g. When the horse moves, the tail should be carried and should swing in a relaxed manner. If it is clamped down or held crookedly in any way, this can be a sign of tension or, possibly, back trouble.

h. The hocks should be "well let down". This means that the first and second thigh are long and well muscled for maximum strength, with the hocks close to the ground. You are also looking for good length from hip to point of buttock.

i. When viewed from behind, the thighs should appear thick. The horse should not appear to have a wide gap going up between its thighs as this is a sign that they lack muscle and are weak.

j. From a side view, with the horse standing square, you should be able to imagine a line that is perpendicular to the ground, running from the point of buttock to the point of hock to the back of the fetlock joint.

k. If the hocks appear to be behind the point of buttock, this is a weakness and the rider will find it difficult to encourage the horse to work with its "hocks engaged".

l. If the fetlock is forward of this line, so that the cannon bones slope forward, these are "sickle hocks" and, again, are weak.

m. If the hind limb appears very straight from a side view, with little curve from thigh round to hock, the horse is said to be rather straight through its hocks. This is a poor feature. Again, the horse

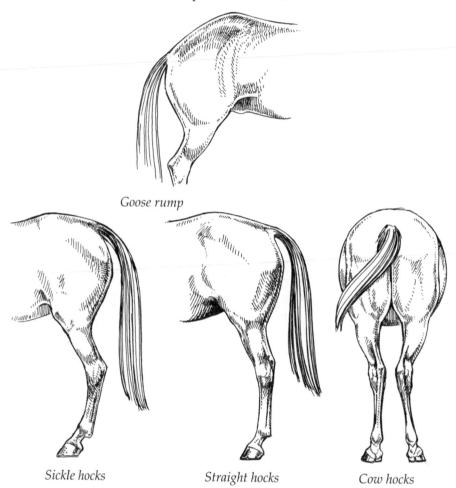

Goose rump

Sickle hocks   *Straight hocks*   *Cow hocks*

is less likely to find it easy to work "up together" with its hind
limbs engaged.

n. From behind, you are looking for straight hind limbs. If the hocks
turn in towards each other, the horse is called "cow hocked". If
the hocks bow out, the horse is "wide behind", "base wide" or
"base narrow", depending on whether the fetlocks are set wide
apart or close together. Any deviation from straight leads to poor
movement and uneven weight distribution.

o. The hock and fetlock joints should be large and clearly defined
with no sign of swelling or puffiness.

p. The hind pasterns and feet should slope at an angle of approximately 50 degrees. Again, a broken foot/pastern axis is not desirable.

q. The gluteal muscles form the main muscle mass over the hindquarters. They flex and extend the hip joint and draw the limb towards the body, as well as being involved in actions such as rearing, kicking and galloping. These muscles extend from the croup, down and over the hip.

r. The biceps femoris, which extends the limb, is a large muscle which stretches from behind the gluteals and on down the thigh. It has several attachments which include the patella and the tibia.

s. The semitendinosus muscle, which extends the hip and hock joints, runs down the back of the hindquarters, behind the biceps femoris.

t. The biceps femoris and semitendinosus muscles are part of the "hamstring" group.

u. All of these muscles need to be well developed in the competition horse, with the gluteal muscles likely to be more prominent in the dressage horse, and the hamstring group more prominent in eventers and race horses.

v. The digital flexor and extensor muscles are found in the hind limb (as they were in the front limb), forming the second thigh.

w. There are many seats of ailments in the hind limbs, ranging from capped hock to spavins, splints, curbs, ring bone and side bone. Again, these may be caused by direct injury or poor conformation, or may be hereditary.

9. Action

Assessment of Action

a. One of the best ways to see how a horse moves in all gaits is to see it loose in a field, showing its paces of its own free will.

b. For a more controlled assessment of the horse's action, it is watched moving in hand on a firm, level surface. The observer should stand where they can see the horse first walk away from them, then towards them and on past them in a straight line, then trot away, then towards and past them.

c. The handler should encourage the horse to move actively and should also keep it on a straight line. At the same time, they should ensure that the horse's head is free to move and therefore must avoid a tight hold near the horse's head.

d. When turning the horse, the handler should walk around the horse, turning it away from them. In this way the horse's hindquarters remain engaged and more control is maintained.

e. As the horse moves away, concentrate mainly on the hind limbs. When it moves towards you, concentrate mainly on the front limbs. As the horse passes you, look at the length and fluency of its stride.

f. The handler should take care to ensure that the horse has returned to walk before turning it and that the horse is straight and balanced in walk before it trots away again. If this procedure is hurried, the horse can easily be made to slip, especially as it is being trotted up on a firm surface.

g. As the horse is turned round in walk, the hind legs should move in a supple way, with the inside hind stepping forward and under. If the horse shuffles or tries to step back, it shows lack of suppleness and may even be a symptom of disease or injury.

h. This same procedure is used when observing a horse to see if it is lame.

The Gaits

a. The horse's walk is a four-time gait. There should be four even beats. The sequence incorporates the hind and front limbs on each side following each other; for example, near hind followed by near fore, then off hind followed by off fore.

b. The trot is a two-time gait. There should be two even beats. The sequence of legs in trot is hind and front limbs moving in diagonal pairs, with a moment of suspension as the horse changes from one diagonal pair to the other; for example, near hind and off fore moving together, a moment of suspension, followed by off hind and near fore moving together.

c. The canter is a three-time gait. There should be three clear beats. The sequence of legs is one hind leg, followed by the other hind leg and the diagonally opposite foreleg together, then, finally, the "leading" foreleg; for example, near hind, followed by off hind and near fore together, followed by the off fore which would be the leading leg. This would therefore be the sequence for right canter.

d. The gallop is a four-time gait. There will be four separate beats. The sequence would be one hind followed by the other hind, then one fore followed by the other fore, with a moment of suspension before the sequence begins again; for example, near hind then off hind, followed by near fore then off fore.

Faults and Different Types of Action

a. In all gaits, the horse should move straight in both front and hind limbs. If they do not move straight, they may be prone to brushing. This is when one limb knocks against the opposite limb, thereby causing injury. This may occur between the front limbs or the hind limbs.

b. The horse may brush very low or higher up the limb, and the injury may be a slight bruise or as severe as an open wound.

c. Young horses often brush due to a lack of balance when learning new movements or when being worked on the lunge. To protect the legs against this type of brushing, boots may be worn on all four limbs.

d. Older horses which brush consistently due to poor action may be helped by simple brushing boots, or may need special shoes if their problem is more severe.

e. Speedy cutting is similar to brushing but tends to happen at faster paces and usually occurs higher up the limb. Again, it may occur between front limbs or hind limbs. In the faster paces, one limb will come across and strike into the opposite limb just below the knee or hock. This generally results in broken skin with bruising. Special boots, which extend a little higher up the limb than normal, are required.

f. Overreaching occurs when a hind foot comes forward and steps on the heel of the front foot. This can result in a severe open wound. Overreaching may occur when a horse is jumping or being ridden through deep going, when it is simply not able to move its front feet forward as quickly as it normally would. Alternatively, it may occur as a consistent problem in a short-coupled horse when

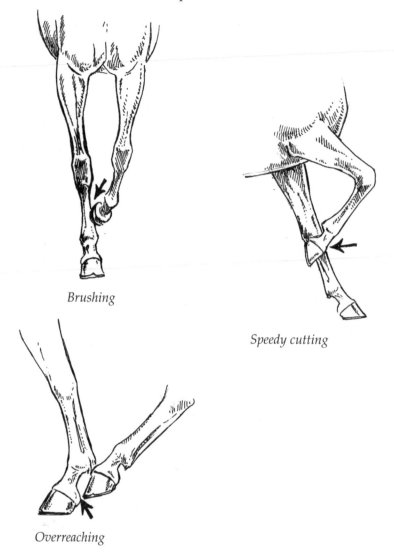

Brushing

Speedy cutting

Overreaching

working in trot and canter because it takes a long stride with its hind limbs. Polo ponies are likely to overreach as they have to stop quickly from fast paces and turn sharply.

g. Overreach boots can be worn for protection or, in more severe cases, special shoeing may be needed.

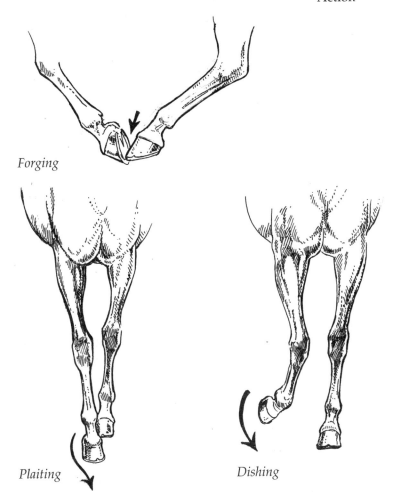

Forging

Plaiting

Dishing

h. Forging generally occurs when a horse is being lazy or has become unbalanced. A clicking sound is heard in walk or trot as the hind foot comes forward just before the front foot has managed to get out of the way. This results in the toe of the hind shoe catching against the toe of the front shoe.

i. Plaiting can occur with front or hind limbs and will not necessarily result in injury unless the horse brushes at the same time. In walk or trot the horse is seen to place one foot across and in front of the other.

j. Dishing occurs in front. The horse is less likely to interfere with an opposite limb with this action fault in which the front limbs, from the knee down, are moved in an outward, circular motion. Pigeon-toed horses are prone to this fault which occurs mainly in trot and to some extent in canter.

k. "Daisy cutting" is a pretty, straight-legged action often seen in show ponies. The toes are flicked forward and straight, close to the ground, knocking the heads off the daisies, hence the name.

l. Other minor problems in action are simply described according to what the observer sees. For example, if the horse moves with its hind legs very close, but is not actually brushing, it would be described as being close behind.

Follow-up Work to Confirm Knowledge and Experience

1. Look at and analyse the conformation of as many horses as possible.
2. Go to shows and observed the characteristics of different breeds in pure bred classes.
3. Visit horse sales where you may see a greater range of horses than you would at home, and observe the condition of these horses. Are they fat, thin, fit, healthy, in poor health, etc.? Also look out for blemishes and see if you can identify any ailments such as splints, spavin, capped hock, etc.
4. Attend horse trials from Novice to Advanced level, showjumping competitions from Novice to Advanced level, and dressage competitions from Novice to Advanced level. Compare the type of horses seen eventing, showjumping and in dressage. See how fit the horses at the lower levels of competition look when compared with those at the higher levels of competition. Likewise, compare the muscle development from lower levels to higher levels, and among dressage, showjumping and event horses.
5. At competitions you will have endless opportunity to observe different types of action.

Helpful Hints and Exam Technique

1. In order to help you to assess how much bone a horse has, measure the span running from the tip of your forefinger to the tip of

your thumb. When you wrap your thumb and forefinger around the horse's cannon bone, you will then have some idea of the measurement of bone. Along the same lines, if you know your own height in hands, then it will help you to assess the height of any horse.

2. If asked to talk about the horse's conformation, stand back and take in an overall impression. This gives you an idea of the type and breed of horse and therefore the job it may be most suited to. This will help your more detailed analysis. For example, if you think the horse looks suited to eventing and then you discover it is a little light of bone and long in the cannon, you may like to comment that it may not stand up to hard fast work without sustaining a tendon injury.

3. When examining a horse with regard to conformation and any blemishes it may have, work logically from head down the neck, shoulder and forelegs (comparing one foreleg with the other), along the back and barrel, over the hindquarters and down the hind limbs (compare one hind limb with the other). Don't forget to view the horse from in front and from behind. By using a logical process you are less likely to miss anything.

4. When talking about particular aspects of conformation, try not to say something is bad or good and leave it at that. Always follow up with why it is a good feature or a poor one.

5. When being examined, take care to approach the horse safely and with due regard for it. If you are the third or fourth person to be asked a question about conformation and the area in question is the hindquarters, don't just step forward and prod the horse's hind limb. Go to its shoulder, speak to the horse and stroke a hand over its body to the area you wish to examine or talk about. Remember that your general approach to your work and your ability to show an affinity with the horse are constantly being examined.

6. Remember, when you are assisting another candidate (for example, holding the horse, trotting it up, etc.), you are still under examination yourself. Keep alert, help the other candidate, stand the horse square. Generally remain involved, even when questions are not being directly aimed at you.

10 The Lower Limb and Shoeing

Understanding some of the farrier's work and the structure of the lower limb and foot will help the horse owner to keep the horse's feet in good condition.

STAGES III and IV

1. The Structure of the Lower Limb and Foot

a. The foot is designed to support the horse, reduce concussion, resist wear and provide grip.
b. Because we demand more from the horse than nature intended, the foot often needs protection to prevent it from wearing down more quickly than it can regrow. By shoeing it, the foot is protected and extra grip is provided.
c. Shoeing can also be used to correct faults and heal ailments and injuries.

The Lower Limb

a. Below the knee and hock joints, the bones of the lower limbs consist of the cannon bone with two splint bones running down the back, the long pastern and the first half of the short pastern, which then goes on into the foot, and the two sesamoid bones at the back of the fetlock joint.
b. Down the front of the limb run the two extensor tendons. The common digital extensor tendon runs from the muscle above the knee down over the front of the knee and on down the limb to

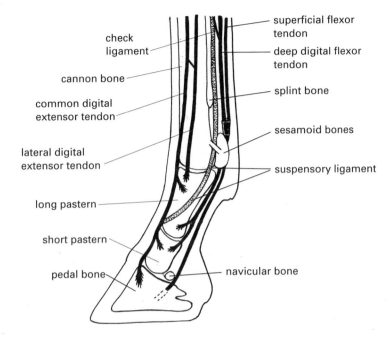

check
ligament

cannon bone

common digital
extensor tendon

lateral digital
extensor tendon

long pastern

short pastern

pedal bone

superficial flexor
tendon

deep digital flexor
tendon

splint bone

sesamoid bones

suspensory ligament

navicular bone

Structure of the lower limb

attach to the top of the pedal bone. It also has small attachments
to the long and short pastern bones. The lateral digital extensor
tendon runs down the limb in a similar way and attaches to the
long pastern bone.

c. Down the back of the limb run the two flexor tendons. The deep
digital flexor tendon runs from the muscle above the knee down
the back of the limb, under the navicular bone and attaches to the
pedal bone. The superficial flexor tendon runs down the limb in a
similar way and branches in two to attach to the long and short
pastern bones.

d. The check ligament supports the back of the knee and attaches to
the deep digital flexor tendon. The suspensory ligament, which is
attached to the back of the cannon bone just below the knee, runs
down the back of the limb, branching to attach to each sesamoid
bone, and then around each side of the fetlock joint to attach to
the common digital extensor tendon.

STAGE III

2. What to Look for in the Newly Shod Foot

a. Each pair of feet should look equal in size and shape.

b. The foot and pastern should slope at the same angle. If this angle differs, it is referred to as a broken foot/pastern axis.

c. The foot should not appear to have been rasped excessively. It should mainly have been rasped around the lower half to tidy the ragged edges.

d. The clenches should all be fairly level, approximately a third of the way up the wall of the hoof.

e. The toe of the foot should not be "dumped" to make the foot fit the shoe. "Dumping" is when the toe has been cut back excessively. The shoe should be made to fit the foot.

f. The heels of the shoe should have good length to support the heels of the hoof.

g. The foot should appear to be flush with the shoe all the way round. There should not be any gaps or apparent unevenness.

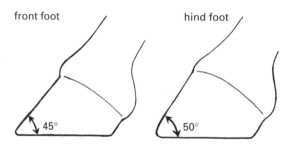

front foot   45°   hind foot   50°

Correct slope and angle of the foot

STAGES III and IV

3. Problems Caused by Poor Shoeing

a. If the horse's feet are not equal pairs, the farrier is altering the natural shape of the horse's feet, unless the horse has some known

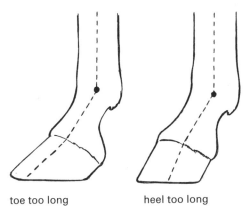

toe too long   heel too long

Broken foot/pastern axis

physical defect like a club foot. Alteration of the natural shape can only lead to unsoundness, as internal structures will be forced to undergo unnatural stresses, causing bruising, inflammation and, eventually, a breakdown of the structures.

b. If the foot/pastern axis is broken, the horse's natural way of moving will be affected. In turn the structures of the limbs and feet will undergo unnatural stresses which will, again, lead to unsoundness. This type of unsoundness will endanger the rider in the early stages as the horse is likely to trip and stumble due to the alterations in its natural gait. The most common fault leading to these problems is when the toe is left too long, throwing the horse back on its heels, straining the flexor tendons and probably causing the horse to trip.

c. Excessive rasping will remove a great deal of periople and leave the foot exposed and unable to regulate the moisture content.

d. Unlevel clenches may be an indication of a nail placed too close to the sensitive internal structures, causing nail bind or nail prick and subsequent lameness.

e. Dumping the foot to fit the shoe causes pressure on the internal structures as the shoe pinches. This will result in lameness.

f. Shoes that are short at the heels do not give sufficient support to the foot. This will lead to collapsed, weak heels and eventual unsoundness.

g. The bearing surface of the foot must be level to provide the horse with even support. Any unevenness results in the weight of the horse being carried unevenly which, in turn, will put unnatural stresses on various structures. A well-prepared foot is generally termed well balanced. The balance of the foot must be perfect in order to carry the weight of the horse evenly.

STAGES III and IV

4. Special Shoes

If the horse has naturally faulty action, or an ailment which can be helped through surgical shoeing, there is a range of designs of special shoes that the farrier can make for the horse. In conjunction with a vet, a farrier can make a surgical shoe tailored specially for a specific problem.

Rolled-toe Shoe

a. This type of shoe is commonly used to help a horse which is inclined to forge or repeatedly overreaches. With both of these problems, the hind foot catches up with the front foot before it can be moved away.

b. When the horse forges, the toe of the hind shoe catches against the toe of the front shoe and a clicking sound is heard. This can happen in walk and trot. It is possible for the horse to begin bruising the sole of the front foot at the toe.

c. When the horse overreaches, the hind foot strikes into the front limb at any point between the back of the knee (high overreach) and the heels (low overreach).

d. If the horse is badly affected by one of these problems, the farrier will endeavour to speed up the "breakover" of the front feet. As the horse takes a step, each hoof is taken forward and reaches a point where it rolls over the toe. The "breakover" point is the point at which the toe of the hoof is lifted and moved forward.

e. To speed up the breakover, the farrier will make the toe a little shorter and fit a rolled-toe shoe.

f. In the case of overreaching, the farrier will also fit the hind shoe a little further back under the toe to help to prevent the shoe from

striking into the front limb. If the horse has only a slight inclina-
tion towards these problems, this may be all that is needed and a
rolled toe shoe is unnecessary.

g. Any ailment which can be helped by speeding up the breakover
   of a front or hind limb can be helped by a rolled-toe shoe.

h. The problem with speeding up the breakover by shortening the
   toe and allowing the heel to be a little longer is that the balance of
   the foot is altered, which could lead to future internal problems,
   as already mentioned.

Feather-edged Shoe

a. This type of shoe is used to help a horse which is inclined to brush
   the inner aspect of one shoe against the opposite leg, causing injury through bruising or cutting into the skin.

b. The inner branch of the shoe is made much narrower and smoother
   than normal and may have fewer or no nail holes. By reducing
   the amount of shoe in this way there is less likelihood of the shoe
   knocking into the opposite limb.

Three-quarter Shoe

For horses which have a particularly severe brushing problem, part of the
inner branch of the shoe can be removed altogether. This leaves a shoe which
extends just three-quarters of the way of a normal shoe around the hoof.

   This type of shoe should only be used if the problem is extreme as it
leaves the hoof partly unsupported.

Grass Tip

This shoe was traditionally fitted to hunters during their summer holidays.
It is a shoe which protects just the toe area of the hoof as this is the area most
likely to split and break if unprotected. Again, as this shoe leaves the heels
unsupported, its use is not so popular now.

Wide-web Shoe

a. This shoe has a broader than normal foot-bearing surface which
   helps to support the hoof and disperse concussion.

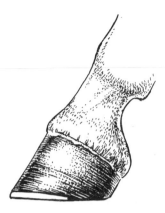

Grass tip

b. It is inevitably a heavier shoe for the horse to wear but can be helpful in preventing concussion-related ailments, such as ring bone and side bone.

c. It is most frequently worn by the competition horse during times when the ground is particularly hard to work on.

d. It may also be used to help to encourage a contracted hoof to expand.

e. A wide-web shoe may also be "seated out" to help to relieve pressure against the sole if the horse also has flat feet. A "seated out" shoe has a narrower foot-bearing surface than ground-bearing surface.

Bar Shoe

a. These shoes are used for a variety of ailments and may be full bar, egg bar or heart bar in design.

b. The horse's weight is distributed over a greater bearing surface.

c. This can be helpful if the horse suffers from corns and it is necessary to remove any pressure from the seat of corn while still offering protection to that area.

d. A bar shoe will also help to prevent too much movement in the heel area, which can be helpful if the horse has any damage to the pedal bone and needs movement to be restricted during the healing process.

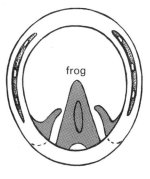 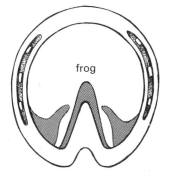

Egg-bar shoe   *Heart-bar shoe*

e. The egg-bar shoe extends further back at the heels than the full-bar shoe. This, in turn, spreads some of the weight of the horse further back and generally reduces compression within the foot. This will help to improve the blood supply and can be helpful in the treatment of navicular. A rolled toe will probably also be used.

f. The heart-bar shoe is used to help to support the pedal bone in cases of laminitis.

g. If the horse is shod with a bar shoe and is sound for work, the heavy clumsiness of the shoe means that the work will probably be restricted to steady flat work on fairly level ground.

Patten Shoe

This shoe is used if the horse has a particularly severe tendon injury. It raises the heel and relieves the tendon of stress while in the initial stages of healing. The horse will not be able to work when shod with a patten shoe and will be restricted to box rest. As the injury heals, the horse will be reshod with a slightly less raised heel shoe, so that the leg is lowered gradually, before returning to normal shoes.

Swan-necked Shoe

This shoe would be used if a tendon had been severed, leaving the leg in need of artificial support. It may be used in conjunction with the leg being put in a plaster cast for extra stability. The horse would obviously be confined to box rest.

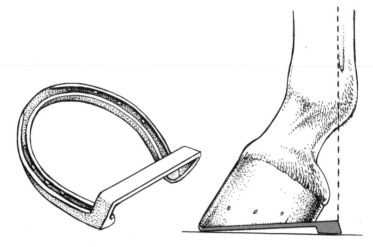

Patten shoe

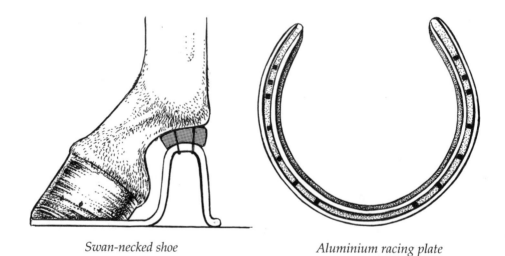

Swan-necked shoe   *Aluminium racing plate*

Racing Plate

a. In order to improve speed and fluency of action, race horses are shod with light aluminium shoes. These are put on just before racing and are replaced with normal-weight shoes for working at home.

b. These shoes are usually made with many more nail holes then you would normally find in other shoes. This helps the farrier to find a suitable position for the nails if the horse has had a fairly new shoe removed recently.

c. These light aluminium shoes are also used for show ponies, to enhance their natural action in the show ring.

d. Some race horses are shod with "light steels" which are a compromise between a normal weight of shoe and the aluminium shoes which wear out quickly and do not stand up to everyday wear.

Plastic Shoes

a. These shoes are glued, rather than nailed, on to the horse's hoof.

b. They are light and very useful in cases where the hoof wall will not take nails. For example, the horse may have problems with the growth of horn which can be protected by a plastic shoe while healthy horn is encouraged to grow through.

c. There are occasional problems with growth and development in foals, which can be helped with the application of a plastic shoe, rather than fitting normal heavy steel shoes to tiny feet.

d. Not all farriers are trained in the skills of applying these shoes.

Pads

a. Hoof cushions can be used to help with the absorption of concussion in cases of ring bone or side bone, for example.

b. As the cushion is fitted between the foot and the shoe, it can cause the shoe to be pulled off the hoof more easily than normal.

c. If the horse has weak soles, hoof cushions are inclined to cause discomfort as they spread some pressure over the sole.

e. Plastic wedges are also fitted between the shoe and the foot. They were initially thought to be a light and simple way of raising the heels in cases of tendon injury recovery or navicular. However, it has now been realised that these wedges create pressure at the heel and cause the heels to collapse.

f. These pads are made in different sizes. The farrier selects the correct size and then trims away any excess plastic once the pad is fitted.

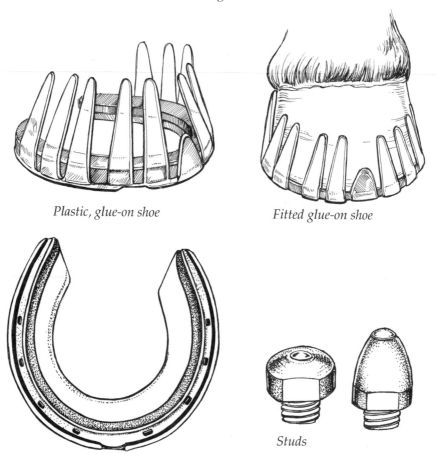

Plastic, glue-on shoe

Fitted glue-on shoe

Hoof cushion

Studs

Studs

a. In order for the horse to wear studs, the farrier will need to put stud holes in the shoes. These holes must be kept clean and oiled when not in use. A good way to do this is to dip cotton wool in oil and then pack it into the hole.

b. A stud "tap' is used as a spanner to screw the studs into the hole and also to clean the thread of the stud hole before the selected studs are screwed in.

c. Studs are generally used in the outside heel (although they can be used in both heels) to help to prevent the horse from striking into itself.

d. They are most often used in the hind shoes as many riders think they will cause damaging by jarring the front limbs if worn in front. Some cross country riders think that they are more likely to be hurt themselves by studs in the front shoes if they have a fall on landing after a fence.

e. Studs should only be worn for the duration of the competition and should be removed as soon as possible afterwards as the studs will unbalance the horse when not sinking into the ground for grip.

f. Thick, chunky studs are used on soft ground, and sharper, pointed studs for hard ground. These studs vary in length and are longer for more extreme conditions.

g. Small, fairly flat studs, called "road studs", are used for general hacking if the rider does a lot of road work on slippery roads.

h. Studs are not used for racing and hunting as they would be too dangerous for both horse and rider. Also, when hunting, the ground conditions would be constantly changing and studs suitable for mud would not be suitable for road work and vice versa.

i. Studs are probably used most widely for showjumping, where precision is vital and one slip can put you out of the competition. They are useful for dressage if the arena is particularly slippery. Cross country riders will weigh up the pros and cons of the help that studs can give and the damage that they can do.

Follow-up Work to Confirm Knowledge and Experience

1. Watch the farrier at work whenever possible, especially when different horses are being shod and if different shoes are being used. Make sure you know and understand each stage of the process.

2. Develop an eye for the well-shod horse by examining as many different shod horses as possible. Look at the wear on the shoes, the angle of the foot and pastern and the action of the horse.

3. Study the different tools available for use by the farrier to make sure you can recognise each one.

Helpful Hints and Exam Technique

1. Carry a hoof pick in your pocket. When talking about shoeing and the horse's shoes, you will find it easier to take out your own hoof pick to pick out feet and examine the shoes rather than having to go in search of one. Don't forget to pick out feet into a skip to keep the yard and bed clean.

2. If talking about specific special shoes, having examined the shoe carefully, hold the shoe with the foot-bearing surface uppermost as it would be when actually on the horse's hoof. This should help you to work out which foot the shoe would be fitted to, which may help you to explain what it would be used for.

11   Travelling

STAGES II and III

1. Preparation

a. Check that the vehicles are roadworthy; for example, road tax, brakes, oil, water, tyres, lights, connections, etc.
b. Park the vehicle in a safe location for loading; for example, an enclosed area from which the horse cannot escape. Use a quiet area with as few distractions as possible. An inexperienced horse may distrust the loading process and attempt to break loose. Distractions may cause the horse to back out of the box or to refuse to go in at all.
c. The ramp must rest firmly and not rock on uneven ground.
d. Both ramp and internal flooring must be non-slip. Rubber matting is ideal. This can be lifted out and washed clean periodically. At the same time, check that the floor underneath is sound and not showing any signs of rotting. Alternatively, straw will provide a good surface, but must be cleaned out frequently.
e. The inside of the box must be free of any protrusions that might cause an injury if leant against or knocked into.
f. Partitions, breast bars and doors must be completely secure.
g. Check that there is string on the tie up rings.
h. Remove loose items, such as buckets, which might move or rattle and become entangled with or frighten the horse.
i. If the horse is likely to be difficult, park the box alongside a wall or hedge. This will help to guide the horse up the ramp. It is also helpful to park the box with its rear towards a slope or bank, if

available. When the ramp is let down, it will rest on the slope, making it level or nearly so. With less of a slope, the horse will walk in with more confidence.

j. Horses may feel claustrophobic and/or cautious about entering an enclosed box. To help, open any top front doors of a trailer, push partitions to one side and make the compartment as airy and light as possible. With a front-unload trailer, keep the front ramp closed or the horse may try to rush in and go straight out of the front opening.

2. Loading

a. The horse, clothed for travelling, should be led out with a bridle over the top of its head collar and rope. A bridle gives you more control when leading. Once in the box, the bridle can be slipped off, leaving the head collar and lead rope to tie the horse up with.

b. The leader must wear gloves, hard hat and strong footwear for protection. It may also be helpful to carry a stick. A quick tap may be all it takes to encourage a hesitant horse.

c. The horse should be led at a purposeful walk straight towards the ramp.

d. An assistant must be available to put up the ramp and also to help if the horse is reluctant to go in. Take care never to stand directly behind a ramp, as it may fall on you if the horse rushes backwards. Two assistants are needed for safe opening and closing of heavy ramps.

e. Always keep looking straight ahead. Never look back towards the horse, even if it stops. You will only discourage forward activity.

f. Once in, hold the horse while the breaching strap is fastened and the ramp or partition is locked in place. The horse is now secure and can be tied up with a quick-release knot.

g. Take care not to give the horse too much rope when tied up. It should not be able to fight with the horse next door, get its head caught under the front of the partition or attempt to turn round.

h. For horses which chew their ropes, have a length of chain tied to the tie up string and clip this to the head collar once the horse is loaded. The lead rope can then be removed.

3. The Difficult Loader

If the horse refuses to enter the box, there are several ways to encourage it. Different tactics work with different horses. Remember to build up the horse's confidence and do not scare it. All handlers should wear protective clothing.

a. An assistant can stand inside the box and offer a small bucket of feed. Allow the horse a mouthful of feed each time it progresses a few steps.

b. Two assistants can hold a lunge line or soft rope around the horse's hindquarters, just above its hocks. Pressure is applied as the assistants walk forward on either side of the horse. This encourages the horse to walk forward. Take great care not to let the horse become entangled in the line.

c. Some horses suddenly gain confidence if each of their feet is picked up in turn and placed a little further up the ramp. In effect, you are moving the horse's legs for it.

d. More experienced but stubborn characters will often respond to a quick tap with a whip on their hindquarters or a quick prod with the brush end of a yard broom.

e. Load a well-behaved and experienced horse into the box first. This may give confidence to the other horse and encourage it to go in.

f. Whatever happens, it is vital that the leader should keep the horse straight. If the horse understands that it cannot escape around the side of the box, it will eventually go forward.

g. Reward the horse with feed once it is inside and secure.

h. Because of the enclosed space in which you are working, and the nature of a frightened horse, loading horses into boxes or trailers is potentially dangerous and every care and precaution should be taken.

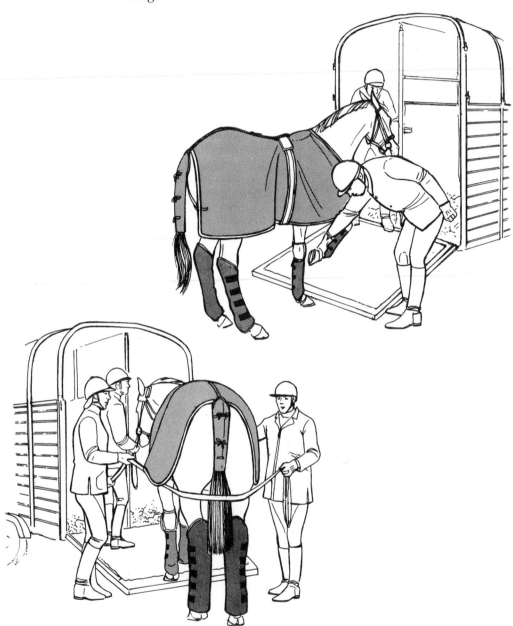

*If a horse refuses to load, there are several ways to encourage it –
placing a foreleg on the ramp may give the horse confidence; a lunge
line behind the horse may help to push it forward*

4. Unloading

a. Untie the horse before the breaching strap is undone, the ramp let down or the partition opened.

b. If the horse is likely to be difficult, slip on a bridle for greater control.

c. With a box or trailer designed for the horse to walk out forwards, simply encourage it to walk slowly. Allow it to stop and take in its surroundings if it wants to. Keep it straight to prevent it from hitting its hips on the side of the box or slipping off the edge of the ramp.

d. If you are using a rear-unload trailer, the horse's main problem is not being able to see what it is backing out on to. Assistants should stand on each side of the ramp and place a hand on the horse's hindquarters to guide it straight and reassure it.

e. The horse may try to turn around which will make it particularly inclined to come out crooked. Once it can see where it is, allow it to look around and take everything in.

5. The Journey

a. If the horse has a smooth and comfortable journey, it will gain confidence and become a willing traveller, walking confidently in and out of the box when required.

b. Stopping and starting at crossings and driving round bends require adjustments in the horse's balance, therefore the driver must make sure there are very gradual changes in speed and direction to prevent injury to the horse or loss of confidence.

c. Be aware that low branches scraping against the roof of the box, or any other unexplained noises, will frighten the horse. Try to avoid this when possible.

d. Young horses should gain confidence from travelling with a companion.

e. It is important to assess the weather conditions along with the type of box before deciding what clothing to put on the horse. When travelling, the horse can generate a considerable amount of heat. If there are several horses in the box and the box is quite enclosed, each horse can become quite hot, especially if the rugs worn are too thick. This can cause the horse to become distressed.

Follow-up Work to Confirm Knowledge and Experience

1. It is a good idea to watch and then assist with loading and unloading horses in order to gain experience gradually. Then practise loading and unloading well-behaved horses. In time, working with a variety of horses, you are bound to come across various horses which are problematical to load and unload. Through these horses you will gain experience and expertise in handling such situations.

2. Try to gain experience with a variety of horseboxes and trailers. Each different type has ramps, fastenings, partitions, fittings and floorings that differ from each other.

Helpful Hints and Exam Technique

1. In the Stage III exam you will demonstrate how to load and unload a well-behaved horse or pony. Treat the horse as if it could be difficult which should make you more aware of demonstrating all the safety procedures and care that should be taken.

12   Health

STAGES III and IV

1. How to Take TPR (Temperature, Pulse, Respiration)

a. Temperature – Shake down the mercury in the thermometer, or zero the reading on a digital model. Grease the bulb end with a small amount of Vaseline. While an assistant holds the horse's head, stand to one side of the hindquarters and hold its tail to one side. Insert the greased thermometer, bulb end first, into the rectum using a rotating action. The inserted section should be angled to rest against the wall of the rectum in order to give a true reading. Take care to hold the thermometer firmly to prevent it from being drawn into the rectum. Remove after one minute, wipe clean and read.

b. Pulse – Press your fingers (not a thumb) gently against the artery located on the lower jaw or inside the foreleg, just in front of the elbow. Use a watch with a second hand and time how many pulse beats there are in 30 seconds, then double this number for the total beats per minute.

c. Respiration – Watch the horse's flanks and count the in-and-out movement of inhalation and exhalation together as one. Time the breaths for 30 seconds and double the figure for the total breaths per minute.

STAGES I–IV

2. Methods of Restraint

a. If a horse is being difficult to restrain (when receiving treatment), the simplest way of keeping it under control is to put on a bridle. This may give you sufficient control.

b. A Chifney bit could be put on for further control. This type of bit seems to help to prevent a horse from rearing and is also known as an anti-rearing bit.

c. A neck twitch can be of help. This entails pinching a piece of loose skin and holding firmly. It can be an effective way of distracting a horse long enough to get it to stand still while the job is done.

d. A twitch can be applied to the top lip if the horse is still too difficult to manage. Care must be taken not to leave the twitch on for more than a minute or two at a time, otherwise the circulation will be cut off and permanent damage done, so this type of twitching is not suitable for a long job. A twitch with a piece of cord on the end or the humane twitch, which is made of metal, can be used. The theory behind this type of twitching is that it causes the horse to release endorphins into its system. These are natural pain-relieving substances and are supposed to have a calming effect on the horse. However, some horses fight against being twitched, which can be dangerous.

e. Sometimes just holding up a leg will be enough to restrain a horse. If examining the near hind, hold up the near fore as the horse will find it difficult to stand on two legs on the same side of its body, but can balance quite well on a diagonal pair.

f. The horse can be sedated for a procedure like clipping if it is particularly frightened of being clipped. By sedating the horse you may help it to become relaxed and accept the clipping process.

g. Hobbles can be used to restrain a horse from kicking. This is sometimes done to mares when being covered to prevent them from injuring the stallion.

h. It is *not* a good idea to hold a horse's ear or tongue to restrain it. If the horse pulls away violently, the tongue or ear can literally be ripped away!

i. Good use of your facilities is important when restraining a horse. For example, check that there is plenty of head room as a horse will panic even more if it throws its head up and hits it on the ceiling. Move the horse over into a corner of its box to make use of the wall to help to keep the horse still.

STAGES II, III and IV

3. Preventive Measures

It is important to incorporate regular inspections into your daily routine. While working around the horses, you must constantly observe them. First thing in the morning, however, the horses will have been unobserved for many hours, therefore this first inspection is vital.

Check water supplies, rugs and signs of health, making sure the horses are safe, happy and healthy. The same applies before and after a lunch break and especially last thing at night when you must make every effort to ensure the horses are securely and safely rugged and stabled with a plentiful water supply. Do the same for your grass-kept horses. In this way, many accidents/illnesses can be avoided.

Apart from good general stable management, various types of routine health care are important in the prevention of ill health.

Worming

a. All horses carry a worm burden. However, an excessive amount will cause disruption of the digestive system, damage to internal organs and general ill health. If untreated, the horse may die.

b. Foals should start being wormed from six weeks of age.

c. To keep the worm burden low, horses should be "wormed" with a recognised brand of wormer on a regular basis. Worm every four to six weeks if your horse is grazing with many other horses on infrequently rested pasture. Worm every six to eight weeks if your horse is stabled and or grazing with few other horses on well-rested pasture that is also grazed by cattle/sheep.

d. Wormers are available in the form of powder/granules, paste and liquid. Different brands will destroy different species of worm.

Worming the horse

Some worms may become resistant to various brands so it is advisable to change your brand once or twice yearly. Ask your vet for advice.

e. The wormer may be fed to the horse in its feed but many dislike the taste and refuse to eat it. Paste and liquid may be squirted directly into the horse's mouth by means of a large syringe. There is usually a guide to dosage on the syringe, which you preset before inserting it into the corner of the horse's mouth (where there are no teeth) then press the plunger, aiming the dose as far towards the back of the tongue as possible. It may be necessary to hold the horse's head up to prevent the dose dribbling or being spat out before the horse has swallowed.

f. There are three main types of wormers for horses, which are sold under a variety of different brand names. These wormers are benzimidazole, pyrantel and ivermectin.

g. The main worms that invade the horse's system are: small redworm (small strongyles), large redworm (large strongyles), roundworm (ascarids), pinworm or seatworm, lungworm, bots and tapeworms.

h. Eggs of the small redworm pass out in the dung. They hatch to release larvae. Within a week the larvae develop if the conditions are warm and moist. Grazing horses ingest these larvae which burrow into the gut lining. From here they emerge as egg-laying adults so the life cycle is complete.

   They pose the greatest threat to the horse because of the damage they can do to the gut. During the summer some larvae develop into adults within six weeks but others remain in the gut wall throughout the autumn and winter. These are called encysted fourth-stage larvae. These larvae can emerge en masse in late winter and early spring, damaging the gut wall and causing colic, diarrhoea, weight loss and general unthriftiness. Not all wormers are effective against the encysted larvae. A five-day programme dosing with benzimidazole should be effective.

i. Eggs of the large redworm pass out in the dung. Larvae can hatch within three days and are eaten by grazing horses. The larvae penetrate the gut wall and migrate through the major arteries which supply blood to the gut. This can cause blood clots and blockages, cutting off blood supply to the gut. The larvae return to the gut and mature into adults. They attach to the intestinal lining and suck blood. At this point the females lay eggs. Large redworm are less of a problem now that modern wormers are better at controlling the larval stages. Ivermectin is effective against the migrating larvae and is most effectively given between October and December.

j. Roundworm eggs pass out in the droppings. The larvae develop within the egg in 10–14 days. The eggs are eaten by the grazing horses and hatch, then burrow through the wall of the intestine. They are carried by the circulatory system to the liver where they develop further. Eventually they migrate to the lungs and work their way through the blood vessels into the airways. They are then coughed up and swallowed, finally maturing into egg-laying adults in the small intestine. The eggs are very resistant to the effects of the weather. They are therefore able to survive and reinfect the horse easily. Foals are particularly prone to infestation which will cause coughing and generally poor growth and condition. Regular worming, combined with removing droppings from the field, is essential to control these worms.

k. Adult female pinworms lay their eggs when they emerge from the anus, on the surrounding skin. The larvae hatch. This makes the horse itch. An infected horse can be seen frequently scratching its tail by rubbing it against walls, fences, etc. The larvae are eaten by the horse, passing to the large intestine where they burrow into the lining and complete their development. Regular worming will control these parasites.

l. Lungworm larvae develop from the eggs passed out in the dung. They need warm, moist conditions to survive. Grazing horses swallow the larvae which burrow through the wall of the intestine and are carried through the blood stream to the lungs. They break out into the air sacs and often fail to develop beyond this stage. If they do develop, the adults lay eggs which are coughed up, swallowed, then passed out in the droppings. They can cause damage, irritation and persistent coughing. Donkeys are the primary host for lungworm. Regular worming is essential.

m. Tapeworms do not affect all horses. In early summer a horse may ingest pasture mites when grazing. These mites may contain tapeworm larvae which will, in turn, infect the horse. A double dose of pyrantel in September is effective against tapeworm.

n. Gadflies pester horses during the summer and lay eggs which they "cement" to the horse's coat. Horses lick the emerging larvae which burrow into the mucous membrane of the gums and tongue. After about a month the larvae migrate to the stomach lining. They stay there until the following spring when they will detach themselves, pass out in the dung, burrow into the ground and pupate. Three to ten weeks later the adult fly emerges. Bots are therefore larvae of the gadfly, rather than worms. Ivermectin given in December is effective against bots which will have reached the stomach by this time in the year.

o. It is possible to have the effectiveness of your worming programme checked by taking a dung sample to a veterinary laboratory for analysis. The egg count will reveal whether your horse is carrying a normal worm burden or not.

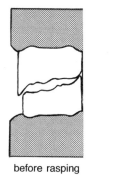
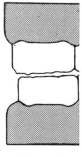

before rasping   after rasping

The teeth should be checked about twice a year

Teeth

a. The horse's top jaw is wider than its bottom jaw. As the horse masticates and its teeth wear down, sharp edges develop on the outer edge of the upper set of molars and also on the inner edge of the lower set. These sharp edges can cut into the horse's cheeks when it is eating or wearing tack. Some of the feed, especially hay and grass, may be partly chewed and then spat out because of the discomfort. This is called quidding. When ridden, the horse may resist the bit or drool from one side of its mouth.

b. A vet or horse dentist should visit and check teeth approximately twice a year. He or she will examine the mouth and rasp off sharp edges if necessary, as well as checking for loose, chipped or infected teeth. If sharp teeth are left unattended, the horse will suffer from poor digestion and loss of condition.

c. You can check for sharp teeth yourself by slipping your thumb up inside the horse's cheek and, taking care not to get nipped, feeling for sharp notches on the first couple of upper molars.

d. As well as checking the teeth, take time to check inside your horse's mouth at least once per week. This out-of-sight area is often forgotten. With one arm and hand around the horse's nose to keep the horse's head still, use your other hand to part the lips gently so that you can examine the gums, tongue and visible teeth. Look carefully at the inner edge of the corners of the lips which sometimes crack and get sore if there is a bitting problem. Look for bruising, sores and signs of teething or injury. If you slip your fingers in the side of the mouth where there are no teeth and gently push the tongue back a little, the horse will usually open its mouth. This is safer than trying to take the tongue out of the horse's mouth. If you are holding its tongue and the horse suddenly pulls away, it is possible for the tongue to be torn. While you are restraining the horse check that the curb groove is clean and free from sores, as sweat, saliva, etc. often collect here, particularly if the horse wears a drop noseband or similar item of tack.

Vaccinations

a. Tetanus is an essential vaccination for all horses. Pregnant mares should be given a booster injection in the last month of pregnancy to help to protect the newborn foal. A foal can then be vaccinated at around three months of age. Initially two injections are given four to six weeks apart, then a third injection one year later. After this, horses should be given a booster injection every two years.

b. Vaccination against equine influenza is not essential but is advisable. For horses taking part in affiliated competitions, it is compulsory. An initial injection is given, followed by a booster four to six weeks later, then a third injection six months after that. The horse then needs to receive annual boosters. For competition purposes, rules state that the first two injections must be no less than 21 days apart and no more than 92 days. The third injection must then be given no less than 150 days after the second one and no more than 215 days. Subsequent boosters must be given no more than one year apart.

c. Flu and tetanus are frequently given as a combined injection.

d. Other vaccinations may be given from time to time under certain circumstances. These include: vaccination against equid herpesvirus 1 (rhinopneumonitis) for pregnant mares, and equine viral arteritis (EVA).

STAGES II and III

4. When to Call the Vet

a. If a wound is bleeding profusely, is more than skin deep or is spurting blood (indicating a cut artery).

b. The horse exhibits any signs of colic.

c. The horse's temperature is more than one degree F higher or lower than normal.

d. If the horse is lame.

e. If the horse is coughing repeatedly and not clearing its nostrils after coughing.

f. If the horse is not responding in its usual way and generally seems off colour.

g. If in doubt, call the vet. It is better to be safe than sorry!

h. A horse suffering from any of the above should not be worked. This may seem obvious but there have been cases where, for example, a horse has shown symptoms of mild colic which then appear to cease. The horse has been ridden soon after and had another colic attack with the rider on board; or a slightly lame horse has been ridden, the lameness appears to wear off but after work the horse has been much lamer than before. So, wait for veterinary advice.

i. If you think a wound may need to be stitched do not apply anything other than cold water as creams, powders and sprays will interfere with the healing process and may make the wound unstitchable.

j. When the vet arrives, he or she should be given the following information if possible and where relevant to the problem: how long the horse has had the complaint; recordings of TPR while the horse has been ill; what symptoms have been displayed; what action has been taken; how the injury occurred, if the horse has staled or passed droppings recently and were they normal; whether the horse has any known disease/problems/allergies/ or allergic reactions to medications.

STAGES II and III

5. Minor Wounds

a. Many minor wounds can be treated without veterinary assistance, providing you have a first-aid kit, including:

- hose and cold water supply
- scissors
- cotton wool
- salt
- warm water
- clean bowl
- wound powder/cream
- antiseptic spray
- gamgee
- veterinary and stable bandages

b. Bruising is accompanied by heat and swelling. This can be effectively reduced by cold hosing, especially if the bruising is on the leg. To make sure you do not frighten the horse, start with a trickle of water and gradually move the trickle from the foot up the horse's leg to the damaged area. The water pressure can then be gradually increased. If there is an open wound with the bruising, hosing will help to remove the mud etc. and clean the wound. Hose above an open wound, to allow the water to trickle over it. Do not hose directly on to an open wound.

c. Bleeding may be stopped by applying direct, firm pressure to the wound with a clean pad.

d. Once bleeding has ceased, any hair overlapping the wound should be carefully trimmed away. This will help you to see the extent of the wound.

e. Warm, salty water works as a safe and mild antiseptic with which you can clean the wound. (Use 1 teaspoon of salt to $\frac{1}{2}$ litre/1 pt of boiled, then cooled, water.)

f. Dip cotton wool into the salty water and clean the wound, working from the middle outwards. Be careful not to rub grit into the wound and use a fresh piece of cotton wool for each wipe, never returning a dirty piece of cotton wool to the clean salt water, nor to the wound.

g. Dry the wound and then apply wound powder, spray or cream.

h. This procedure can be followed for all minor wounds, whether it is a saddle sore, scratch, kick, etc. Hosing can only really be used on the lower part of the body as higher up would involve soaking a large part of the horse, which would certainly be inappropriate in cold weather.

i. If the wound is within the mouth, clean by irrigation with salt water, and do not use a bit if it is likely to interfere, until the wound has healed. If the horse has a split in the corner of its lip, clean with salt water and then apply Vaseline.

STAGES III and IV

6. Isolation Procedure

If the horse has an infectious or contagious disease, it will need to be isolated. This also applies when a new horse arrives in the yard as it could be harbouring disease.

a. An isolation box should be detached from the other stables and should preferably be downwind.

b. In some circumstances it may be more appropriate to leave the horse in its normal box and move other horses away from it.

c. The isolation box should have provision for a separate set of equipment for caring for the horse.

d. The isolated horse should have a set of mucking out equipment, grooming kit, rugs and tack if in work.

e. A separate groom should care for the horse, taking care to wear overalls, headscarf/cap, boots and gloves which are removed before they approach any other horses.

f. Any medication or equipment required for treating the horse must be kept separately and only handled by the groom taking care of the horse.

g. Soiled bedding should go to a separate muck heap and be burned.

h. If the public have access to the yard, the area should be fenced off and signs erected to warn people to keep away.

i. The vet will advise how long the horse should be isolated. At the end of this time, all used equipment must be thoroughly disinfected/washed/cleaned/burnt as appropriate.

STAGES II and III

7. Nursing a Sick Horse

a. The horse should have very frequent visits to check that there is no deterioration in its condition but visits should be made with a minimum of disturbance.

b. A regular check should be made and written records kept of its TPR and other general points to do with its condition; for example, how much it is eating, if there is more or less swelling, whether the horse is lying down more or less, etc.

c. Remove droppings frequently and keep the bed level, with good high banks. Short straw, or shavings, allow for ease of movement. Shavings will stick into wounds, however, and should be avoided for this type of ailment. Full mucking out may not be possible if the horse has limited movement. Use the deep litter system in this case.

d. Keep the stable well ventilated but free from draughts.

e. Keep the horse warm but not weighed down with heavy clothing. Use leg bandages, and possibly a hood, to keep extremities warm. Use light, quilted rugs.

f. Do not groom vigorously if the horse is weak. Pick out the feet twice daily. Sponge eyes, nose and under the dock each day. Lightly brush over, being careful not to let the horse get cold.

g. If worn, remove bandages daily and hand massage the legs to improve the circulation.

h. Monitor how much water is drunk and keep the supply very fresh.

i. Give light, tempting but laxative feeds. Remove any uneaten food immediately. Stale food and water will discourage the horse and possibly delay recovery.

j. Follow veterinary instructions carefully.

k. If the horse has an eye injury, keep the stable darkened and avoid bright lights.

l. Unless the vet advises otherwise, give an ad lib supply of hay.

STAGES II and III

8. How to Recognise Lameness

a. When lame in a front limb/foot, the horse will be reluctant to put its weight on the lame leg. In order to keep as much weight as possible off this leg, the horse will raise its head up as it puts this leg to the ground. When it puts its sound leg to the ground, it will put extra weight on it and drop its head down as it does so.

b. Walking straight towards you, on firm, level ground, you may observe the head and neck of the sound horse bobbing gently in rhythm with the walk. Trotting straight towards you, the head and neck of the sound horse will be held level.

c. If you watch the head and neck of a horse that is lame in a front limb, in either walk or trot, you will notice it raise its head high when the lame leg comes to the ground and drop its head low when the sound leg comes to the ground.

d. The extent to which the horse raises and lowers its head will depend upon the degree of lameness, varying from a slight nod to a very pronounced movement up and down.

e. Hind leg lameness can be more difficult to detect. Watching a sound horse from behind, the hindquarters should rise and fall evenly as the horse walks or trots away from you on a straight line.

f. A horse that is lame behind will drop one quarter lower and raise one quarter higher. This may be difficult to see if the lameness is only slight.

STAGES III and IV

9. Poulticing, Tubbing and Bandaging

There are a number of ailments for which the treatment or method of applying/administering treatment is similar. It is important to know how to poultice.

a. Poulticing is the application of heat and moisture in some form to an injured area. A poultice is generally applied to the limbs and feet where it can be fairly easily secured. For other parts of the body a hot fomentation can be used. This involves immersing a towel or cloth in hot water, wringing it out and then holding it over the affected area. Remove the towel and repeat the process every few minutes. The same could be done with cold water.

b. Poultices can be used to clean a dirty wound, draw out infection, protect the wound and encourage a flow of blood, with its healing properties, to the affected area.

c. An Animalintex poultice is a sterile dressing which can be applied either dry or warm and wet. The treated side is placed directly over the wound and is secured in place with a veterinary bandage. If on the lower limb, a stable bandage can be placed over the top for extra security. Bandages should be checked, removed and replaced at least every 12 hours to prevent pressure sores and aid circulation. The use of Velcro fastenings helps to prevent pressure points being created by tapes being tied too tightly.

    To wet the poultice, trickle boiled and cooled water over the untreated side until the whole poultice is damp. Test the temperature of the dressing on the back of your hand before you apply it. If it scorches your hand, it is definitely too hot to apply to the horse. A layer of plastic can be placed over the poultice to help to retain heat and moisture before bandaging. Animalintex is a good poultice for cleaning dirty or infected wounds. It should be used for one or two days only, unless your veterinary surgeon advises otherwise, as it tends to keep wounds open and encourages proud flesh to form.

d. Kaolin poultice is a clay mixture with excellent drawing properties. It is a useful aid in reducing swelling and minimising the effects of bruising. It can also be used for wounds, being especially useful on cracked heels and other areas where there is a good deal of movement, as the oil in the clay keeps the skin very supple.

e. A warm kaolin poultice is prepared by heating a quantity of kaolin in a microwave oven or in a water bath of boiling water. Spread a layer of kaolin on a piece of brown paper or a cloth of suitable size to cover the affected area. Test the heat of the poultice on the back of your hand. If it is a comfortable heat, it can then be applied to the horse. Bandage in place with a veterinary bandage and a stable bandage, if appropriate, for extra security. The poultice can be applied cold, in which case it is prepared and then placed in the fridge before application.

f. A bran poultice is sometimes used on the foot if there is bruising to be drawn out. It is not an appropriate poultice for open wounds as the bran would get trapped in the wound and make it difficult to clean. A quantity of bran is damped with boiling water. The mixture is allowed to cool a little and is then packed on the sole of the foot. A tough plastic bag or hessian sack is placed over the foot and more bran can be placed in the sack around the foot. A veterinary bandage is used to secure the poultice. Alternatively, a poultice boot, which is stronger and easier to handle, may be used if available.

g. One of the greatest drawbacks of the bran poultice is that the horse is tempted to try to eat it. In so doing, it may eat some of the sack or bandage used to secure it. Some horses will try to chew any bandages applied. In this case a bib should be worn, as eating plastic, bandages or sacking could lead to a serious colic.

h. All poultices and bandages should be removed and replaced at least every 12 hours unless your vet advises otherwise

i. Tubbing is another way of cleaning a wound or drawing out bruising from the foot or coronet area. The horse's foot is placed in a shallow, plastic bucket. Deep buckets are more difficult to get the foot into and can cause the horse to panic. Warm water is poured gently into the bucket to the required depth, and salt, Epsom salts or potassium permanganate crystals are added to the water. This procedure would help to cleanse a punctured sole, for example. The horse may be tubbed for 10–15 minutes, then the foot is removed and bandaged or poulticed to keep it clean.

j. When bandaging a dressing over a wound or keeping a poultice in place, gamgee or Fybagee should always be used under the bandage. This helps to spread pressure evenly. Bandages must be applied firmly to prevent them from slipping. Velcro fastenings are best but if the Velcro fails to stick then tape can be used. Tie-up tapes must be tied carefully to prevent uneven pressure, and a fold of the bandage should be turned down over the bow to prevent it from being rubbed or knocked undone.

k. To bandage the knee or hock joint, a figure-of-eight bandage is needed to allow for joint movement. When applied to the knee, the bandage should not cover the pisiform bone at the back of the knee. This bone is easily rubbed and a pressure sore would then form. The bandage can be made to cross at the side of the knee or over the front of the knee, depending upon whether you need to keep pressure off the front of the knee or not.

For the hock joint, the cross of the bandage is usually at the side, but discretion is needed according to the wound and treatment being applied. Again, there must be some form of padding under the bandage, and in this case gamgee is usually best as it is more pliable than Fybagee. The gamgee should be a little loose over the point of hock particularly, otherwise, as soon as the horse flexes its joint, the gamgee will pull out from the bandage, so allow for joint movement even though the horse's movement is going to be restricted to some extent. Bandages are available which have been specifically designed for keeping dressings or poultices on joints. They are made of elasticated material and shaped to fit a hock, knee or fetlock.

l. As the horse is likely to rest its wounded limb and carry extra weight on its good limb, the opposite limb should be supported by a stable bandage. If a knee or hock bandage is used, the lower limb and opposite limb will both need to be supported by stable bandages. This also helps to prevent swelling in either limb.

STAGES III and IV

10. Ailments

Types of Wound and Common Ailments Involving Wounds

Contusion – This is a bruise, a very common type of wound, and may be caused by a kick or blow to the area. Sometimes the skin is broken but often there may just be swelling or a painful reaction from the horse. Cold hosing, poulticing or fomentation are the most likely treatments.

Incision – This is a clean-cut wound that has been caused by a sharp object like glass or a knife. It is not a common occurrence. The edges of

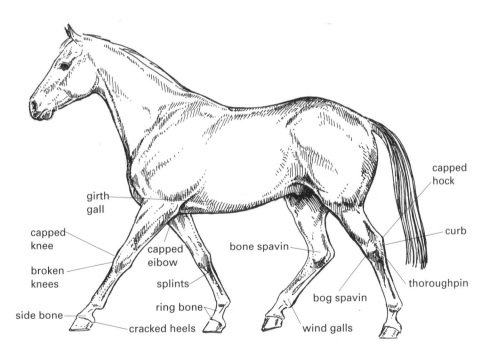

Seats of ailments

the wound will be regular and there will often be copious bleeding. This type of wound is likely to need veterinary attention and will probably be stitched. Incisions usually heal well as the skin edges can be drawn close together where they knit with minimum scar formation. This is called healing by first intention.

Laceration – This is a tear to the skin, again caused by a sharp object, but one that leaves jagged edges rather than a clean cut. This is a more common type of wound, being caused by broken fencing, a protruding nail, barbed wire, etc. There will be bleeding but not as much as with an incision. The vet may be able to stitch the wound or it may need hosing/poulticing to help to clean it. This type of wound may take longer to heal and scar tissue may form as the edges of the skin do not come so neatly together. This is called healing by second intention as granulation tissue quickly forms to cover the exposed area, and then, more slowly, the skin (epithelial cells) gradually grows in from the edges.

Puncture – This is a particularly troublesome type of wound, being caused by an object that pierces the surface, leaving only a tiny entrance hole, but which may go deep into the underlying tissues. A nail or thorn may be the most common cause of a puncture wound. Once the object has been removed, the puncture will need to be poulticed to draw out any dirt that is trapped inside. The entrance of the puncture must be kept open to allow the wound to heal from the inside outwards. If the surface heals too quickly, infection may be trapped inside.

For all wounds check that the horse has up to date tetanus cover.

Girth Galls – These are sores found in the girth region, usually just behind the elbow.

Cause – A dirty or hard girth rubbing against a soft-skinned or dirty horse.

Symptoms – The hair is rubbed short just behind the elbow. A swelling or small lump will appear, which will eventually become a sore if not treated. The horse will show signs of discomfort when being girthed up.

Treatment – Remove the cause by not riding. Clean the girth, change to a softer type or use a girth sleeve. Treat the gall as a minor wound if the skin is broken, or hot foment if there is swelling. When both sore and swelling are healed, harden the skin with surgical spirit or salt water.

Prevention – Groom the horse throughly before girthing up. Use a clean, soft girth. Harden the skin of an unfit horse before riding and accustom its skin to the girth gradually by not riding for too long in one session.

Broken Knees – This is broken skin over the front of the knee.

Cause –   The horse falling on its knees on a hard surface. Falling on the road would cause a lot of damage.

Symptoms – Swelling, bleeding from open wounds. The horse may or may not be lame.

Treatment – Cold hose, aiming the water above the knees and allowing it to run down over the wounds to help to wash away grit that will be in the wound. Warm, salt water may be needed to clean the wounds throughly, but take care not to rub grit further in. Trim hair away from the wounds to help to reveal the extent of the damage. As the wound is on a joint, the constant movement of the horse tends to slow the healing process and proud flesh is often a problem with broken knees. To keep proud flesh to a minimum, restrict the horse to box rest and bandage the knees using a non-adherent dressing. This will help to keep the wounds moist and prevent drying and cracking of the wounds. Healing of more severe damage can be accelerated with the use of laser treatment. Make sure your horse's tetanus cover is up to date.

Prevention – Take care when riding on rough surfaces. Use knee boots for any horse inclined to trip. Keep the horse well shod as long toes will cause stumbling. Don't allow the horse to "slop" along on a long rein; keep it alert and between leg and hand.

Cracked Heels – These are sores which sometimes develop into deep cracks in the area at the back of the pasterns. Cracked heels and mud fever are one and the same thing, just in slightly different areas.

Cause – Damp conditions, particularly wet and mud in the winter months, can make the skin soft and sore. If a small wound goes unnoticed, infection can easily set in in these conditions and quickly lead to cracked heels. Excessive washing of the legs, particularly if they are then rubbed dry, can make the skin sore and more prone to cracked heels. Some horses seem more prone than others to this problem.

Symptoms – Scabs and sores form at the back of the pastern. Cracks run horizontally and may become very deep. The skin is "weepy" and there may or may not be swelling. The horse is often lame, as movement makes the cracks open.

Treatment – Clip away any excess feather and clean the area thoroughly. Keep the horse in clean dry conditions and keep the skin supple with an oil-based cream. Kaolin poultice is very effective at removing scabs and leaving clear skin which can then be protected with cream. It may be necessary for the vet to give antibiotics if there is a great deal of inflammation. Dermobian is a soothing cream which also contains an antibiotic and is an effective, although rather expensive, way of treating this problem.

Prevention – Make sure grass-kept horses are brought in periodically to allow their legs to dry. Brush the legs thoroughly and inspect for any signs of sores/scabs. If the horse is prone to this problem, apply an oil-based barrier cream to protect the skin. Horses with heavily feathered legs can be more prone as the feathering seems to hold wet and mud. Clip the feathers to facilitate cleaning and drying the legs on a regular basis.

Mud Fever – This is the same problem as cracked heels but is found most commonly on the lower limbs, although it can be anywhere on the leg or even on the belly.

Cause –   As for cracked heels.

Symptoms– Swollen limbs with scabs and sores. The skin is "weepy". The horse may or may not be lame.

Treatment – Gently remove the scabs and clean the affected area. Again, kaolin or Animalintex poultice may help to clean the skin. Clip away hair and treat as for cracked heels.

Prevention – As for cracked heels.

Interfering – This is an overall term for any of the problems caused mainly by faulty action: brushing, overreaching, speedy cutting. The nature of these problems and their prevention has been covered in previous chapters. The treatment of any resulting wounds is the same as for any minor skin abrasion. An overreach may result in a more serious wound and could require veterinary attention, poulticing and antibiotics. Always check that tetanus inoculations are up to date.

Ailments of the Foot

Bruised Sole

Cause –   The horse treading awkwardly on a flint or other hard, uneven protrusion in the ground. Thin, flat-soled horses are most prone to this problem.

Symptoms – The horse may be immediately lame, then go sound and lame again the next day, or stay lame from the moment it bruises its sole. Hoof testers can be used to apply pressure to the sole. When the bruised area is put under pressure, the horse will react, showing its discomfort.

Treatment – A bran or Animalintex poultice will usually relieve the bruising within a couple of days. Once the foot has been allowed to harden up after poulticing, the horse can be reshod.

Prevention – For horses prone to bruising, a wide-webbed shoe may help to give some protection. In some cases a pad over the sole will protect it. This depends a little on the shape of the horse's sole. If it has very flat soles, a pad sometimes puts too much pressure on the sole and aggravates the problem. It is also more difficult to care for the horse's feet when pads are worn.

Nail Prick/Bind – If the farrier drives a nail into the sensitive structures of the foot, it is a nail prick. If the nail is driven very close to the sensitive structures, putting undue pressure against them, it is a nail bind.

Cause –   Poor farriery, although, in some cases, a horse with very thin walls to its feet may be particularly prone to nail bind as the farrier has very little room for placing the nail.

Symptoms – If the nail has pricked the sensitive structures, the horse will be lame. When the offending nail is removed, there is likely to be a trace of blood on the end of the nail. If it is a nail bind, the horse may be lame a short time after being shod. There will probably be some heat in the foot and if the wall is tapped over the site of the nail bind, the horse will react with discomfort.

Treatment – Immediate removal of the nail will reduce the likelihood of any subsequent bruising and inflammation. In the case of a nail prick, the site should be flushed out with a strong antiseptic solution, such as dilute hydrogen peroxide, to prevent any infection. Poultice the foot to help to relieve bruising and reshoe when the horse is sound.

Prevention – Regular shoeing by a good farrier who is familiar with your horse's feet and any problems it may have.

Corns – These are deep-seated bruises to the sole in the area of the seat of corn.

Cause – Pressure on the seat of corn from a badly fitted shoe or one that has been left on for too long. Horses with low, weak heels may be more prone to bruising in this area.

Symptoms – The horse will be lame but it may only be intermittent, for example when turning corners and placing more weight on this area. When the shoe is removed and some of the sole is pared away from this area, a red area may be visible where blood vessels have broken. If the corn has been there for some time, there may be black, dead tissue to pare away before the bruise is exposed. Again, hoof testers can be used to test the seat of corn for a reaction to discomfort from the horse.

Treatment – The shoe is removed and the sole pared away to expose the bruise and relieve pressure. A poultice will ease the bruising or draw out infection if the corn is so bad that it has become infected. Once the horse is sound, it can be reshod.

Prevention – A good farrier will leave the shoe quite long at the heels, which helps to support the heels and prevents the shoe from pressing into the seat of corn. Make sure your horse is shod regularly every four to six weeks, especially if it is prone to corns.

Laminitis – Inflammation of the sensitive laminae tissues of the foot.

Cause – Most commonly seen in overweight ponies eating large amounts of grass, especially in the spring. Also excessive work on hard ground. The normal blood flow to the foot is interrupted so the laminae tissues do not receive an adequate supply of blood. This causes the tissues to become inflamed and die.

Symptoms – The pony has severe pain, usually only in the front feet. This results in a reluctance to walk and a tendency to rest back on its hind limbs which it draws further underneath it while stretching its forelimbs out in front of it to relieve the pressure. If made to walk, the pony will take short, pottery steps and is particularly uncomfortable on hard or uneven ground which puts pressure on the soles of its feet. The respiratory rate increases with the distress. The feet will feel hot, especially at the coronary band, and a strong pulse can be felt in the arteries that supply blood to the feet.

Treatment – Remove the pony from the cause and restrict its diet. It must still receive nourishment and plenty of fresh water. The vet will probably administer a course of phenylbutazone to relieve the pain. The pony should be encouraged to exercise gently to help to improve the blood supply to the feet. In severe cases the pedal bone, which is normally supported by the healthy laminae tissues, may rotate and point downwards, sometimes even protruding through the sole. In this case, the pony may be shod with a heart-bar shoe which will help to support the pedal bone. The whole of the front of the foot may need to be cut away in order to remove the dead tissues and rebalance the foot.

Prevention – Once a pony has suffered from laminitis it is likely to be prone to it in the future so take great care to limit the pony's time at grass, especially in the spring. In the case of more chronic laminitis, the feet easily become misshapen and the farrier will need to trim the feet regularly to try to improve their balance and shape.

Navicular – A deterioration and roughening of the navicular bone, causing the horse pain. The reasons for the pain may be many, for example the roughened bone rubbing against the deep flexor tendon.

Cause – The exact cause of navicular is not known but it may be due to a breakdown in the blood supply to the bone, causing it to deteriorate and become rough. Poor conformation of the foot may be the initial cause or there may be many other reasons.

Symptoms – Initially, the horse may begin to trip very frequently. This is due to it altering its stride because of the slight discomfort. This discomfort may lead to it refusing to jump obstacles it has previously been happy to jump, and no longer being willing to extend its stride. There may then be intermittent lameness, for example on circles or on hard ground.

Treatment – First the diagnosis must be confirmed. Initially, the horse will probably be nerve blocked. If it moves freely and is sound as a result of a nerve block to the back part of the foot, the horse will then be sent for X-rays. These X-rays are not always conclusive but should help the vet in his or her diagnosis. Treatment can then be a case of trial and error as each case is a little different. If caught in the early stages, the farrier can greatly improve the condition. The heels can be supported with a bar shoe and should be encouraged to spread, not contract, as this will only limit the much needed blood supply to the foot. For the same reason, exercise is important and phenylbutazone may be given to relieve pain and help the horse to work. Warfarin has been used to lessen the effect of blood clotting and to try to improve the blood supply to the bone. However, it is a dangerous drug to use as the horse needs its blood to clot in the event of an accident, otherwise it could bleed to death. Isoxuprine may be used to dilate blood vessels and improve the blood supply in this way.

Prevention – A good farrier and regular attention to the feet are most important. Contracted heels, low, weak heels, heels not fully supported by the shoe and the toes being left too long are all faults which could bring about the onset of navicular disease. A good farrier will not allow this to happen. Exercise is also of vital importance for good blood supply. Horses restricted to long periods of inactivity in their boxes are more likely to be prone to navicular.

Seedy Toe – Separation of the sole from the hoof wall in the toe area.

Cause –   Not really known, but may be due to the toes being left too long.

Symptoms – The horse is not usually lame. Dead tissue with a cheesy smell will be noticed at the toe between the wall and the sole. It may only be apparent when the farrier removes the shoe.

Treatment – The farrier should pare away the dead tissue. The resulting hole can be filled with Stockholm tar and cotton wool. The area will gradually grow out and be replaced with healthy horn providing the horse is being well cared for and is receiving a good diet. Some horses seem to be prone to the problem, in which case it will tend to recur.

Prevention – Good stable management and regular attention to the feet by the farrier.

Thrush – An accumulation of degenerative material in the cleft of the frog.
Cause –   Poor stable management, leaving the horse standing in damp dirty bedding. It may also occur in the field-kept horse left standing in damp conditions.
Symptoms – Unpleasant smell from the foot. Black, moist material in the cleft of the frog. When probed, the cleft of the frog is soft. If left untreated, the horse will become lame.
Treatment – Thoroughly clean the foot. Dilute hydrogen peroxide can be used to rinse out the cleft of the frog. Have the farrier trim away any dead tissue. Spray the feet with antibiotic spray which will help to harden them. Make sure the horse has clean, dry conditions to stand in.
Prevention – Good stable management. Keep the bed clean and pick out the feet and clean them thoroughly every day.

Quittor – An abscess on the coronary band.
Cause –   An infection in the foot which needs to work its way out through the first soft tissue area it can find.
Symptoms – The horse is usually lame. A soft painful area will be apparent at some point on the coronary band, usually towards the heel area. Heat in the foot. The abscess will eventually open.
Treatment – Poultice the abscess to draw out the infection. Tubbing can also be useful. The farrier may be able to find a site on the sole of the foot that can be pared away to allow the infection to drain out through the bottom of the foot. This may happen in the case of a corn.
Prevention – Take good care of the horse's feet.

Skin Diseases

Lice – Small parasites which spend their whole life cycle on the horse.
Cause –   Lice tend to infest horses which are not groomed on a regular basis, particularly when their coats are long in the winter.
Symptoms – The horse is seen to rub itself, scratching its neck and hindquarters particularly. This results in a patchy coat with rubbed areas and maybe sections of mane almost completely rubbed away. It

may be possible to see the lice and/or their eggs if you part the hair and look carefully.

Treatment – Washes and sprays are available, which need to be applied not only to the infected horse, but also to any horses that have been in contact with it. After the initial treatment, the horse will need to be treated again two to three weeks later, as eggs will hatch that were not initially destroyed by the first treatment.

Prevention – Groom horses regularly and do not use rugs or other clothing from an infected horse on any other horses as the lice may be transferred from one horse to another in this way.

Sweet Itch – An allergic reaction to biting midges.

Cause – During spring, summer and early autumn, midges are abundant in the evening and early morning. These midges will bite ponies out at grass. For reasons unknown, some ponies are allergic to these bites.

Symptoms – It is mainly ponies that are affected by this complaint. When the midges begin biting, the pony develops an itchy allergic reaction and will rub itself on any available object, particularly in the neck and tail region. It may be seen rubbing itself vigorously on trees, fencing, gate posts, etc. This rubbing causes the skin to become sore in places and the mane and tail will quickly be rubbed away. The skin tends to become thick and wrinkled.

Treatment – The ideal would be to keep the pony in a midge-free environment but this is not often possible. It will help if the pony is stabled when the midges are most active, which is early morning and through the evening. Benzylbenzoate should be applied daily to the rubbed areas and sore patches. This lotion heals the sores and soothes the itching, while discouraging the midges.

Prevention – There is no way of preventing the problem but keeping the pony away from midges and providing shelter are essential. It is not a good idea to breed from a pony with sweet itch as it will probably pass the allergy on to its offspring.

Ringworm – Skin disease causing patchy loss of hair mainly in the head and neck area.

Cause – A fungus.

Symptoms – Raised patches of hair, varying in size, fall away, leaving a scaly area that may become scabby and infected. This problem generally affects young horses as older horses gradually gain an immunity.

Treatment – As ringworm is very contagious to both people and horses the horse should be isolated. Any patches of hair should be removed and a fungicidal cream applied to the affected areas for several days, taking care to look for any new patches forming. Ringworm can survive in buildings, wood and clothing for some time so stables should be cleaned by pressure hosing and all equipment and tack that has been in contact with the horse must be disinfected.

Prevention – A difficult problem to prevent as it can easily be picked up at horse sales, shows and during transport, so always isolate new arrivals to the yard in case they have picked up the disease.

Photosensitisation – Sensitivity to sunlight, generally on the muzzle, causing sore skin.

Cause – Grazing horses eat plants which cause the skin to become sensitive to sunlight. St John's wort is thought to be one of the causes.

Symptoms – Pink skin is most affected, particularly if there is little hair covering the area. The horse's muzzle tends to be the area most affected, and sometimes the lower limbs. The skin begins to look red and then a bluish, bruised colour. For this reason, the problem is sometimes called "blue nose". Scabs form and the nose may swell.

Treatment – Susceptible horses should be kept out of bright sunlight. If St John's wort is known to be the problem, do not allow the horse to graze where this plant is growing. The pink skin can be covered with a sunblock cream each day, which proves very effective.

Prevention – As soon as bright sunny weather arrives, use a sunblock and restrict daytime grazing.

Diseases of the Respiratory System

Equine Influenza – A very infectious disease causing a high temperature and a cough.

Cause – A virus.

Symptoms – The first indication that the horse has flu is a harsh cough. However, it may have been noticed that the horse has not been performing at its best shortly before the cough begins. The horse will have a raised temperature and may go off its feed and seem generally depressed. There may be some nasal discharge.

Treatment – The horse must be isolated, have plenty of fresh air and be rested. It is a good idea to lead it out gently in hand each day to help to maintain good circulation – if this is possible without increasing the risk of spreading the disease. Once the horse has recovered, usually after a period of about two weeks, there should be a gradual return to exercise.

Prevention – Horses can be vaccinated against flu and, although this may not always stop them from being infected with the virus, it generally reduces the severity of the attack.

Chronic Obstructive Pulmonary Disease (COPD) – This is a chronic respiratory condition.

Cause –   The horse develops a sensitivity to dust and mould spores in the air, hay, bedding, etc. This generally occurs if the horse is stabled and constantly exposed to large amounts of dust and spores. Some horses are more susceptible than others.

Symptoms – Initially, the horse coughs intermittently, often at the start of exercise but also when in its stable. Quantities of thick yellow mucus are coughed up from time to time. There is no temperature with COPD, which helps to distinguish, initially, between COPD and flu, and the horse will usually continue to have a good appetite unless the condition is allowed to progress to an extreme. If untreated, the horse will cough more frequently and begin to wheeze. It will show difficulty in exhaling and a "heave" line will develop from the double expiratory effort required. Its capacity for exercise will be reduced. The sensitivity causes narrowing of the tiny airways in the lungs, resulting in the horse having difficulty in taking in air and expelling it again.

Treatment – The cause must be removed, so the horse needs plenty of fresh air and as little dust in its environment as possible. This usually necessitates bedding the horse on paper or shavings and feeding well-soaked hay or Horsehage. The horse should be kept out as much as possible. Stabling next to other horses which are on dry hay or straw bedding is enough to spark off the sensitive reaction. The horse can be given drugs in its feed, which help to open the tiny airways and remove the excess mucus.

Prevention – Be aware of the importance of keeping dust to a minimum with all horses. Try to provide an environment with plenty of fresh air and clean, good quality bedding and feed.

Whistling and Roaring – A noise made by the horse during inhalation, particularly at fast paces.

Cause –   One side of the larynx, usually the left, becomes partially or completely paralysed due to degeneration of the nerve which supplies the muscles on that side.

Symptoms – During faster work the horse is heard to be making a whistling or roaring noise as it breathes in. In more severe cases the horse may become distressed and exercise will need to be reduced. Some horses appear unaffected by the problem.

Treatment – If the horse does not become distressed, no treatment is needed, but if it finds exercise difficult then an operation may help to open up the airway. The Hobday operation is often used. In extreme cases, the horse may be tubed. This involves putting a tube in its neck so that the airway can be opened up for fast work.

Prevention – This problem cannot really be prevented. It sometimes occurs after a severe case of flu, for example.

Bony Enlargements

Splints – Small bony enlargements in the area of the splint bones, most commonly just below the knee on the inner aspect of the forelimbs.

Cause –   Work on hard ground, or overwork in a young horse, may cause movement between the splint bones and cannon bones and result in the formation of extra bone. A direct blow to the limb can also cause a splint, as can an imbalance in the calcium/phosphorus ratio in the diet.

Symptoms – Slight lameness, particularly in trot and on hard ground. When a splint first begins to form, it can be very difficult to detect. There may be some heat and a tender area may be found. There could be very slight swelling. If due to a blow, it will be more obvious as there could be a mark where the horse has been struck into.

Treatment – Rest the horse and cold hose to reduce inflammation. It may be necessary to box rest for as long as six weeks. In more severe cases anti-inflammatory drugs, such as phenylbutazone, may be given, or a substance known as DMSO may be applied to the site of the splint and will be absorbed into the underlying tissues. A firm bony lump will eventually form, which is the resulting splint. Most splints gradually reduce in size over a period of time.

Prevention – Use brushing boots on young horses inclined to strike into them-selves and do not work young horses hard or fast, particularly on hard ground.

Bone Spavin – A bony enlargement in the hock joint, or degenerative joint disease in the hock.

Cause –   General wear and tear in a working horse.

Symptoms – The horse may be lame on one hind leg or, if both hocks are affected, it may shorten its stride and work less fluently. It could become reluctant to jump or show lameness on circles. Due to a reluctance to flex its hocks, it is likely to drag its toes and wear its shoes unevenly. Holding up the hind limb and flexing the hock for 30–45 seconds prior to asking the horse to trot away may re-veal increased lameness. This is generally known as a spavin test, although it flexes all the joints of the hind limb, not just the hock. An X-ray will be needed to confirm diagnosis. As the disease progresses, extra bone forms in the hock as nature's way of re-ducing movement between the bones where the cartilage is break-ing down. Once the bones have completely fused together, the horse may become sound again.

Treatment – The horse should be shod with a rolled-toe shoe to help the breakover. Fusion of the bones should be encouraged, so work-ing the horse while it is receiving painkillers can help to acceler-ate the process. Jumping, schooling to a more advanced standard and any work which particularly stresses the hock should be avoided until the fusing process is complete.

Ring Bone – Bony enlargements in the pastern joint, or degenerative joint disease of the pastern joint.

Cause –   General wear and tear.

Symptoms – The horse will be lame. Any of the limbs can be affected. There may be some heat, and sensitivity if the joint is flexed and moved. There will be swelling. An X-ray will show the formation of new bone which may occur anywhere from the lower joint between the long and short pastern and the upper end of the long pastern.

Treatment – There is no real treatment. There may be some fusion and, if no more bone forms, the horse may become sound again.

Side Bone – Ossification of the lateral cartilages of the feet.

Cause –   General wear and tear, more common in heavier types.

Symptoms – Side bone does not tend to cause lameness. Where the cartilage extends above the coronet band, it will feel hard rather than slightly spongy.

Treatment – If the horse is not lame, none is necessary. If there is lameness, the farrier must check the balance of the foot and a wide-webbed shoe may help to spread the effects of concussion.

Bursal and Synovial Enlargements

Bursae are small sacs containing synovial fluid, which act as cushions where tendons and muscles pass over bony places. Synovial fluid is contained in joint capsules to nourish and lubricate the joint.

Bog Spavin – A swelling of the joint capsule of the hock joint.

Cause –   May appear spontaneously or be a sign of disease within the hock.

Symptoms – A soft swelling is seen over the front and inner aspect of one or both hocks. The horse is not usually lame.

Treatment – If there is lameness, further investigation is necessary to find out if there are problems within the hock. If the horse is not lame, no treatment is necessary and the problem will usually resolve itself.

Windgalls – These may be tendinous, which is an enlargement of the tendon sheath just above the fetlock joint, or articular which is a swelling of the fetlock joint capsule.

Cause –   General wear and tear in the working horse.

Symptoms – There may be swelling around the fetlock joint (articular wind gall), or just above and to the rear of the joint (tendinous wind gall). This swelling may increase with work and decrease when the horse is rested. There may or may not be some heat. The horse is not usually lame. Wind galls may occur on the front or hind limbs.

Treatment – No treatment is necessary if there is no lameness.

Thoroughpin – Enlargement of the deep flexor tendon sheath above the hock.

Cause –   General wear and tear.

Symptoms – A swelling is seen, usually on the outer aspect of the hock to-
           wards the rear. This swelling can be pushed from the outer aspect
           to the inside and back again. There is not usually any lameness.

Treatment – None is necessary.

Capped Hock/Knee/Elbow – A swelling over the point of hock, front of the
           knee or point of elbow.

Cause –   Frequent knocks to this area. For example, a horse lying down in
           its stable may constantly knock the point of hock and elbow on
           the hard floor. If it lies down with its feet tucked up underneath
           it, it may bruise its elbows with its shoes. A horse which frequently
           knocks solid obstacles with its knees when jumping will be likely
           to have swellings over the knees.

Symptoms – Soft swellings varying in size. There may be some heat. The
           horse is not usually lame, the swellings are just unsightly.

Treatment – Try to remove the cause. Provide the horse with extra bedding
           or, in the case of capped elbow, a sausage boot may be worn in
           the stable to act as a buffer between shoe and elbow.

Prevention – Note early signs and take action as quickly as possible to pre-
           vent a persistent problem.

Strains

In general, to treat the strain of any tendon or ligament, cold applications
will help to keep the initial inflammation under control. Bandaging the limb
will also help to keep swelling down. Phenylbutazone is usually given as
an anti-inflammatory and as a pain killer to keep the horse comfortable. An
ultrasound scan can reveal the extent of the damage and is used subsequently to help to check the extent of the healing. Box rest, with gentle walking in hand, is the usual course of action, followed by a long period of
convalescence.

Strained Tendon – Tendon strain is most common in the superficial tendon
           which runs down the back of the forelimbs.

Cause –   It most frequently occurs in the muscles of a tired or unfit horse
           lacking smooth co-ordination at speed, when jumping or when
           moving on uneven ground, causing a sudden force on the tendon
           which is then strained as a result.

Symptoms – In some cases a slight strain can be present without lameness, but there may be slight heat and swelling. If not noticed at this stage and work is continued, it is likely to result in a severe strain. A severe strain will result in the horse becoming immediately lame and there will be considerable swelling down the back of the limb between knee and fetlock. The more swelling there is, the more severe is the damage.

Treatment – Try to minimise inflammation by cold hosing and then applying ice packs. It is important to keep swelling to a minimum so that the tendon will begin to knit together with the tendon fibrils in normal alignment. The ice packs will need to be bandaged in place and removed and replaced frequently to keep the leg cold. Phenylbutazone is usually given to act as a pain killer and anti-inflammatory.

The horse will need to be kept on box rest, with the leg bandaged, until the initial stages of inflammation have subsided. Box rest should then continue but the horse could be walked out gently in hand daily to help to encourage the tendon to knit in a uniform manner. Providing the horse is sound, after some six to eight weeks gentle ridden exercise could commence at walk. The walking period is built up and trotting is gently and gradually introduced. The horse should then be turned away to rest for at least nine months. During this time ultrasound scanning can be used to examine the extent of the damage and the progress of healing. The horse may appear to be sound and completely recovered but an ultrasound scan may reveal that the tendon is still not fully repaired and therefore the horse needs more time.

Prevention – A good fitness programme to tone and strengthen muscles and which keeps fast work to a minimum, especially if the ground conditions are not ideal.

Curb – A strain of the ligament that runs down the back of the hock.

Cause – Poor conformation may lead to curbs, as may undue strain on the hock joint.

Symptoms – Curbs do not often cause lameness but in some cases the horse may be slightly lame. There will be a small swelling approximately 10 cm (4 in) below the point of hock at the back of the limb.

Treatment – Rest if lame, otherwise none is necessary.

Other Ailments Commonly Encountered

Colic – Abdominal pain.

Cause – There are many possible causes, such as worm damage to the gut; feeding too soon before or after exercise; eating large quantities of unsuitable feedstuffs; distress brought on by travelling, moving yards, etc.; a twisted gut.

Symptoms – These may vary from slight to violent. The horse may lie down and get up frequently. It is likely to stand with its head down and look round at its stomach. It may kick at its stomach. It may roll violently and throw itself around. There could be an increase in respiration, and patchy sweating if the horse is very distressed. These symptoms may come and go, the horse not wanting to eat when in pain and then eating again when the pain appears to have subsided. It will probably not pass any droppings.

Treatment – If symptoms persist for more than 10–15 minutes, call the vet. Remove feed from the stable. Keep a constant watch on the horse. If the symptoms are only mild, the horse may benefit from gentle walking in hand. However, care should be taken as a sudden bout of pain may cause the horse to try to lie down and roll wherever it happens to be. If this is a concrete yard, it could damage itself quite badly. If possible, try to walk the horse on grass or in an indoor/outdoor school. Otherwise, leave the horse in its box. Let it lie down if it wants to but you may have to try to restrain it or get it to stand up if it tries to roll violently as it could damage itself as it thrashes around.

    The vet will try to determine what type of colic the horse has. He or she will probably give a muscle relaxant which may be all the horse needs to solve the problem, as in the case of spasmodic colic when the muscles of the intestinal wall go into spasm and cause the pain. If the horse has an impaction, a stomach tube will be used for the administration of large quantities of liquid paraffin to help to move the blockage. In the case of a twisted gut, an operation is the only option, so the horse will have to be rushed to the nearest surgery that is equipped with an operating theatre. The vet's diagnosis will be aided by any information you can give about the horse with regard to what it has been doing and eating in the preceding hours.

Prevention – Good stable management.

Azoturia – Stiffness and pain in the muscles, particularly over the hind-quarters. It is a problem that is not completely understood and is often called by different names, such as setfast and tying up.

Cause – The exact cause is unknown but the muscles become damaged and lactic acid is released into the muscles, causing pain.

Symptoms – During exercise, sometimes very shortly after exercise has commenced, the horse seems to begin "seizing up" behind. It appears to be lame and reluctant to go forward. If it is quite badly affected, it will show discomfort if the muscles over the loins and hind-quarters are touched. These muscle areas may feel hard. In less severe cases, the horse will just appear stiff behind. Some horses seem prone to this problem but it is most likely to occur in fit, stable-kept horses on a high concentrate ration. In more severe cases, the muscle pigment myoglobin is released into the blood. This is then filtered out through the kidneys, resulting in dark-coloured urine.

Treatment – Exercise must cease, especially if the horse is reluctant to go forward. Keep the horse warm. Phenylbutazone is usually given to reduce pain and as an anti-inflammatory. Rest and give a laxative diet for a period of time, depending upon the severity of the attack. A blood test will confirm the diagnosis and the degree of severity as enzymes from the muscle cells leak into the blood when damage occurs and the concentration of these enzymes in the blood will tell the vet how severe the attack has been. He or she can then advise on the rest period and how gradual the return to work should be.

Prevention – Susceptible horses usually improve if their concentrate ration is cut or changed to one less high in protein. Before and during a day off the horse should be fed a laxative diet and be turned out if possible. On return to work, exercise should progress slowly, with at least half an hour of walk first.

Filled Legs – Swelling in the lower limbs.

Cause – A stabled horse standing in for long periods with restricted amounts of exercise.

Symptoms – General filling in both forelimbs or both hind limbs, or in all four legs. If swelling is only in one limb, this is likely to be due to an injury or infection and further investigation is necessary.

Treatment – When the horse is exercised, the filling generally disappears. Stable bandages could be used to minimise swelling when the horse is standing in. More exercise and time in the field will help to reduce the swelling.

Prevention – Try to establish a routine which breaks up the day and therefore keeps the horse's circulation active. Make sure the horse is not being overfed with concentrates.

Strangles – This is a disease of the upper respiratory tract mainly affecting young horses, although it can occur at any age. It is highly contagious and may spread quickly among horses at a sale or show. Horses already suffering from a slight virus may be more susceptible.

Cause –   Streptococcus bacteria.

Symptoms – The horse will have a temperature, appear depressed and probably be off its feed. It will probably have a soft cough and swellings will appear under and behind the lower jaw. These swellings make swallowing difficult and can restrict breathing. The horse will poke its nose forward and have a rather stiff head carriage as a result. The swellings will eventually burst open or will require to be lanced, releasing a thick pus. It may take up to two weeks for these swellings to rupture. There will also be a thick nasal discharge. It is in the lymph nodes that the abscesses form and, occasionally, the bacteria will spread through the lymphatic system, causing swellings in the abdominal region. This is called "bastard strangles".

Treatment – The horse should be isolated and a strict isolation procedure followed. When the abscesses burst, the pus will spread the disease, so infected bedding, clothing, etc. should be burnt or disinfected. Feed a soft laxative diet, giving the feed at ground level where it will be easier for the horse to feed. The swellings can be hot fomented to encourage them to mature. The nostrils should be cleaned frequently to help breathing. The horse may be given antibiotics. Diagnosis can be confirmed by a bacterial culture.

Prevention – New arrivals in the yard should be isolated and any horses known to have suffered from strangles or to have been in contact with a horse with strangles should be isolated for up to one month as the bacteria can remain in the environment for some time.

Tetanus – This is not a common disease but horses are particularly susceptible to tetanus which, if contracted, will usually prove fatal, hence the need for vaccination.

Cause –   The toxin *Clostridium tetani*, which is present in the soil, enters the body via a wound, where it causes spasm and paralysis of the voluntary muscles. Puncture wounds are most likely to be the site of infection.

Symptoms – There is a general increase in muscle stiffness. The third eyelid is seen stretched partway across the eye. Jaw movement may become restricted. The horse becomes extra sensitive to light and noise. There may be muscle spasms as well as paralysis, the horse looking anxious, with pricked ears, rigid limbs and tail held out awkwardly. The horse may fall down and eating and swallowing may become progressively more difficult as the muscles cease to work.

Treatment – The horse should be isolated in a quiet, dark environment. Large amounts of penicillin will be given. The wound where the toxin entered should be cleaned very thoroughly to prevent further amounts of toxin being absorbed. If muscle spasms are bad, the vet may give tranquillisers, muscle relaxants or sedatives.

Prevention – Vaccination. After the initial dose of two injections four to six weeks apart, a booster is given after one year and then every two years after that.

Follow-up Work to Confirm Knowledge and Experience

1. To gain experience in all matters to do with the horse's health, it is essential to have worked with a large number of horses and ponies. Until you have actually seen a variety of diseases/wounds and have been involved in treating and nursing these horses, you cannot be completely aware of the problems involved and the signs to look for. Each horse or pony will react a little differently and the circumstances in which the horses are kept will have a bearing on how each problem is tackled. For Stage IV level students particularly, it is essential to have worked in a fairly large commercial yard to have enough experience for this level.

Helpful Hints and Exam Technique

1. The subject of health may come up in various different parts of the exam, both when working with the horses and during theoretical discussion. Some candidates make the mistake of forgetting the obvious with this topic. The examiner is usually looking for basic practical answers, not complicated veterinary knowledge which is best left to the vets themselves.

2. In the Stage III exam there is a written paper, lasting 45 minutes, in which five questions must be answered. The answers are expected in note form rather than as an essay.

Sample question: Your horse is lame after shoeing.

    a) Name possible causes.

    b) What can you do to make your horse more comfortable?

Sample answer:

    a) 1. Nail prick or nail bind.

        2. The foot has been made to fit a shoe which is too small and therefore pinching.

    b) Determine which foot is affected. Have the farrier return and remove the shoe. Check the nails to see if there is any blood which would indicate a nail prick. Poultice the foot with a bran or Animalintex poultice and rest the horse on a laxative diet. If you have taken prompt action, the horse should be sound again within one or two days and can be reshod.

    Try to write neatly and spell correctly as this makes the examiner's job of understanding your paper much easier. This, in turn, should help you to receive a favourable result.

13 Breeding

STAGES III and IV

At Stage IV level the candidate is hoping to qualify as an Intermediate Stable Manager. They may subsequently find themselves running an establishment with a variety of interests. They are more than likely to come across stallions, in-foal mares or owners who wish to breed from a mare. A basic understanding, along with some hands-on experience of horse breeding, is essential.

1. Making the Decision to Breed from your Mare or Stallion

The Mare and Facilities

a. It is quite common for mare owners to breed from a mare just because the mare is no longer able to do any other work. This is not a good enough reason. There are too many unwanted, mediocre horses and ponies and care should be taken not to add to those numbers.

b. A mare should be chosen because she has excellent conformation, a good temperament, a proven performance record and, preferably, registration papers which detail her own breeding.

c. The owner must consider what market or work they intend to produce the offspring for. Although breeding is always a gamble, is the mare likely to produce the type wanted?

d. If the decision is made to go ahead, have you the necessary facilities for mares and youngstock?

207

- You will need a large foaling box, approximately 5.5 sq m (16 sq ft). Even if you send the mare to stud to foal, an in-foal mare needs plenty of room when stabled and mare and foal may need to be stabled together when they return from the stud.
- Good grazing is essential for healthy early development, along with safe fencing. Remember that young foals are likely to race about and could easily run into a fence. Also, if they lie down near to the fence and roll over, they can easily end up on the wrong side of the fence if the bottom rail or wire is too high.
- Facilities for weaning the foal need to be considered. Are there other youngsters that your foal could run with, and is there somewhere you can put the mare where she will be out of ear-shot of the foal at weaning time?
- Accommodation for the youngster must be considered. It will need grazing and stabling for whatever period of time you intend to keep it.
- The cost, both financially and in time, must be considered. There will be vet's fees as well as stud fees, extra feed, worming, innoculations and farriery attention. A youngster needs time and patience in order to make sure it is well handled and will be manageable in the future.
- If you intend to have the mare foal at home, you should have a certain amount of knowledge and experience of foaling, as well as someone capable to assist you. Time must be made to keep a check on the mare when she is due to foal, which can mean a number of sleepless nights. If you send the mare away, there are more costs to consider but you should have peace of mind that both mare and foal are in capable hands should anything go wrong. If you wish to have the mare put in foal again straightaway, it will save time if she is already at the stud when she foals.

The Stallion and Facilities

a. A male horse should only be left entire if he has excellent conformation, comes from a breeding line with a proven performance record, has a good temperament and is approved by the breed society with which he is registered.

b. Stallions like to be kept where they can be involved in the activities of the yard and not be completely isolated. Their tendency to be more boisterous leads to a requirement for a high bottom door with a grid at the top, which can be removed or replaced as necessary. The box should be a generous size as the stallion may have to be confined a little more than the other horses on the yard.

c. Suitable turn out facilities for a stallion include a paddock close to his box, so that he will not have to be led any great distance, and high, secure fencing as a stallion is more likely to try to jump out of his paddock than other horses, in order to get to a mare for example.

d. A competent and experienced rider must be on hand to keep the stallion well exercised. The horse will need to be fit for the covering season, and a ridden stallion can advertise his own abilities if he does well at competitions.

e. To keep the stallion well mannered and content in himself, a good handler is required who will keep the stallion in line without being too easy going which could lead to the horse getting out of hand, or too overly firm, which could lead to the horse being miserable and possibly becoming aggressive.

2. Preparing to Go to Stud

Choice of Stallion/Stud

a. Having decided what type of offspring you are hoping to produce, you will have an idea of what type of stallion you are looking for. How much you are prepared to spend and the location of studs will then help to narrow down the choice. If you choose a stud too far from home, it will make visiting difficult and extra transport costs will be incurred.

b. Having made your initial selection of studs, do go and visit to see the stallions and their offspring. Take note of the stallion's temperament, how he is handled and the conditions he is kept in, as well as assessing whether his type and conformation are to your liking. If your mare has any weak points, make sure they are not also weak points in the stallion and, likewise, if the stallion has any weak points, they should not coincide with weak points in the mare. For example, if your mare is a little light of bone, choose a stallion with really good bone.

c. The National Light Horse Breeding Society (formerly the HIS), runs a scheme for inspecting and grading both mares and stallions. The stallions are mainly Thoroughbred, although they do approve others from time to time. Approved stallions stand at stud in allocated areas. If you are a NLHBS member and/or if you choose an approved stallion in your area, the stud fee will be quite low, giving you the opportunity to put your mare to a quality stallion at low cost. The offspring will be eligible for registration. The Horserace Betting Levy Board contribute to the NLHBS, enabling them to run their premium scheme.

d. Ask to see where the mares will be kept and note the condition of the fencing and grazing, as well as the way the yard is kept. All of these factors will help you to decide if the stud has high standards and will do a good job.

e. Find out if the stallion of your choice has a good fertility rate. If you choose a young stallion in his first year at stud, the stud fee may be cheaper as there will be no offspring to see or fertility rate to assess. If this is the case, find out how many mares they intend to cover with this stallion, as it should be no more than approximately six to ten. An experienced stallion around five years of age may cover 20–50 mares in a season. Older stallions are likely to have a lower fertility rate and the number of mares they cover each season should be reduced.

Preparing the Mare

a. Mares are less likely to get in foal if they are in very poor condition or very overweight. The best condition for a mare going to stud is if they are gradually improving in condition. This is how they would be likely to be in the wild as they would have been through the winter on poor grazing and would then be grazing spring grass as they come into the breeding season.

b. Longer daylight hours and warm weather stimulate the oestrous cycle. This cycle lasts an average 21 days, oestrus being for five days followed by 16 days of dioestrus. During the winter the cycle normally ceases altogether and this period is called anoestrus.

During oestrus, when the mare is receptive to the stallion, she is generally referred to as being "in season". As spring approaches, watch the mare carefully to see when she begins coming into season and make a note of her cycle.

c. The mare must have up-to-date vaccination records for flu and tetanus.

d. The hind shoes should be removed and it is best if her feet have been recently attended to.

e. The usual worming programme must be continued but the mare will be wormed again on arrival at the stud.

f. You will need to ask the vet to swab the mare. Initially, he or she will take a clitoral swab to test for contagious equine metritis (CEM). Another swab will be taken when the mare is in season. This is a cervical swab to check that there are no uterine infections. The vet must be asked for a certificate to show that the mare has been tested clear for CEM as this is needed as proof when the mare arrives at stud.

g. Having chosen your stud and stallion, a nomination form will be filled out. This is an agreement between the owner of the mare and the stud. It will detail various points, including most of those made above: the mare must have flu/tetanus/ and CEM certificates; hind shoes must be removed and the farrier will be called as necessary while the mare is at stud; the mare will be wormed on arrival and at regular intervals during her stay; the stud fee/cancellation fee; conditions such as "no foal no fee"; costs that the owner is responsible for, etc.

h. It is best for the mare to live out while at stud. It will be cheaper for the owner and more relaxing for the mare, so make sure the mare is roughed off.

i. Send the mare with a minimum of equipment, usually just a leather headcollar with the mare's name printed clearly on a name plate. The mare will probably wear this headcollar the whole time she is at stud, so make sure it is of good quality and comfortable.

j. With all these things to organise, it is helpful if you start preparations early in the year in order that the mare can go to stud and, with luck, get in foal around April/May. The foal will then be born in March/April the following year and should be able to enjoy the best of the spring grass.

k. Thoroughbred mares, producing for the racing industry, are encouraged to come into season early by being stabled, kept warm and having lights left on in their stables to make them feel as if the days are getting longer and spring has arrived. The mares can then be covered early so that they will produce as early as possible in the year as all Thoroughbreads are aged as one year old from the 1st of January following their birth. The earlier the foal is born, the more mature it will be by its first birthday, giving it an advantage over late foals when they all begin racing as two year olds. However, in this situation extra facilities are needed in the form of heated stables and foal rugs to keep the foals warm at this time of year.

3. At Stud

a. When the mare arrives, all the relevant paperwork will be checked, so the mare owner must remember to take flu/tetanus certificates etc. The mare will be settled in.

b. The mare will be checked regularly to see when she comes into season. Different studs use a variety of methods. A stallion may be ridden out past the mares' field to see which mares show an interest. It may be necessary to bring the mares to a "teasing board" where a stallion is led up to the mare to see if she is receptive. The board protects both the stallion and his handler from being injured if the mare kicks out, while allowing the "teaser" (a less valuable stallion that is easy to handle, perhaps a pony stallion) to nuzzle the mare and see if she appears to be in season.

Signs of a Mare in Season

- The mare shows an interest in the stallion if it is ridden or led past the field.
- Stradling her hind legs.
- Lifting her tail and "winking" the vulva.
- Willing to stand for the stallion.
- If the vet makes a manual examination of the mare to see if she is ready for covering, he will insert his hand into the rectum and feel for the ovaries through the wall of the rectum. If he can feel a well-developed follicle (a sac containing the egg), this is a good

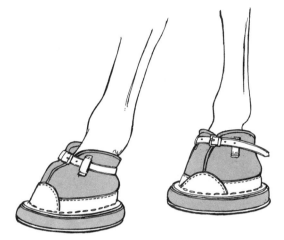

Felt kicking boots

time to cover. Some mares show more obvious signs than others but an experienced stud groom should recognise the signs.

c. If the mare is in season, she will be prepared for covering. A tail bandage will be put on. The area under her tail and around the vulva should be washed with warm water. The handler should wear strong footwear, gloves and a hard hat and should lead the mare out in a bridle to the covering area. The mare will then have felt kicking boots put on to prevent her from injuring the stallion should she kick out.

d. The covering area may be similar to a small indoor school, with a good non-slip surface.

e. The stallion's handler also needs to wear strong footwear, gloves and a hard hat and will lead the stallion out in a bridle and lead rein.

f. The mare will be covered every second day until she no longer shows signs of being in season.

g. Most mares come into season every three weeks. If the mare does not come into season again approximately three weeks after she was last covered, it is assumed that she is in foal. Once the mare has been tested to see if she is definitely in foal, she can return home.

Pregnancy Testing

Scanning – An ultrasound scanner can be used around three weeks after the last covering date to see if the mare is in foal. This method can be used as early as 15 days after the last covering date.

Manual Examination – The vet can feel through the wall of the rectum to see if one of the uterine horns is swollen, which would indicate pregnancy. This can be done at around six weeks.

Blood Test – From around 45–90 days, a blood test taken from a pregnant mare would contain gonadotrophin.

Urine Test – After about 100 days a urine sample from a pregnant mare would contain high levels of oestrogen.

Ultrasound scanning is the most reliable of all these tests, and would also show if the mare was pregnant with twins, in which case the vet would try to "pinch out" one of the twins as mares seldom manage to give birth to twins without serious problems.

4. Care of the In-foal Mare

a. When the mare returns from stud, she should be turned out on good pasture, preferably with other in-foal or barren mares, and be treated as a normal horse at grass. The usual daily checks should be made, along with regular worming and visits from the farrier. Before using a wormer, check the manufacturer's notes to make sure it is a safe wormer for mares in foal. This is especially important in the very early stages. As the grazing becomes poor and colder weather sets in towards Christmas, she can be given hard feeds and hay to keep her in good condition. She should not be allowed to get overweight.

b. Once the embryo has had time to become secure, there is no reason why an in-foal mare cannot be ridden if the owner wishes. It is probably best to cease riding after about seven months.

c. Although the mare has been tested in foal before leaving the stud, there is sometimes cause for the mare to abort or resorb in the early stages. It is wise to have the mare scanned again around the end of September as most studs offer terms of "no foal fee returned" or "no foal free return" if there is evidence that the mare is no longer in foal. This means the stud fee will be returned or the owner can have a second covering, free of charge, the following year. The cost of livery is not reimbursed, nor is livery free if the mare returns to be covered again. The date set for this arrangement is 1 October, so the mare must be checked before this date and a veterinary certificate produced to state that she is no longer in foal if this is the case.

d. It is during the last three months of pregnancy that the foal makes its greatest increase in size, therefore, if the foal is due at the conventional time of year, in the new year the mare's belly will increase in size significantly. At this point, stud nuts or a stud mix can be introduced into the diet to make sure the mare is receiving the correct amount of protein.

e. The mare may already be being brought in at night if the weather is poor. If not, and you wish to have the mare foal indoors, you should start bringing her in at night to the box you intend her to occupy for the foaling. She needs to be able to establish a routine and feel relaxed and comfortable in her surroundings. Remember, as the mare reaches the end of her pregnancy she will become increasingly cumbersome in size and will need plenty of room to turn and manoeuvre, especially in doorways. Many mares become particularly placid and quiet when in foal.

f. During the last month of pregnancy, the colostrum, the first milk, which contains antibodies to help to protect the young foal against infection in its first weeks of life, begins to form in the mare. During this last month, therefore, the mare should receive a tetanus booster so that this protection can be passed on to the foal in the colostrum. Likewise, if the mare's flu vaccination is due in the last month of pregnancy, this is also quite helpful. She can be wormed as normal right up to foaling and will continue being wormed after foaling.

g. If a mare arrives in your yard a few months before she is due to foal, it will be necessary to make notes of as much background history as possible. Check: last covering date; previous foaling history; medical background; flu/tetanus and worming status;

and the usual information about her feeding, character, handling problems, etc. The average length of pregnancy for a mare is 340 days, so you can work out the date the mare is due from her last covering date. However, they can foal several weeks late or be early, so don't be caught out.

5. Foaling

Preparation

a. As already stated, a large foaling box is required, with a good, deep and clean straw bed. As with all boxes, there should be no obvious projections as the mare will get up and down during foaling.

b. Closed-circuit television is an ideal way of observing mares through the night. Alternatively, use a foaling alarm which is a device strapped to a roller worn by the mare, which detects a rise in temperature when she is due to foal. If you haven't got either of these devices, you must visit the mare every 20 minutes, making sure you cause a minimum of disturbance. You may still find that the mare manages to foal between your visits, however, so this is not ideal.

c. If the mare is to foal in a field, short of camping out with her, it is more difficult to check her. However, a field can still be used, providing there is no water in which a foal could drown, and very secure, safe fencing. As already mentioned, a foal can easily end up on the wrong side of a fence.

d. In order to be prepared for any eventuality, the following equipment is required:

- The vet's telephone number and a phone – The vet will probably be aware that you have a mare due to foal from previous visits to your yard. If, due to previous history, the foaling may be complicated in any way, you should have discussed this with your vet and given him or her some warning of the event.
- Telephone number of the National Foaling Bank – If either mare or foal should die, or if the mare rejects the foal, this organisation can help with foster mares and give general advice.

- String – After foaling, the mare may not cleanse immediately and the afterbirth should be tied up to prevent it from being stepped on and torn.
- Clean towels, soap and water – The foal can be rubbed down with towels to help to dry it. You may need to wash your hands.
- Antiseptic/iodine spray – The stump of the umbilical cord should be sprayed as soon as the cord has broken naturally, to prevent any infection from entering at this vulnerable site.
- Rugs – If the foal is born early in the year, it may be necessary to put a rug or jumper of some sort on it for warmth. Likewise, after foaling the mare may feel cold and need rugging up.
- Feeding bottle/mare's milk replacer/frozen colostrum – If the worst should happen and the mare dies, you need to be prepared to feed the foal. Or, if the mare and foal have problems with suckling, you may need to milk some colostrum from the mare and feed it to the foal.
- Tail bandage – If the mare's tail is bandaged, it will not become entangled with the foal during presentation.
- Any other equipment, such as foaling ropes, should only be used by an experienced stud hand or vet.

The Early Signs

a. One of the first signs that the mare's time to foal is near is the udder beginning to swell and fill with milk. Sometimes milk will run from the udder and traces can be seen on the hind legs.
b. Due to the mare being very large and heavy in these last few weeks, she may stand quietly and not move around much, which could result in filled legs. Walk her gently in hand each day if this is the case.
c. When a waxy substance appears on the end of each teat, referred to as "waxing up", she is likely to foal quite soon, although this can happen two or three weeks before foaling. However, a close watch must now be kept.
d. The muscles over the hindquarters become soft and dip down, making the quarters look poor, and the vulva appears to slacken.
e. Some mares show the above signs well before foaling, while for others these signs mean that they will foal very soon.

The Birth

a. The majority of mares foal at night, often in the early hours between midnight and 3 a.m. The mare seems to be able to control
   the time of birth to some extent as it is often the case that she will
   foal when there are no humans watching over her.

b. When the foaling begins, the first stage for the mare is the initial
   contractions. She will show similar signs to those of colic, looking
   round at her flanks, pacing around the box, possibly sweating
   and getting up and lying down. This first stage is over when the
   waters break, which is the moment the placenta breaks and
   allantoic fluid gushes from the vulva.

c. Once the waters have broken, it should be no longer than approximately half an hour before the foal is born, which is the second
   stage. First a whitish sac will appear, then the foal's first front
   foot, with the second front foot just behind it. The sac surrounding the foal (the amnion) will soon rupture and, indeed, needs to
   do so in order that the foal can breathe. If the sac does not rupture,
   someone must step in to break the sac so the foal can take its first
   breath.

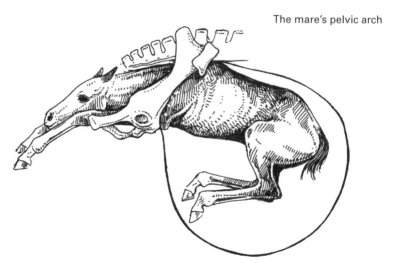

The mare's pelvic arch

The correct presentation of the foal

d. After the two feet, the foal's nose will be visible. During this time the mare continues to have contractions and is likely to get up and lie down. This is a natural process and helps to move the foal into the right position for birth. Most mares will foal lying down but some will do so standing. Once the head and shoulders of the foal are out and you have checked that the foal's nostrils are clear for breathing, leave the mare to rest if she wishes. She may lie there for a while and, during this time, blood is passing through the umbilical cord into the foal. This process is vital as much-needed oxygen is passing into the foal. Eventually the cord will break naturally and the birth will be completed as the mare moves and the hind feet of the foal come clear. Remember to spray the umbilical stump with antiseptic/iodine spray.

e. Depending on the experience of the mare, you may now assist by rubbing the foal to help to dry it and, if the mare is still lying down, pull it round towards its mother's head. The bonding process will begin. Mare and foal often whinny to each other, and the mare will begin to lick the foal dry.

f. The third stage is the cleansing. The mare may cleanse straightaway. Cleansing is the expulsion of the umbilical cord, amnion and placenta (afterbirth). If she does not cleanse immediately, tie up the afterbirth, then, once she has cleansed, which should take no more than five to six hours maximum, check it is all intact. If in any doubt, call the vet. He or she can examine the afterbirth and attend to the mare if there is a problem. If you do not act promptly, it could be fatal.

g. The mare and foal should not be left unattended until the foal has found its feet and learnt to suckle. Again, this should take no longer than five to six hours maximum, and usually happens within a couple of hours.

h. The mare could be gently washed, under her dock and down her back legs, and have the tail bandage removed. Check the vulva for tears.

i. Within the first 24 hours the foal must pass the meconium. This is a fairly hard black substance which collects in the bowels of the foal before it is born. The foal sometimes has problems passing the meconium, in which case it will need an enema from an experienced person.

j. Most foalings take place with no complications and no assistance needed. However, if any of the expected stages of foaling, or subsequent events, do not occur within the times stated, it is vital that the vet is called immediately as complications can result in particularly severe problems.

k. If the worst does happen and the mare or foal dies or the mare rejects the foal, contact the National Foaling Bank, Meretown Stud, Newport, Shropshire. Tel: Newport 811234. This centre probably has more experience with foster mares and rearing orphan foals than anywhere else in the country.

A dead foal should not be taken away from its mother. The mare should be left with it for up to two days. If the mare is to foster another foal, the skin of her own dead foal will be wrapped round the orphan foal to try to get the mare to accept it. If a foal is to be hand-reared, once it has had the colostrum (which may have been milked from the mare) which is probably best fed to it from a bottle, it should be encouraged to drink its milk from a bucket which is easier in the long run.

6. The Foal's First Weeks/Months

a. Both mare and foal should be watched carefully on their first day to make sure that all is well and that they generally appear happy and in good health. Check that the foal appears to be feeding normally and that it is getting enough milk. If a foal goes to feed and milk is not forthcoming, it will tend to butt the mare and keep changing from one teat to the other. Sometimes mares are ticklish or tender and inclined to move away from the foal or warn it off at first. It may be necessary to pin the mare in the corner of the stable and hold up a front leg while she gets used to the idea.

b. If the foal was born out in the field, it may be necessary to bring the mare and foal into a stable to check them thoroughly and observe their behaviour. It will also be necessary to put a foal slip on the foal in the first few days, which will probably be more easily done in the stable.

c. Foal slips should be made of leather so that they will break in an emergency rather than leaving the foal struggling and caught up on some sort of projection. Once fitted to the foal, they will need to be readjusted more or less every week as the foal will grow quickly and it is easy to forget that the foal slip is becoming tight.

d. If the foal was born in a stable, it can be turned out on the second day, either with other mares and foals or on its own with its dam. Foals can run loose after the mare but it is a good idea, and often easier, to begin leading from the start in order to teach control right from the beginning. At this stage, the foal is too young to be led from its head. The best way is to slip a soft scarf around the foal's chest and hold this in one hand by the withers, while placing an arm around the foal's quarters. In this way you can encourage the foal from behind but control the forward movement too as it can be a little erratic at first. Guide the foal along beside the mare and it will soon learn the routine.

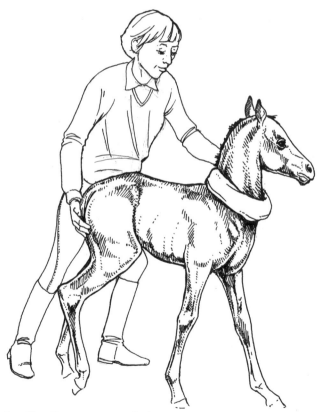

Leading the very young foal

e. While the foal is small and of a manageable size, it is quite easy to familiarise it with grooming and having its legs touched and its feet picked up. It will not be long before the farrier is needed to trim its feet and most farriers will be happy to allow the foal to get used to him and the trimming process providing the foal has learnt the basics first.

f. Approximately seven to ten days after foaling, the mare will usually come into season. This is known as the foaling heat. Sometimes a mare will be covered again at this stage but the conception rate is usually quite low. Also, the mare may not yet have completely healed from the birth, so if time is not too tight it is probably best to wait until the next time she comes in season. During this foaling heat, the foal will often scour. This is quite serious as a small foal can easily become dehydrated. The vet will supply treatment for this common problem. Sometimes foals scour because the mare's milk is too rich or the foal is too greedy. The foal may have to be muzzled for periods throughout the day in order to regulate the amount of milk taken.

g. The foal will quickly learn to feed by sharing the mare's daily ration. The mare should be fed from a large, handle-less bucket which their two heads can easily fit into. At the same time, the foal will also begin grazing. When the foal begins eating a reasonable quantity of feed, it should be given its own ration from a foal creep, a manger or feed bowl with bars over the top through which its small muzzle can fit but not the larger muzzle of the mare. This ensures that the foal has a reasonable ration and the mare doesn't get to eat too much.

h. It may be necessary to travel the mare and foal in a horse box or trailer, perhaps to a show or stud, for example. Don't attempt to put any protective clothing on the foal; at this stage it should travel loose with the mare and use her for support. Put a minimum of clothing on the mare so that there is nothing the foal is likely to get tangled in should it panic at any point. For the same reason, do not use a haynet.

To load mare and foal, two people should guide and partly lift the foal in first and the mare will follow. If the mare is loaded first, she is likely to try to rush straight out as the foal will hesitate at the bottom of the ramp, not knowing how to negotiate it. As the mare will not want to leave her foal she should follow it in calmly which will instil confidence in the foal. Make sure the compartment is large enough for the two and check that there are no gaps through which the foal could squeeze, causing them to become separated. Remember that the foal is likely to find the journey quite tiring.

i. The foal must be eating well and independently before it is weaned. It should also have had its flu/tetanus inoculations and a worming programme should have been started. Foals are generally weaned at around six months of age unless the mare is having problems with providing milk, for example. Various methods can be used depending upon your facilities. If there is a group of mares and foals living out together, then one mare at a time may be taken away until just the foals are left, with perhaps one or two barren mares for company. When separated, mare and foal should not be able to hear each other. Calling to each other will only cause more distress and encourage both mare and foal to try to break out to get to each other. If suitable facilities are not available, it may be necessary to shut perhaps two foals in a box and take the mares away.

   Either method will be easier if the foal has learnt to leave its mother gradually. Mare and foal could be separated for short periods each day, for example while the mare is being ridden. This teaches the foal a little independence and makes the final separation less traumatic. The mare should not be too well fed immediately after weaning, to help her milk to dry up. Exercise also helps the drying up process.

j. A colt foal will need to be castrated. If he is going to race or has been bred specifically to breed from in future, he will obviously be left entire. In this case the breeder should have made sure that he or she has suitable facilities to keep the colt separate from mares, both as a foal and as a mature horse. If facilities are limited, the colt should be castrated at around six months if both testes have descended. In some cases, the owner may like to delay castration in order to allow the colt to become better developed physically. However, it must be remembered that the colt will require confident and experienced handling if he is not to become unmanageable.

k. Through its first years, the youngster must be well fed but not overfed. Unlimited hay and two feeds a day, of a stud mix or cube specially formulated for youngsters, through the winter, and good spring and summer grazing should strike the right balance. An overfed, fat youngster is likely to have growth-related problems which can be very serious. Good management with regard to shelter, worming, attention to feet, etc. play a major part in uncomplicated development.

Follow-up Work to Confirm Knowledge and Experience

1. It is essential to have been involved in the care of a mare from when she goes to stud to when she foals in order to be able to talk confidently about mares, foals and foaling. Likewise, you need to visit a stud and see what goes on in a typical working day.
2. If you are able to find a friendly vet who is dealing with brood mares and is willing to take you with him or her on their rounds, you would gain invaluable experience from seeing a variety of horses and their problems.

Helpful Hints and Exam Technique

1. The breeding section of the Stage IV exam is mainly dealt with in theory. It is easy to begin quoting facts from the book in this situation so try to avoid this by recounting events from your own real experience.

14 Assessing the Horse's Age

STAGE IV

In previous chapters I have mentioned the need to inspect the horse's teeth on a regular basis in order to make sure that they are in good condition. Apart from being an essential part of the digestive process, a horse's teeth are also our best means of assessing the horse's age.

1. Structure of the Teeth

a. The part that is situated in the jaw bone is called the root.
b. The middle section surrounded by gum is the neck.
c. The visible section above the gum is the crown.
d. Inside the tooth, extending most of the way up, is the pulp cavity.
e. Around the pulp cavity is the dentine.
f. The visible portion of the tooth is covered with enamel.
g. The permanent teeth grow to their full length by the time the horse is around five years old. From then on the existing tooth is gradually pushed up through the gum as the surface wears down in the process of grazing and mastication. In this way, different portions of the teeth gradually come into wear.
h. The flat tops of the teeth are called the tables. On these tables marks can be seen which help to identify the horse's age. These marks are the infundibulum, which is like a hole going down into the tooth, and the dental star which is the appearance of the pulp cavity.

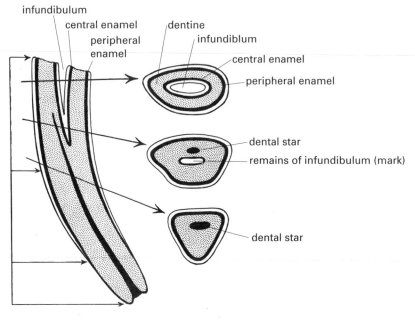

Structure of the teeth

2. Temporary Teeth

a. The temporary, or milk, teeth consist of six incisors in the upper jaw and six in the lower jaw, and three premolars in each side of the upper and lower jaws. This makes a total of 12 incisor teeth and 12 premolars.

b. When the foal is born, it may already have its premolar teeth but the first two incisors (the centrals) generally appear after a week or so.

c. By the time the foal is approximately six weeks old, the temporary centrals (two in the top jaw and two in the bottom jaw) will have reached their full size and the four laterals will have appeared.

d. At around nine months of age, the laterals will have reached their full size and the corner teeth will have appeared.

e. There are no temporary tushes.

3. Permanent Teeth

It is the permanent teeth which give us the best indication of the horse's age, the incisors being the best guide as they are quite easy to see. In most cases, up to the age of eight years an accurate assessment can be made. However, it is possible for some horses to be backward in their tooth development and exhibit, for example, a three-year-old set of teeth when they are actually four years old, therefore even the teeth cannot be totally relied on as a guide to age. Once the horse is over eight years old, it is even more difficult to be accurate. At this stage an assessment could easily be five or ten years over or under the horse's real age.

    a. At two and a half years, the temporary central incisors are shed and the permanent central incisors make their appearance. At the same time there will now be two of the permanent molar teeth on each side of the upper and lower jaws.

    b. At three and a half years, the temporary lateral incisors are shed and the permanent lateral incisors make their appearance. By this time the centrals have reached their full length and are in wear against each other. Two more molars will have appeared, pushing out the first two temporary molars, making a total of four permanent molars and one temporary one in each jaw.

    c. At four and a half years, the temporary corner incisors are shed and the permanent corner incisors make their appearance. By this time the laterals have reached their full length and are in wear against each other. The last two permanent molars will appear around this time, one of them pushing out the last temporary molar. There will now be a total of six molars on each side of the upper and lower jaws. The corner incisors will be their full length by the time the horse is five years old, and will be coming into wear against each other from five to six years.

    d. At around four years of age, the tushes will have appeared in male horses. Female horses do not usually have tushes, although some will have small ones. The tushes will be fully grown by the time the horse is five to six years old.

    e. The adult male horse therefore has 40 teeth and possibly additional wolf teeth. In the absence of tushes, the adult female has 36 teeth with the possible addition of wolf teeth.

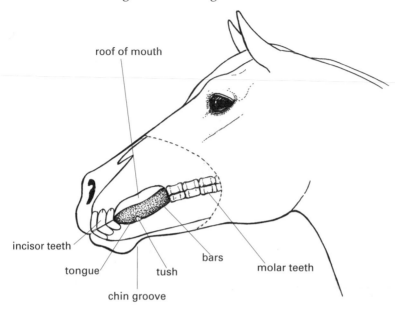

roof of mouth

incisor teeth

tongue

chin groove

tush

bars

molar teeth

The structure of the mouth

From four and a half years of age, the tables of the lower set of incisors are used to tell us more about the horse's age.

    f. At six years of age, the tables of the corner incisors will show a large dark hole which is the infundibulum. By now the infundibulum will have disappeared from the central incisors and be growing smaller as it disappeares from the laterals. On the tables of the central incisors there will now be a dark brown line which is the dental star. The dental star will also be in evidence on the tables of the laterals, between the front of the tooth and the disappearing infundibulum.

    g. At seven years of age the infundibulum will have disappeared from the centrals and laterals, while it is becoming smaller in the corner incisors. The dental star will be more obvious in the centrals and laterals. On the upper corner incisors, a hook will appear on the back corner, due to uneven wear. This hook disappears at around eight to eight and a half years of age.

From eight years onwards it becomes increasingly difficult to be accurate about the horse's age. However, there are a few other pointers to look for.

h. Up to eight years, the tables of the horse's teeth are oval. From eight or nine onwards, starting with the centrals, the tables gradually become triangular, then, finally, when the horse is around its late teens onwards, they become rounded.

i. Sometimes a second, more pronounced, hook appears at around nine to 13 years. This should not be mistaken for a seven-year-old hook, which illustrates why all other factors should be considered when making an assessment of a horse's age. This second hook is likely to stay as a permanent feature.

j. Some horses have a Galvayne's groove. This is a groove which begins to appear at the top of the tooth in the middle of the upper corner incisor. It may first appear at around ten years of age, extending halfway down the tooth by the time the horse is 15, then right to the bottom by the time the horse is 20. It then begins to disappear from the top of the tooth downwards so that it is half-gone by the time the horse is 25 and completely gone at 30.

k. As the horse gets older, the teeth appear to be longer and more forward sloping, rather than short and upright as they are in a youngster.

l. The dental star gradually becomes less of a line at the front edge of the tooth as the teeth wear. It finishes up as a dot in the middle of the tooth.

4. Other Indicators of Age in the Horse

a. Youngsters tend to have a long-legged, immature look. Up to almost two years of age, the short foal tail can be a good clue to age.

b. If you look and feel along the lower jaw of a youngster, it is often bumpy with the roots of the teeth that have not yet fully erupted.

c. The hollows above the horse's eyes become more sunken with age.

d. Older horses often begin to grow grey hair over their faces and around their muzzles.

e. Young horses usually have fairly straight backs and less signs of wear and tear on their limbs, while an older horse may have a sunken back and blemishes, such as wind galls etc., on their limbs.

f. The general demeanour of an old horse can be a clue when compared to that of a more lively youngster.

As already mentioned, the ageing of horses is not an exact science. Although the age of a youngster up to seven years old can usually be checked quite accurately, there are always exceptions to every rule. Every possible factor should be looked at and considered before a decision is reached.

Follow-up Work to Confirm Knowledge and Experience

1. Having read the information on teeth and ageing, it will be necessary to look at as many different sets of horses' teeth as possible. If a vet or horse dentist visits to check a horse's teeth, they will probably use a Haussman's or Swales gag to help them with their inspection. This is an ideal time to take a really good look at the teeth with someone who can point out the different marks you should be looking for. The Swales gag would be the best design for looking at the incisors, as the Haussman's gag will cover the tables of the incisors.

2. When you think you know what you are looking for, begin practising on horses whose ages you already know. Look for the marks, teeth, hooks, etc., that should be present at that age, as well as other signs of age in the horse. From this you will gradually build up knowledge that you can use when looking at the teeth of a horse whose age is not known to you.

Helpful Hints and Exam Technique

1. In a Stage IV exam it is necessary to check the age of all horses you are dealing with, whether you are tacking them up, taking their temperature, riding them, etc., as it has a bearing on your approach to the horse and assessment of its behaviour. The examiner will ask you how old you think the different horses are.

2. If you check the sex of the horse first it will help you when ageing as, if it is a male horse and there are no tushes, you could

immediately assess it as four years or under, making sure that you check all other possible factors. However, if it is a mare, the lack of tushes would not have any bearing on its age.

3. When first approaching the horse to age it, begin by just gently parting its lips to look at the angle of its teeth etc. Don't dive straight in and grab its tongue as you don't know how it may react. When you are ready to look at the tables of its teeth, gently slip a couple of fingers over the bar of its mouth and push its tongue back a little. This is usually enough to make it open its mouth without risking any accidents by holding its tongue.

4. Always look at both sides of the horse's mouth as they can often present very different pictures. For example, you may look at a horse who chews at one side of its stable doorway, which has caused its teeth to be worn and difficult to assess on one side, but which still appear normal on the other side.

15   The Respiratory System

STAGES III and IV

The process by which oxygen passes from the air into the blood stream, while carbon dioxide is expelled, is referred to as respiration or breathing. This exchange of gases (oxygen and carbon dioxide) takes place in the lungs.

1. The Respiratory Process and Basic Structure of the System

a. The nostrils – Air enters the nasal passages via the nostrils. They are capable of expanding when there is a greater demand for oxygen, for example during exercise.

b. Nasal passages – These are separated from the mouth by the hard palate. It is here that air is warmed.

c. Pharynx – The nasal passages lead into the pharynx which is an area through which air passes on its way to the larynx.

d. Larynx – This is the voice box. It also controls the passage of air into the trachea. The epiglottis closes over the opening of the larynx to prevent food and water from passing into the lungs.

e. Trachea – This is the wind pipe which runs from the larynx down the neck to the chest and into the lungs.

f. Bronchi – The trachea divides into two bronchi. These bronchi then branch, going one into each lung.

g. Bronchioles – These are subdivisions of the bronchi, which end in alveolar sacs.

h. Alveoli – By the time the air reaches these sacs, it has been warmed and moistened. Here the exchange of gases takes place.

i. The air is then expelled back along the same route, and the process begins again.

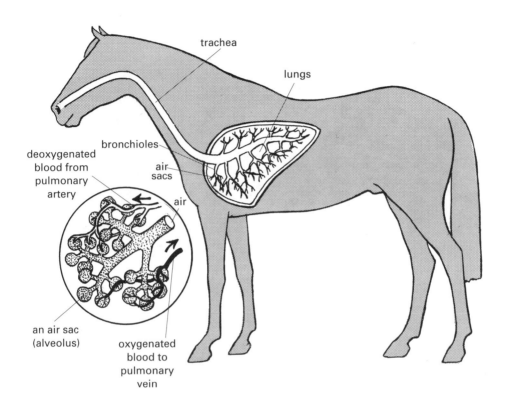

trachea

lungs

bronchioles

deoxygenated
blood from
pulmonary
artery

air
sacs

air

an air sac
(alveolus)

oxygenated
blood to
pulmonary
vein

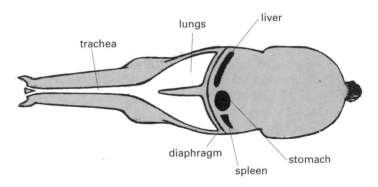

lungs

liver

trachea

diaphragm

spleen

stomach

The respiratory system

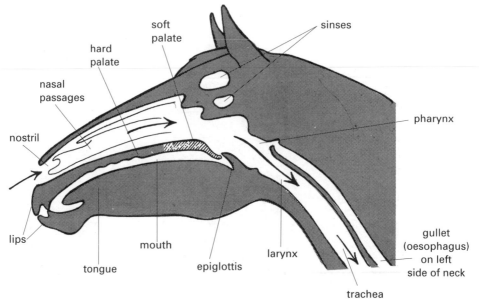

The upper respiratory tract

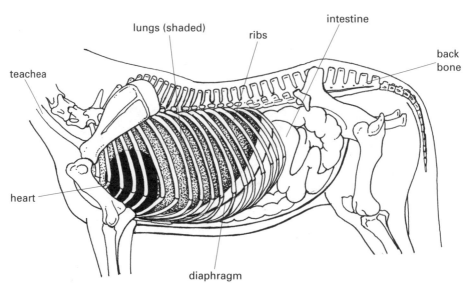

The lower respiratory tract

2. Additional Information

a. Other functions of the respiratory system include: temperature control by breathing out warm air and taking in cool air; voice production; the sense of smell.

b. A horse does not breathe through its mouth.

c. Inside the nasal passages are tiny, curling bones called the turbinate bones. They increase the surface area within these passages, which aids the warming of the inhaled air.

d. Sinuses are the air-filled cavities at the front of the skull, which connect with the nasal cavity.

e. The respiratory tract is often referred to in two sections. The upper respiratory tract refers to the parts leading to the trachea. The lower respiratory tract refers to the section from trachea to lungs.

f. The trachea is kept open by rings of cartilage. It is lined with a thin film of mucus and tiny hair-like projections called cilia. The cilia move and keep the mucus moving over them. This traps foreign particles and moves them back up to the throat.

g. Mucus is a slimy substance which lubricates the mucous membranes, like those inside the eyelid. If these membranes become inflamed, an excess of mucus is produced. Inflammation in the respiratory system will result in excessive mucus draining out via the nostrils.

n. The pleura is a smooth membrane which surrounds the lungs and prevents friction.

i. The diaphragm separates the chest cavity from the abdominal cavity. It is a thin sheet of muscle attached to the inside of the rib cage. It starts just in front of the loins and slopes forward and downward to the breastbone.

j. The chest cavity expands when the diaphragm and rib cage muscles contract. This draws air into the lungs. As the muscles relax, air is expelled.

k. The diaphragm is dome-shaped when relaxed. When the muscles contract, it flattens. Movement of the diaphragm will be restricted by a full stomach (the stomach is situated just behind the diaphragm), hence the need to feed the horse well in advance of exercise.

l. At rest, the horse has a respiration rate of 8–12 breaths per minute.

Follow-up Work to Confirm Knowledge and Experience

1. As with the other systems, try building a model to which you can relate visually to help you to remember the respiratory process.
2. Practise saying the unfamiliar words aloud until you are comfortable with them. Use word association to help you to remember words which are particularly difficult for you. For example, if you find the word trachea difficult to remember, think of it as the track to the lungs so that the word track gives you the beginning of the word trachea.

Helpful Hints and Exam Technique

1. Try not to become flustered if you forget the names of various parts of the system under the pressure of the exam situation. The examiner will give you time to think and come back to a point you have problems with.
2. Try to learn the basic system and avoid confusing your memory with too many extra details. Don't worry if other candidates come out with details you don't know about, as they have probably managed to learn much more than they need to know for the exam.

16   The Circulatory System

STAGES III and IV

The circulatory system is responsible for transporting oxygen, water, nutrients, hormones and defence cells to various parts of the body, as and when
required. It also transports waste products away from various areas, and
helps to regulate body heat.
    The circulatory systems consist of:

1. The Heart

a. The heart is situated in the chest cavity, between the two lungs.
b. It is a muscular organ which acts like a pump.
c. The heart is divided into a right and left side. Each side is then
    further divided into an upper collecting chamber and a lower
    pumping chamber. Non-return valves control circulation between
    these chambers.

2. Arteries

a. Arteries are the strongest of the blood vessels. They carry blood
    away from the heart.
b. Artery walls are capable of expanding with the volume of blood
    pumped along them, then contracting again to their original size.
c. The arteries branch out into smaller and smaller vessels as they
    reach the tissues and organs. When they become very small, they
    are called arterioles. When even smaller, having reached their
    destination, they are called capillaries.

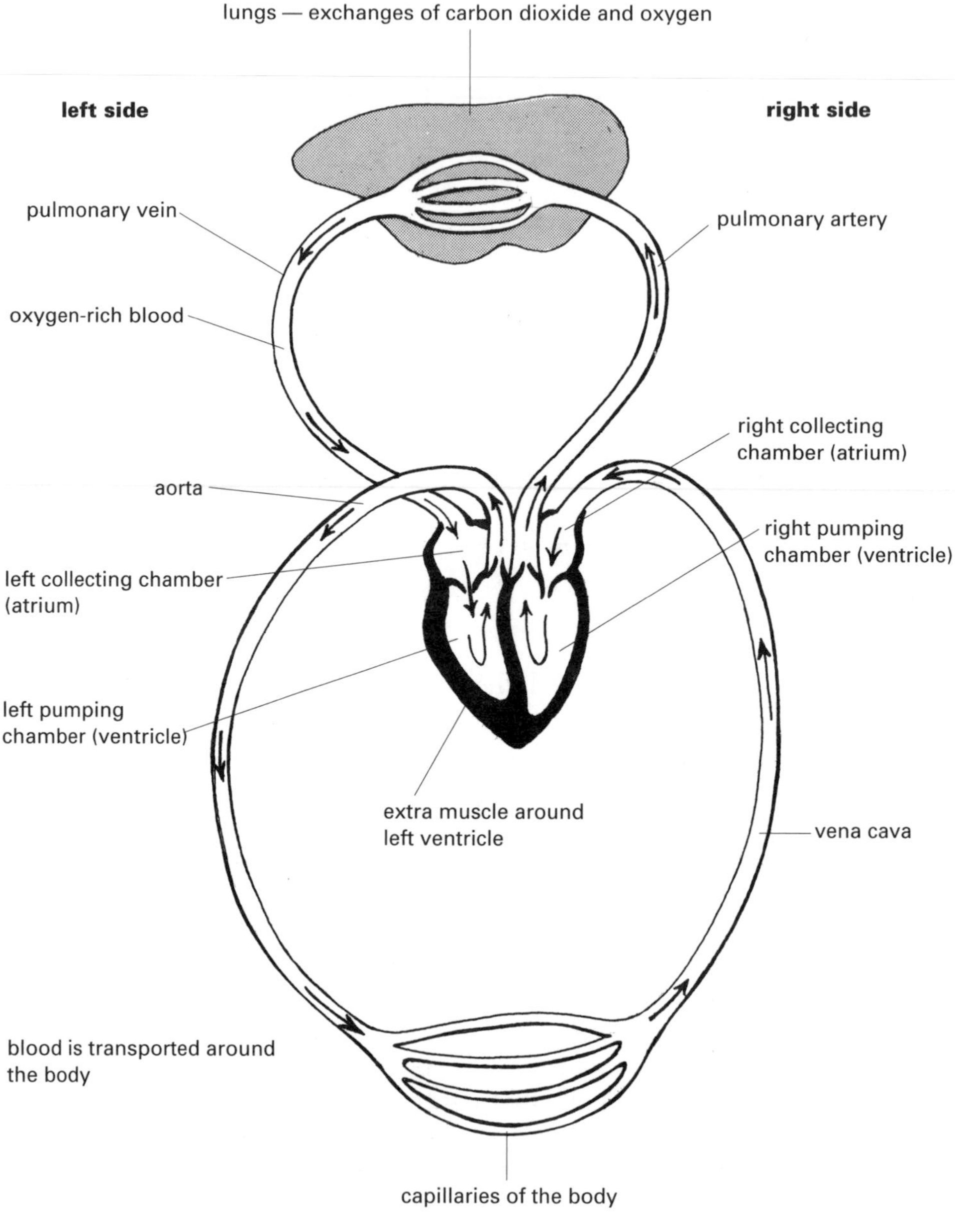

The heart and its circulation

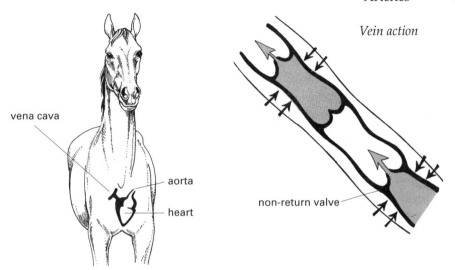

Vein action

vena cava

aorta

heart

non-return valve

The location of the heart

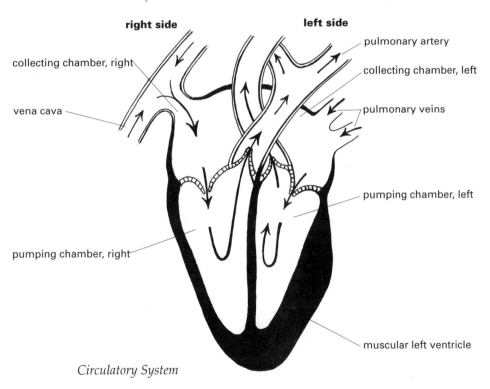

right side

left side

collecting chamber, right

vena cava

pumping chamber, right

pulmonary artery

collecting chamber, left

pulmonary veins

pumping chamber, left

muscular left ventricle

Circulatory System

3. Capillaries

a. Capillaries are very small blood vessels, only one cell thick.
b. The thinness of the capillaries allows the exchange of fluids and gases, to and from tissues of the body, to take place.
c. Arterial capillaries lead into venous capillaries.

4. Veins

a. Veins are very small vessels which join the venous capillaries and gradually become larger.
b. Veins carry blood back to the heart.
c. Valves in the veins prevent the blood from flowing in the wrong direction.

5. Blood

a. Blood consists of a transparent, straw-coloured fluid called plasma, in which are suspended red and white cells.
b. Blood is the transport system of the body, carrying nourishment to all the tissues and transporting waste products away.
c. A red pigment called haemoglobin is present in the red blood cells and is the main carrier of oxygen.
d. White blood cells are responsible for fighting infection and re-moving germs and dead cells.

6. Circulation

a. Oxygenated blood is pumped out of the left pumping chamber through the aorta which is the main artery taking blood to the body.
b. The blood travels through arteries, arterioles and capillaries to all parts of the body, bringing life-giving nutrients and taking away waste products.
c. The blood returns along capillaries and veins and enters the right collecting chamber via the vena cava.
d. It is propelled through a non-return valve into the right pumping chamber.

e. From this chamber, the blood is pumped along the pulmonary artery to the lungs where an exchange of gases takes place and the blood is re-oxygenated.

f. It leaves the lungs and returns to the left collecting chamber via pulmonary veins.

g. Here it is propelled through a non-return valve into the left pumping chamber to begin the whole cycle again.

7. Additional Information

a. The system of circulation throughout the body is called the systemic circulatory system. The system of circulation to the lungs is called pulmonary circulation.

b. When blood leaves the heart, it is pumped with great force. This enables it to reach all parts of the body. If an artery is cut, the blood will come out in strong spurts due to the strong pumping action of the heart.

c. The horse's pulse is the blood being pumped rhythmically through the arteries, and should be approximately 35–45 beats per minute when the horse is at rest.

d. As the left pumping chamber needs to be strong enough to pump blood around the whole body, it is more muscular than the right pumping chamber.

e. A collecting chamber is called an "atrium", and a pumping chamber is called a "ventricle".

f. As veins carry blood back to the heart, there is no strong pump to help the blood on its way. For this reason veins are equipped with non-return valves to stop the blood from flowing the wrong way. General body movement helps to massage the blood back along the veins. If a vein is cut, blood will flow, rather than spurt, out.

g. When caring for your horse, it is important to remember that body movement aids circulation. Horses that are confined to their stables for long periods may be prone to circulatory problems. For example, filled legs may be caused by inactivity, leading to a collection of lymph in the lower limb.

h. The lymphatic system, which consists of a network of tubes and vessels similar to blood vessels, also relies on body massage to keep the lymph fluid moving. Unlike veins and arteries, the tubes have blind ends. However, in a similar way to veins and arteries, they join up into increasingly larger channels. The lymph fluid drains towards the heart and is helped on its way by valves which prevent backflow. The lymphatic system is responsible for draining off excess fluid from all parts of the body. It also plays a part in defending the body against infection and has glands at various points which filter off unwanted substances.

Follow-up Work to Confirm Knowledge and Experience

1. As with the other systems, try building a model to which you can relate visually to help you to remember the circulatory process.
2. Practise saying the unfamiliar words aloud until you are comfortable with them.

Helpful Hints and Exam Technique

1. Try not to become flustered if you forget the names of various parts of the system under the pressure of the exam situation. The examiner will give you time to think and come back to a point you have problems with.
2. Try to learn the basic system and avoid confusing your memory with too many extra details. Don't worry if other candidates come out with details you don't know about as they have probably managed to learn much more than they need to know for the exam.

17 Other Systems

<u>STAGE IV</u>

It is helpful for Stage IV level candidates to have a working knowledge of the systems of the horse. They should already have a good knowledge of the respiratory, circulatory and digestive systems, as well as the systems of support and movement. The rest of the systems include: nervous and sensory system, skin, reproductive, mammary and urinary. A basic understanding of physiology and anatomy, not complicated veterinary knowledge, can help in the care of the horse and prevention of disease. Physiology is the normal function and workings of the system, while anatomy is the structure of those systems.

1. **Systems of Information and Control (Nervous and Sensory)**

   Basic Functions of the System

   a. To take in information via ears, eyes, mouth, nose and skin, in the form of hearing, seeing, tasting, smelling and feeling (the senses).
   b. To control various functions and movements of the body.
   c. To process and evaluate information.

   What the System Consists of

   a. The central nervous system – Made up of the brain and spinal cord.

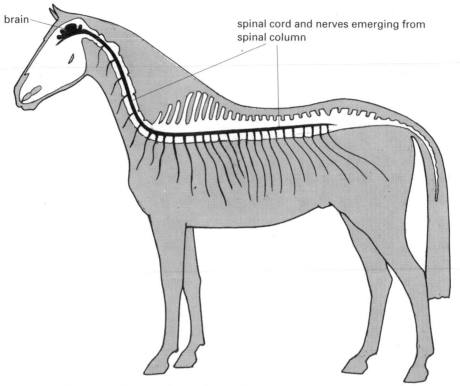

Systems of information and control

- The brain is encased in the skull for protection. It receives messages from all the senses of the horse.
- Messages are sent down through the spinal cord which is encased in the backbone for protection.
- Horses can store information, which they have learnt through their experiences, in their memory for future use.
- Messages are received through the five main senses noted above, as well as through a "sixth" sense. This "sixth" sense is the term used to describe a horse's ability to sense things like human feelings and imminent changes in the weather. They may demonstrate their sixth sense by refusing to go down a certain path which subsequently turns out to be a deep bog and not safe.

b. The peripheral nervous system is made up of all the other nervous tissues in the body. Nerves will respond to some stimuli with a reflex action, for example flinching away from pain, or coughing as a result of irritation. A reflex action occurs without conscious effort.

c. The autonomic nervous system – This controls involuntary activity, such as movement of food along the gut, breathing and the heart rate.

d. Instinct – This is a natural ability to do certain activities without prior learning. For example, all the activities a foal performs in its first hours of life, like walking, sucking and keeping close to its mother.

e. The endocrine system – This is made up of a number of ductless glands which secrete hormones directly into the blood stream. Hormones are chemical messengers. These glands include: hypothalamus, pituitary, thyroid, adrenal, pancreas, uterus, ovaries, thymus, parathyroids and testes, and they control all the basic functions of the horse. If any of these glands fail to function properly, the horse's behaviour and/or systems will be affected. For example, the horse may become thin, fail to reproduce or have a lower than normal performance level.

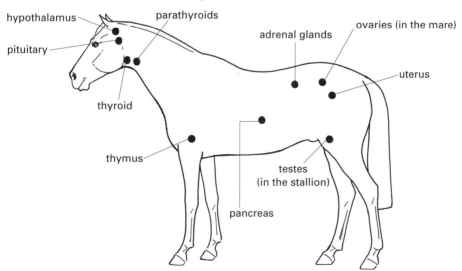

The endocrine glands

2. The Skin

a. The skin is the largest organ of the body. It covers and protects the whole body. Apart from protection, its functions are many, including: prevention of dehydration, preventing foreign bodies from entering the body, helping to control body temperature, secreting, carrying sensory nerves and synthesising vitamin D.

b. It consists of:

- Hair – which helps to regulate body temperature.
- Epidermis – which is the outer layer where cells die and scale away.
- Dermis – which contains blood vessels, glands and nerves.
- Sebaceous glands, sweat glands and hair roots – which are located in the dermis.
- Pores – which are in the outer layer of skin where these glands and hair pass out to the surface.
- Nerve fibres – located in the dermis.

c. The skin varies in thickness over the body and is elastic. The hooves are part of the skin. The oil secreted from the sebaceous glands keeps the hair oiled, while the sweat discharged from the sweat glands evaporates away from the skin, having a cooling effect.

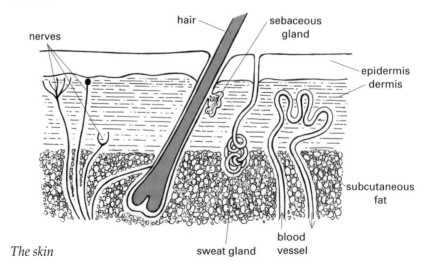

The skin

3. Reproductive System

a. The reproductive system of the male horse is designed to produce sperm which will unite with the female egg to fertilise it. The reproductive system of the female horse is designed to produce the egg with which the sperm will unite and then to provide nourishment for the resulting embryo along with a suitable environment in which it can grow.

b. The male system consits of:

- The testes which hang in the scrotum, located between the hind legs.
- Spermatozoa form in the testes from where they pass into the epididymis.
- The epididymis is a long, coiled tube.
- The sperm are stored in the tail of the epididymis prior to ejaculation, at which point they leave and enter the vas deferens.
- The vas deferens is part of the spermatic cord.
- The two tubes, one from each testis, run past the two seminal vesicles which produce seminal fluid.
- Sperm and seminal fluid form semen, which passes out through the penis via the urethra.
- The urethra is a common duct for both semen and urine.
- The penis is enclosed in the sheath.

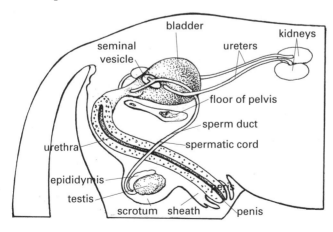

The reproductory system of the stallion

c. The female system consists of:

- The ovaries which contain ova or eggs. At birth, the female already has all the egg cells she needs for her lifetime, and no more are produced. The ovaries are situated just behind the kidneys, approximately under the fourth or fifth lumbar vertebra.
- Two Fallopian tubes run from the ovaries to the two horns of the uterus or womb.
- The cervix closes the other end of the uterus.
- The vagina runs from the cervix to the vulva which is covered externally by the labia or lips of the vulva.
- The mare's oestrous cycle is controlled by the pituitary gland which secretes the hormone FSH (follicle-stimulating hormone). A follicle develops in the ovary and matures to the point where an egg is released into the Fallopian tube. At the same time, the ovary secretes the hormone oestrogen which brings the mare into season. The egg matures as a result of the pituitary gland secreting LH (luteinising hormone). At the site the egg has left, a yellow body forms which secretes the hormone progesterone. At this point oestrous ends and becomes dioestrus.

4. The Mammary System

a. The mammary system consists of two glands situated between the mare's hind legs. These are modified skin glands. Each gland ends in a teat in which there are two small holes through which the foal will suck milk.
b. Its main function is to supply the young foal with nourishment.
c. Mastitis is a painful condition of the udder caused by some sort of infection and would need treatment by the vet.

5. The Urinary System

a. The urinary system consists of the kidneys, which are located in the lumbar region. Ureters run from the kidneys to the bladder. The bladder empties via the urethra.
b. Its main function is to maintain water and electrolyte balance within the body and to filter out unwanted substances. To do this,

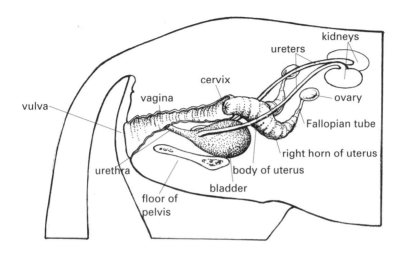

The reproductory system of the mare

the horse's blood is filtered through the kidneys and waste products are removed.

c. A urine sample can be tested for drugs or abnormal substances to help to aid diagnosis of ailments like azoturia or cystitis.

d. The horse's urine is usually pale yellow or slightly brown in colour. Observation of the colour of the urine is an aid to monitoring the horse's health.

Through learning about the systems of the horse it becomes obvious that each system is very much interdependent on the others. This is why a little knowledge of each helps in the overall understanding of maintenance of good health in the horse and observation/awareness of ill health which may not always be obvious to the inexperienced.

Follow-up Work to Confirm Knowledge and Experience

1. Having learnt a little about each system, try to put that knowledge into practice in everyday situations by observing the horse in good health and seeing how these systems function, then compare this with malfunction of the system when the horse is not in good health.

Helpful Hints and Exam Technique

1. Try not to get bogged down with complicated anatomy and physiology. Examiners are usually looking for the simplest and most basic explanation in answer to their questions. This shows that you have practical experience of the subject rather than that you are good at learning about the system from a book. You should be trying to show that the basic knowledge taken from the book has been put into practice and related to everyday work with the horse.

18 Aspects of Yard Management

STAGES I, II, III and IV

1. Accident Procedure and Reports

It is advisable for everyone to have first-aid training, whatever their occupation. The following is the procedure to take in the event of an accident, rather than how to administer first aid.

Accident Procedure

a. First, remain calm as it is important to think clearly.
b. While the injured person is your first priority, you must make the situation safe while you make your way to them. If someone has been kicked, move the horse away. If someone has fallen off, halt the rest of the ride and send a responsible person to catch the loose horse. Each situation will be a little different, so use common sense.
c. Go to the injured person. Reassure them and tell them to keep still.

If Conscious

d. Encourage them to breathe deeply and calmly. (They may be winded and panicking about getting air.)
e. Ask them if there is any pain. Can they move their fingers and toes?
f. Make a mental note of what they say; it will be helpful information to give the doctor or ambulance staff, should they be needed.

251

g. Keep talking to the person. If they appear to be talking nonsense, they may have concussion and will need to be taken to a doctor.

h. If they cannot move their fingers or toes or have pain in the neck, back or limbs, do not move them. Ask for an ambulance to be called. Keep them warm with a blanket or jackets. Do not try to remove hat or boots etc.

i. Obvious bleeding should be stemmed by applying direct pressure with a handkerchief or clean pad.

j. If they feel fine and want to get up, allow them to do so on their own. Stand near in case they feel faint and need support. Do not allow them to remount if you feel there is any chance they may faint, or if they have hit their head.

k. Allow them to walk for a while before remounting, and continue with an easy, confidence-giving exercise, or let them sit quietly before resuming their work which should be of an undemanding nature.

If Unconscious

l. Check that there is no blockage in the mouth that may prevent breathing and carefully loosen any tight clothing around the neck.

m. Do not move the person unless they are in danger of choking and need their airway kept clear by putting them in the recovery position (this should be done with great care to keep the spine straight). Send for an ambulance. Anyone who has been unconscious must be examined by a doctor in case of skull damage.

n. Keep talking to them; this may help to bring them round. Keep them warm.

o. Remain calm and also reassure the rest of your ride as soon as possible. Once the injured person has been taken to hospital, you may resume the work, hack or lesson.

Further Points

a. Be prepared for accidents. Have the telephone number of your local doctor and vet clearly displayed by the telephone. Dial 999 for an ambulance. Have a human first-aid kit on the yard and also one that can be taken out when hacking.

b. If you have a pay phone, keep money for emergencies in an obvious place beside the phone. When hacking, take money for the phone.

c. If an accident occurs on the road, someone should be posted on each side of an injured person to redirect traffic around them. With luck, there will be a motorist with a car phone who will be able to summon help. It is obviously important to catch the loose horse as it may cause further accidents.

On return home, you should fill in a British Horse Society accident report form. This helps the Road Safety Development Officer of the BHS to compile statistics on road accidents involving horses.

d. If an accident involves injury to human and horse, take care of the human first but attend to the horse or send someone else to do so as soon as possible.

Accident and Incident Reports

a. In all yards an accident book should be kept in which all incidents and accidents are recorded. You could have two books, one for minor incidents and one for more serious accidents.

b. Records should include: date, place and time of incident, name of person or persons involved and what they were doing at the time, what happened, what injuries (if any) were sustained, what horses (if any) were involved, whether the person was taken to hospital/doctor/home etc. It is also a good idea to draw a sketch of the incident. For example, the position of jumps and other riders when a person fell off during a lesson.

c. When possible, any one who witnessed the accident should be asked to sign the report.

d. The law requires that certain accidents have to be reported to the enforcing authority under Health and Safety regulations. This generally means sending a written report to the local Environmental Health Department within seven days of the occurrence. In the case of really serious accidents, the Environmental Health Department should be contacted by phone immediately. The type of accident which needs to be reported is one resulting in broken bones, the person being detained in hospital overnight, the person being off work for three or more days, or death.

e. The Health and Safety Executive publish a number of booklets which give full details to employers and employees about accident and incident reporting.

f. The type of incident that would need to be reported would be one which, potentially, could cause serious injury; for example, if a building collapsed or a boiler blew up. Obviously, a horse kicking out could cause serious injury but this is in the nature of horses and would not be a reportable incident. However, if a building collapsed, it would be due to negligence on the part of the owner and is therefore a reportable incident.

g. Sometimes an accident can occur in which the injured party seems only a little bruised or shaken. Then, later in the day, because of continuing pain, they go to a doctor or hospital and are found to have, for example, a broken bone. It may then be necessary to report this accident to the enforcing authority. If a good report was written at the time of the accident, it will be easy to pass on the information. So, however small the accident appears to be initially, a record should always be made.

h. The accident book should be available for staff and clients to look at if they wish and should therefore be kept in an accessible place in the office or similar room.

i. An accident book will also bring to the manager's notice any horse, pony or worker who seems to be frequently involved in accidents. If this is the case, the point should be followed up to find out why this is happening. It may be necessary to give extra training to a staff member, to reschool a horse, or to make sure novice riders no longer ride a certain horse, etc.

STAGE IV

2. Communications/Routine Organisation

a. A yard routine is essential if jobs are going to be carried out efficiently and be completed within a given time. A haphazard approach to work is bound to lead to important tasks being missed out and forgotten. Yard workers, whether there are two of them or 22, should start the day knowing what they are expected to do. They should know if they are to muck out, catch field-kept ponies or feed stabled horses. In this way, each important task will be taken care of.

b. The person in charge should agree a yard routine with their workers and allocate tasks according to experience. The employer or person responsible for organising the workforce must make sure that each employee/helper/or client has the necessary skills to be able to carry out their given tasks safely and effectively. They must provide training whenever it is needed. Each person's level of fitness should be taken into consideration. Yard work can be very tiring for new workers. They will get fitter, rather than over-tired, if tasks are allocated according to their ability.

c. Good communication and observation are essential. Without them, the person in charge will not know if each worker understands their jobs for the day and knows how to complete them. In the same way, the workforce must also understand the importance of communication and observation. They must be trained to report problems with horses and equipment. For example, if person A fails to tell anyone that a particular horse tried to kick them when they went to catch it, then person B may well get kicked and injured by the same horse when they go to catch it. Similarly, if person B breaks a yard broom and doesn't tell anyone, then when person A goes to sweep the yard there may not be enough brooms to carry out the task.

d. For the yard to run smoothly, with a happy workforce, the leader of the group must have good organisational skills and be prepared to listen to their workforce. For example, the manager may be allocating too much time to one task and not enough to another. By listening to the workforce, they will be able to pinpoint problems and make adjustments.

e. The manager must also be flexible and be able to prioritise when problems arise. For example, half an hour may have been allowed for catching field-kept ponies. However, when one pony decides it will not be caught, it may take an hour or more of the person's time. The manager must be able to decide how to reallocate that person's tasks or which tasks can be left for another day.

STAGE IV

3. Collecting and Collating Information

By keeping good clear records, time and money can be saved and the yard will run more efficiently.

a. Details of each horse should be kept. The simplest system would be to start a file for each horse when it arrives, and keep the files in alphabetical order of horses' names. Details should include: date of arrival, age, height, colour, markings, sex, freeze mark/brand and any other distinguishing features. Any previous history of the horse should be included, along with details of feed, inoculations, registration papers, and any other available information. These files can then be easily accessed whenever information is needed.

b. As each horse will need regular attention from the farrier, it is easier to keep shoeing details in one book rather than in each horse's separate file. The shoeing book will include a list of all the horses along with the date they were last shod and what was done. The person in charge of shoeing then needs to establish a routine time for checking this book in order to make sure that the farrier is booked at suitable intervals. At the same time, if a horse loses a shoe, the book can be checked to see if any other horse needs attention while the farrier is there to replace the shoe. This book should be accessible to all staff so that records can be kept up to date when the person normally in charge is away for any reason.

c. The same system could be used for flu/tetanus inoculations, although each horse's own record card will need to be kept in their file. As an added reminder, a note could be made in the office diary, saying "inoculations due", in advance. This will act as a reminder for someone to check the flu/tetanus book, or the shoeing book, so that the vet or farrier can be called.

d. Each horse needs to be wormed on a regular basis. To have an effective programme, all the horses in the yard should be wormed at the same time. Worming records are probably most easily kept in the yard diary. After each worming, write in the next date when they will be due.

e. A yard diary is a must for recording all forthcoming events. The type of diary used will depend on how large the yard is in terms of horse and staff numbers.

f. As already discussed, an accident book is required by law.

g. In yards with a fairly large workforce, each staff member will need a personal file. This will include: home address, contact name and number and their contract. In the case of students training, personal details, such as date of birth and examinations attained, will help when planning their next exam and training programme. Holiday and sick leave could also be noted in their files.

h. Staff holidays could be recorded in the yard diary if there are only a few staff, but a year-planner wallchart may be needed for larger numbers of staff in order that the manager can see at a glance when people are going to be away.

i. For yards with a regular clientele, records of each person's name, address and telephone number are needed. A simple card index in alphabetical order of client surnames is probably the best system.

j. For livery clients, a system is needed for recording any items that need to be charged to their account. These could be noted in the yard diary which would then be checked at the end of each month before the client's bill was made up. Alternatively, another book could be kept, with the livery horses listed in alphabetical order, and all items could be entered there.

k. Many yards will have computers into which all the above information could be entered and regularly updated. The number of horses, clients and staff will dictate which system is most appropriate.

l. Whichever method is used, it is vital that a good routine is established to make sure that records are kept up to date, that all relevant information is collected and stored in an easily accessible system and that action is taken, to call the farrier etc., when appropriate.

STAGE IV

4. Insurance Cover and Legal Matters

a. Anyone running a business and employing staff is required by law to have employer's liability insurance. As mentioned above, it is the employer's duty to provide safe working conditions. This insurance will cover accidents to employees due to the employer's apparent negligence. The insurance certificate must be displayed in a prominent position to prove to the employee that their employer has taken out this insurance.

b. If the yard has regular visits from members of the public, the law requires that there is public liability insurance for the same reasons.

c. Any vehicles must have third party insurance, although it is probably best to have a comprehensive policy.

d. The above are the only legal requirements for insurance but it may be a wise move to insure horses, tack, buildings, hay and straw and any other expensive items of equipment. If you have any livery horses, make sure that the owners understand that they must insure them and their equipment themselves.

e. Before making any alterations or additions to your yard, make sure you have planning permission. If you are in doubt about whether or not it is needed, it is best to contact the local planning officer just in case.

f. If you are running a business and employing staff, you must make sure you record your income and outgoings, and that you make arrangements for tax and national insurance contributions to be paid.

g. For your own sake, make sure that your yard and fields are really secure. If a horse strays and causes damage, it is the responsibility of the person who is caring for it. So even if it is a livery horse, you will still be responsible for it if it escapes and damages property or causes an accident.

h. As a professional you are responsible for keeping risks to a minimum. For example, even if a rider says they are OK riding without a hat, you must still make sure that you don't allow them to ride unless they are wearing a suitable standard of hat for riding, otherwise you could be said to have neglected your "duty of care".

STAGES II, III and IV

5. Stable Construction and Maintenance of Facilities

Site

a. If you are able to choose the site, the stables should be positioned with their backs to the prevailing wind.
b. Choose an area that should drain well. If at the bottom of a dip, the stables and drains may flood in wet weather.
c. Large trees too close to the building may pose a problem in stormy weather if a branch or the whole tree falls.
d. Other considerations include accessibility for vehicles, electricity and water.

Drainage and Flooring

a. Drains are generally laid to take all water away from the stables towards the rear.
b. When the floor is laid, a slight slope towards the front or rear is incorporated to aid drainage. If the slope drains into a front channel it is visible and easy to keep clear. However, as horses often stand at the front of their boxes, this may lead to them standing in the wettest area. If the slope drains into a back channel, it will be less visible and may become blocked but the horse will usually be standing in a drier area. Each individual must weigh up the pros and cons.
c. Drainage channels and covers must be swept clean daily.
d. Concrete, with little ridges on the surface for grip, is the most commonly used flooring. The concrete is laid a metre or so (3 ft) wider than the floor area needed. This allows for hard dry standing immediately outside the boxes.

Walls

a. Wooden walls are frequently used and can be purchased in sections ready to erect.

b. Brickwork, one or two bricks high (or more), is put down as a base for the wooden structure. This helps to prevent rotting and invasion by vermin.

c. The higher the brick base, the more expensive the structure becomes. For this reason, complete brick-built boxes are not often erected these days.

d. Breeze blocks are a cheaper alternative and may be used as a compromise between brick and wood. The advantages of brick/breeze block over wood are that they are more durable and also fireproof.

e. A small hole must be incorporated in the base of the wall for drainage.

f. Walls should be approximately 240 cm (nearly 8 ft) high to the eaves to allow for head room.

g. Walls and doors need to be lined with kicking boards. This will protect both the outer walls and the horse from each other. Kicking boards also provide insulation and strengthen the walls. They are usually 120 cm (4 ft) high.

Dimensions

a. A box 300 × 300 cm (10 × 10 ft) would provide enough room for a pony up to 14.2 h.h.

b. 300 × 360 cm or 360 × 360 cm (10 × 12 ft or 12 × 12 ft) provides enough room for a 14.2 – 16 h.h. horse.

c. 360 × 420 cm or 420 × 420 cm (12 × 14 ft or 14 × 14 ft) would be a suitable size for a horse 16.2 h.h. or over.

d. Boxes for very large horses, or for foaling, should be 480 × 480 cm (16 × 16 ft).

e. Doorways should be 120 cm (4 ft) wide, with a bottom-door height suitable for the size of horse. Horses of 14.2 h.h. and above will usually have a bottom door 120 cm (4 ft) high, with a top door of 90 cm (3 ft), making a total doorway height of 210 cm (7 ft).

f. Pony boxes will have lower bottom doors and will not require as much head room in the doorway.

Roof

a. A pitched roof gives more head room and air space inside the box and also drains well.

b. The roof should overhang the front of the boxes by approximately 90 cm to 1 m (about 3 ft). This will keep the horses dry and give shade when they have their heads over the door.

c. Air vents may be put in the roof to aid good circulation of air.

d. Roofing felt provides an attractive and relatively inexpensive roof covering. However, its insulation properties are poor and it is not fireproof. As it is inclined to expand and contract in hot and cold weather, cracks will gradually appear, leading to leaks.

e. Slate is more expensive, but is attractive, insulates well and is fireproof. However, it does crack easily.

f. Tiles are more expensive still, but are strong, attractive and have excellent insulation properties which keep the stables warm in winter and cool in summer. They are also fireproof.

g. Corrugated sheets of plastic, iron, onduline and other modern materials can provide a cheaper form of roofing. Iron is the worst of these. It is hot in summer, cold in winter and very noisy when it rains. Plastic is a useful addition to all types of roof as it provides an extra source of light. The other materials are fireproof and provide reasonable insulation. Obtainable in large sheets, this type of roof is quick to erect but whole sheets will need replacing if damaged.

Fittings

a. Stable doors, particularly the top door which is rarely closed, need hooks to secure them when open.

b. When closed, they need strong bolts to secure them. On the bottom door use a bolt design that your horse cannot open at the top and a kick bolt at the bottom.

c. A metal strip along the top of the lower door can prevent the horse from chewing the wood. The upper part of the door frame may also be covered with metal to prevent chewing.

d. Windows should be located on the same side of the box as the door. This prevents through draughts, while providing light and fresh air.

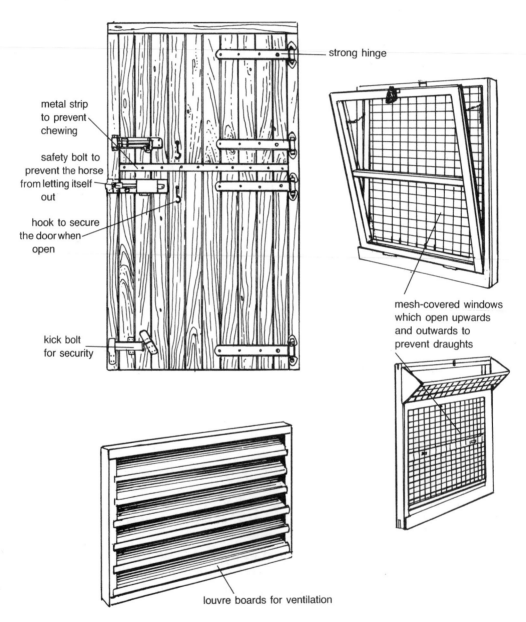

strong hinge

metal strip to prevent chewing

safety bolt to prevent the horse from letting itself out

hook to secure the door when open

kick bolt for security

mesh-covered windows which open upwards and outwards to prevent draughts

louvre boards for ventilation

Safe stable fittings

e. Windows that hinge at the bottom to open outwards prevent draughts. They should be covered with wire mesh and be glazed with wired safety glass.

f. Louvre boards can be used to provide further draught-free ventilation, and are usually positioned fairly high up on the wall.

g. Tie-up rings should be positioned towards the front of the box. Then, when the horse is tied up, you will be able to enter the box with the horse's head towards you, rather than its hindquarters. Fix the ring approximately at horse's eye level.

h. Further fittings, such as automatic water bowl, hay rack, feed manger, are optional. If used, there should be no sharp edges and each item should be high enough to prevent the horse from getting its legs caught.

i. Strip lighting or bulbs can be used. Position these well above the horse's head height. They must also be covered to prevent shattered glass from falling into the bed. The light switch should be outside the stable, out of the horse's reach. Obviously, all electrical wires must be well insulated and covered to keep them away from horses and protected from weather and rodent damage.

Converted Buildings

Many buildings are converted from their original use for use as stables. It is important to check that these conversions will provide a safe environment for the horse. Each situation will vary but the following points should be considered.

a. Buildings and dividing walls must be strong enough to withstand being kicked and leant on by the horse. Badly built walls crumble and fall easily, while flimsy wood panels will splinter.

b. There must always be plenty of head room in the doorway and inside the building. Old barns with low beams may not be suitable.

c. Dividing walls that do not reach up to the ceiling must be high enough to stop the horse from fighting with its neighbours. Bars could be used so that the horses can still talk to each other.

d. Check that there are no protrusions that could damage the horse; for example, old nails, hooks, etc.

The Layout of the Yard

Safety and efficiency should be the main considerations when planning the layout of the yard. The hazard of fire should be a first consideration.

a. If two rows of buildings facing each other are favoured, then the central space will need to be at least 20 m (66 ft) across as fire spreads easily across small spaces. If a square of buildings is to be erected, there must be plenty of gaps for fire exits. Always consider how you would get people and horses from any part of the yard to a safe area if there was a fire.

b. The muck heap needs to be easily accessible and not too long a walk from any of the boxes. It also needs to have access for farm machinery or a lorry which may be used to dispose of it. However, being a fire hazard, it should not be too close to any of the buildings.

c. A tack room and feed room will be needed. These also need to be within easy reach of all the boxes, so a central location is helpful. However, the proximity of the feed room to any stabled horses should be considered, as it may lead to some horses constantly banging their doors.

d. Hay and straw barns need to be easily accessible, while the fire hazard factor must also be considered.

e. There should be several watering points in the yard to reduce the need to carry heavy water buckets any great distances, to help in the event of fire and to reduce the amount of water spilled in cold weather.

f. If an office and telephone are to be incorporated in the design, these also need to be quite central to enable anyone to get to the phone quickly, unless a full-time secretary is to be employed.

Internal Layout

a. Feed rooms should be large enough for storage of feed unless a separate feed store is available. Within the feed room a system must be established for using feed by its use-by date and not letting new feed be fed before older feed. One wall needs to be free for a feed chart listing all the horses' feed requirements. Vermin-proof feed bins must be easily accessible. A water point needs to

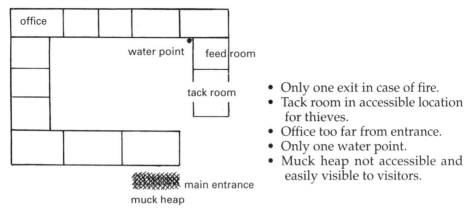

- Only one exit in case of fire.
- Tack room in accessible location for thieves.
- Office too far from entrance.
- Only one water point.
- Muck heap not accessible and easily visible to visitors.

Poor yard layout

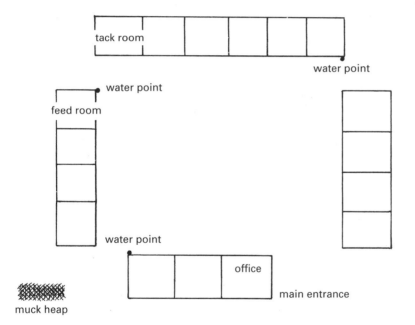

- Several exits in case of fire.
- Office at entrance to receive visitors.
- Accessible muck heap but not immediately visible to visitors.
- Several water points.
- Tack room away from easy access for thieves.

Good yard layout

be nearby but it is probably best not to have a tap in the feed room in case of flooding.

b. The tack room may be organised to include space for rugs and all other equipment, or larger yards may require separate rooms for rugs and storage of tack. Rugs can be hung on hooks or folded and stored on deep shelves. Storage rooms should be vermin-proof and warm enough not to be damp. Within the tack room saddles and bridles can be arranged in various ways according to the number of horses and type of yard. For example, riding schools should take care to put small ponies' tack on low pegs for small children to reach. A sink with hot and cold running water and a washing machine large enough to take rugs are useful additions to any tack room as tack, boots and rugs will need regular cleaning.

STAGE IV

Maintenance

All stable buildings and equipment are expensive so, apart from maintenance for safety, good maintenance is essential to prolong the life of the equipment.

a. Yard surfaces must be kept level and non-slip to prevent accidents involving people tripping and falling. Running water and puddles quickly erode the surface, so good drainage and care with the use of water and hose pipes is very important. Any holes appearing should immediately be filled.

b. Wooden stables can get attacked by vermin and chewed by the horses. Preserve the wood initially with regular applications of creosote or other wood preservative. Cover tops of stable doors with metal anti-chew strips. Replace any broken panels immediately before a horse is harmed by sharp edges or splinters.

c. Keep doors working smoothly by having hinges adjusted if the door drops so that it does not drag on the ground. Keep door bolts and hooks working easily and firmly fixed so that no one has to struggle to open or close a door – essential in case of fire and time saving on a daily basis.

d. Wooden fencing needs the same care as wooden buildings, and wire fencing must be kept taut for safety reasons.

e. Electrical fittings must be well maintained. Wires are best encased in metal tubes to prevent damage by vermin. Trip switches should be incorporated into the system.

f. All water pipes should be lagged where possible, thereby preventing freezing and all the subsequent problems.

g. Riding surfaces, indoors and outdoors, need to be raked regularly. A track inevitably develops around the edge of the school. This must be levelled daily to prevent damage to the membrane and underlying structures and to maintain a safe and level surface to work on. The surface should also be kept damp. Dust is a hazard to the health of both human and horse. Doors and gates to school areas should be kept free-moving and close securely.

7. Knowledge of the British Horse Society (BHS)

As all candidates for the BHS examinations must be BHS members, it is important to understand the aims and objectives of the society, along with how it benefits them and others (not just examination candidates) to be a member.

STAGE III

a. Examinations are taken care of by the Training and Education Policy Committee. They have an exams department which can be contacted directly for information. This committee is also responsible for training and trying to set and improve standards. They also have a department responsible for the approval of riding establishments. BHS-approved schools receive regular random checks from a BHS representative. The BHS publishes a book called *Where to Ride* which lists all the approved riding schools in the UK, along with the level to which they are capable of training.

b. The Welfare Policy Committee tries to iron out problems where cruelty and neglect are concerned. Regional representatives are on hand to visit and try to educate owners as well as to help neglected horses and ponies.

c. The Safety Policy Committee has a department that is responsible for administering the Riding and Road Safety Test.

d. The Access and Rights of Way Policy Committee have regional representatives who work to preserve existing bridleways as well as to open up new, safe routes for riders.

STAGE IV

a. The BHS has a structure of regional and county committees. Each county committee has a chairman, a secretary, a bridleways officer, a road safety officer, a welfare officer, a press officer and a number of district representatives. Together, they try to promote the aims of the society, encourage membership and provide advice at a local level. These committees also raise funds by running local events such as showjumping competitions, dressage, etc.

b. The Instructors' Register is updated and published each year. For a small fee, qualified instructors are entered into the register which provides proof of their qualifications. Registered instructors agree to abide by a code of conduct and are required to attend a BHS training day to update their standards at least once every three years. It is also compulsory for registered instructors to have a current Health and Safety at Work First Aid Certificate. For freelance instructors, not covered by an insurance policy within a riding establishment, public liability insurance is provided, the cost being part of the registration fee. This register can be used by the instructor as a means of providing proof of their qualifications, as an identity card is also issued, as well as providing the customer with the knowledge that the instructor is trained to a certain level, has first aid training and insurance, and has agreed to a code of conduct to provide professional training.

Follow-up Work to Confirm Knowledge and Experience

1. Through working in an equestrian establishment, it should be possible for any student to observe how important safe working procedures are. Unfortunately, accidents will happen but it is hoped that each individual will learn by their mistakes.

2. For Stage IV candidates particularly, working in a variety of yards

will enable them to see different systems for records, routines, equipment and yard layouts. Having gained some experience in different situations, they will be able to select those that suit them best for any yard they may subsequently be in charge of.

3. Students at all levels need to train themselves to ask the questions "Why?", "How?", "What is it?" and so on, about everything that goes on around them. In this way they will learn more and have a much deeper understanding of all aspects of yard work and management.

Helpful Hints and Exam Technique

1. The subjects of safety, accident procedure and knowledge of the BHS will be examined at all levels. Candidates must show a really thorough knowledge of safety and accident procedure if an examiner is going to have confidence in their ability to work safely and sensibly with horses. While the candidate is unlikely to fail an exam due to lack of knowledge of the BHS, it does not give a very good impression if a person is a member of a society about which they know nothing! For your own sake, read the members' yearbook and see what you can gain from the BHS, rather than just being a member for the sake of your exams.

2. When talking about routine, communications, records and stable construction, do use examples from your own experience. Describing methods or designs that you have seen in use, and highlighting both good and bad points, will immediately show the examiner that the candidate really has been involved in working in a yard and that they therefore have the practical experience which is so important.

Index